The Business of Consumer Magazines

by
Benjamin M. Compaine

Knowledge Industry Publications, Inc.
White Plains, NY and London

Communications Library

The Business of Consumer Magazines

by Benjamin M. Compaine

Library of Congress Cataloging in Publication Data

Compaine, Benjamin M.
  The business of consumer magazines.

  (Communications library)
  Bibliography: p.
  Includes index.
  1. Periodicals, Publishing of. 2. Publishers and publishing. I. Title. II. Series.
  Z286.P4C63   070.5'72   82-180
  ISBN 0-86729-020-X   AACR2

Printed in the United States of America

Copyright © 1982 by Knowledge Industry Publications, Inc., 701 Westchester Ave., White Plains, NY 10604. Not to be reproduced in any form whatever without written permission from the publisher.

Table of Contents

List of Tables and Figures iv

Preface viii

1. Introduction 1
2. Size and Structure of the Industry 7
3. Circulation and Distribution 23
4. Advertising 55
5. Magazine Audience Research 77
6. How Special Interest and General Interest
   Magazines Differ 89
7. Entrepreneurship and Magazine Publishing 105
8. Group Ownership and Competition 123
9. Production, Paper and Printing 139
10. Outlook and Conclusions 147
11. Profiles of Selected Consumer Magazine Publishers 157

Appendix A: Circulation for Selected General
           and Special Interest Consumer
           Magazines, 1973 and 1978 183

Appendix B: Consumer Magazines Published
           by Major Groups 187

Selected Bibliography 192

About the Author 193

Index 194

List of Tables and Figures

Tables

2-1	Value of Industry Shipments in the Print Media Industry, 1973 and 1980	7
2-2	Value of Periodical Industry Shipments Compared to Gross National Product, Selected Years, 1960-1980	8
2-3	Consumer Magazine Circulation in the United States, Selected Years, 1954-1980	9
2-4	Annual Advertising Expenditures, by Medium, Selected Years, 1935-1980	12
2-5	General Magazine Advertising Revenue (in Current and Constant Dollars), Pages and GNP, Selected Years, 1929-1980	14
2-6	Operating Revenues and Costs for Consumer Magazines, 1965 and 1980	18
2-7	Advertising and Editorial Linage Ratios, Selected Publications, Selected Years, 1961-1979	19
2-8	Editorial Cost as a Percentage of Revenue for Magazines of Varying Size	21
3-1	Subscription and Single-Copy Sales of A.B.C. General and Farm Magazines	24
3-2	Largest 100 A.B.C. Magazines with More Than 50% Single-Copy Sales, 1980	25
3-3A	Profit Analysis of Single-Copy Sales at Alternative Levels of Draw	26
3-3B	Marginal Analysis	27
3-4A	Profit Analysis of Subscription Revenue at Alternative Levels of Acquisition	27
3-4B	Marginal Analysis	28
3-5	The Cost of Magazines to the Reader	29
3-6	Outlets for Consumer Magazines in the United States, 1978	35
3-7	Economics of Subscription Acquisition and Fulfillment	42

3-8	Cost of Mailing a Magazine, 1971, 1972, 1977, 1979	44
3-9	Hypothetical Cost and Savings Using Private Delivery of 13 Magazines in the Washington, D.C. Metropolitan Area	47
3-10	100 Largest Circulation A.B.C. Audited Consumer Magazines, 1980	50
4-1	Cost per Thousand for Selected Magazines and Categories	56
4-2	Relationship Between Cost per Thousand and Circulation Size	60
4-3	Trends in Magazine Advertising Rates and CPMs Selected Years, 1961-1980	61
4-4	Media Cost Index, Unit of Advertising, 1970-1981	61
4-5	Media Cost Index, Cost per Thousand, 1970-1981	62
4-6	Major Media Shares of National Ad Revenue	62
4-7	Effect of Increased Circulation on Total Revenue, at Constant CPM and Pages	63
4-8	Leading National Magazine Advertisers 1979, 1980	65
4-9	Advertising Pages by Selected Category, 1974-1978	67
4-10	Brand Awareness as Result of Advertising Exposure	72
4-11	Brand Awareness in Unaided Recall	72
4-12	Summary of Five Studies of Advertising Recall	72
4-13	Advertising Readership Averages of Magazines Above and Below Total Survey Norms for "Associated" Intensity	74
4-14	Unit Sales of Seagram's Brands Compared to Total Category, August 1977-January 1978	75
5-1	Comparison of In-House and Simmons Readership Studies for *Us,* 1977 and 1978	83
5-2	Demographic Profile of Adult Magazine Buyers and Non-Buyers	84
6-1	Circulation Changes in General and Special Interest Magazines, 1973 and 1978	96
6-2	Subscription and Single-Copy Prices for Special and General Interest Magazines, 1973 and 1978	96
6-3	Subscription Price as Percentage of Single-Copy Price	98

6-4	Ad Pages in Selected General and Special Interest Consumer Magazines, 1973 and 1978	99
6-5	Examples of Special Issue Magazines, 1978	102
7-1	Selected Consumer Magazine Start-ups Since 1969, by Entrepreneurs and by Publishers	112
8-1	Concentration in the Periodical Publishing Industry, 1947-1977	124
8-2	Selected Characteristics of Group-Owned and Independently Published Magazines, 1980	126
8-3	50 Largest Circulation Consumer Magazines and Their Owners, 1980	127
8-4	Largest Consumer Magazine Publishers in the U.S., by Revenue, 1980	128
8-5	Largest Consumer Magazine Publishers, by Number of Magazines Owned, 1980	129
8-6	Largest Consumer Magazine Publishers, by Total Annual Circulation, 1980	131
8-7	Circulation Size of Consumer Magazine Groups, 1980	131
8-8	Selected Consumer Magazine Acquisitions by Major Publishers	134
9-1	Selected Profit Criteria for Paper Product Manufacturers in *Fortune* 500, Selected Years, 1971-1980	140
9-2	Selected Measures of Profitability for Leading Paper Manufacturers, 1980	140
9-3	Production Costs for Different Size Magazines	145

Figures

2-1	Percentage of Advertising Expenditures by Medium, 1950 and 1980	11
2-2	Comparison of Changes in Circulation and Advertising Pages, Selected Years, 1950-1980	15

3-1	Flow of Magazines and Receipts in Single-Copy Distribution	32
3-2	How Wholesalers Streamline Single-Copy Distribution	33
5-1	The Media Imperative Matrix	86
6-1	Consumer Magazine General-Special Interest Matrix	92

Preface

It is strange to be writing about magazines when the attention of the media world is riveted to the so-called "new media." The telephone and cable lines are supposed to be buzzing with data, creating text and video on our ubiquitous cathode ray tubes. Video cassettes and discs are the new paper; personal computers are the new file cabinets; satellites the transmitters which make short work of long distances.

This is all true. Such technology will indeed be increasingly used in furthering (though not always in a socially beneficial way) communication and information creation, gathering, storage and transmission. It is to be neither feared nor worshiped. Rather, if history has any bearing on the future, new and newly combined technologies will create additional needs and wants, while not necessarily replacing those that are filled by older media formats.

Thomas Edison is on record as having predicted that his movies would shortly make books obsolete in the classroom. Wrong. In 1873, the Postmaster General of the United States wrote that before the 20th century dawned, telegraph and telephone would make physical delivery of mail obsolete. Wrong. The advent of television encouraged some futurists to pronounce dead the radio broadcasting industry. It thrives. And despite the convenience of watching the television set at home, Hollywood has continued to make money cranking out theatrical films.

And so it has been with consumer magazines. Three times in this century the magazine was viewed as a dying institution, most recently in the early 1970s, following the suspension of the venerable *Life* close on the spine of *Colliers, The Saturday Evening Post* and then *Look*. But publishers bobbed and weaved. They found new market niches, new advertisers. Special interest magazines multiplied, often serving the interests of audiences being captured by the presumed competition. Television, after all, spawned the largest selling magazine of all time, *TV Guide*. Other magazines, newspapers and even books have benefited from television programming in sports and drama. Magazines for video enthusiasts, home computer owners and cable subscribers fill niches created by declines in the old romance and movie star magazines.

So while magazine publishers sort out the threats and opportunities being presented by the electronic media, perhaps it is not so whimsical to take a fresh look at consumer magazine publishing. Apparently, there are still interests to be satisfied, writers and editors more than willing to provide the content, and advertisers eager to deliver their messages to a well-defined audience. Some publishers go so far as to co-opt much of the new technology to put out magazines that look better than ever, are more timely as well, and remain affordable.

This, then, is a study of the magazine business. It is not an attempt to glamorize the personalities or, indeed, the product. It is rather something of a snapshot of what the industry looked like in 1981. As a snapshot, it naturally cannot reflect changes made since it was "taken." However, it has been composed to show, in its depth of field, much of the industry's past. This book concentrates on the contemporary state of the industry: how does it work, how is it changing, in what ways does it stay the same.

As such, I am indebted to the many publishers, editors and knowledgeable analysts I have met while researching and writing this book; as might be expected, they are too numerous to name individually. They include people at most of the major magazine publishers and many at some of the less well-known ones. You know who you are. Thank you.

Three sources have been especially crucial, however. For many of the years I have been hunting data on magazines (for earlier studies as well as this one), the staff at the Information Center of the Magazine Publishers Association has been most accommodating. For much of that time, Dorothy McGowan was in charge of the library. Second, Gil Maurer, president of Hearst Magazines, provided insights into particularly arcane facets of the business that substantially furthered the analysis presented in this book. And finally, I wish to acknowledge an early participant in this work, David Orlow. He provided a unique contribution of both concepts and details that has proved invaluable in analyzing the structure and developments in the industry.

I also appreciate the help of Robert Maginn who helped me update the many tables in this volume. Of course, no one but myself can be held accountable for its content.

Benjamin M. Compaine

Cambridge, Mass.
January 9, 1982

To two important influences in my life:
My grandfather and
Aunt Jenny

1
Introduction

Magazine publishers have weathered well the media wars. They have experienced real growth, not just growth measured in inflationary dollars. Advertising pages, a more valid measure of financial vitality than revenue per se, are well above the levels of the mid-1970s. The skeptical futurists who proclaimed the magazine dead a few years ago are quiet now. They talk now of a media mix, with magazines playing an important role. Advertisers have been pleased, too. Consumer magazine advertising has been a useful escape valve from the astronomical leaps in the cost of their favorite medium, television. Many have rediscovered magazines and found they work. And advertisers of specialized goods and services never had abandoned the publications appropriate to their products.

Consumers also appear satisfied. They recognize that they are being asked to pay more—significantly more—for their magazines than they did a few years ago. But they seem to accept this as part of the rise in price of everything. In the meantime, circulation growth has apparently not been affected, since circulation per adult has increased slightly. Consumers can find a publication concerning virtually any interest they have, from vegetarian eating habits to skin diving. They also have more alternatives for light reading, with the return of *Life* on a regular basis, the ubiquitous weekly tabloids like the *Star* and the newer *People* and *Us*.

But not even the best of times is good for everyone. Some magazines have failed, even those that were well-planned, managed and financed. *New Times* gave up in 1978 when it ceased being a viable editorial product. *Argosy,* almost 100 years old, changed owners and was suspended, at least temporarily. A host of ambitious new titles, such as *Pizzazz* for youths, *Vital* for the "me" lifestyle folks, *Human Nature* targeted to the intellectuals, and *Your Place,* an imitation of the established *Apartment Life,* all came and went. For the most part, they were from experienced publishers, and their failure cannot be explained by undercapitalization. Thus, publishers have also learned that they cannot just throw anything out on glossy paper and expect it to stick: a magazine has two constituencies, consumers and advertisers, and the product must be acceptable to both.

Even the successful publishers have had to keep working, despite the advertising rolling in. Paper and postage costs have had to be watched closely. Subscription liabilities have had to be controlled with an eye on rising costs. Single-copy and subscription sales ratios have needed adjustment for optimum yield. But in general, life for consumer magazine publishers has been good although a trough was hit in 1975.

FACTORS IN THE MAGAZINE REVIVAL

At least five times in the 20th century certain "experts" forecast the demise of the printed magazine. First, after World War I, as the automobile became a common vehicle for the average citizen, analysts thought that people would no longer have time to read consumer magazines. Soon thereafter, in the mid-twenties, a new technology—radio—was viewed as the replacement for entertainment and information supplied by magazines. Still later, "talkie" motion pictures were supposed to be another nail in the coffin. Then television would eliminate the need for magazines, thought the futurists.

For the first time, there did seem to be an element of truth here, as the visual impact of this new mass medium occupied an increasing amount of the population's leisure time and began to draw away advertising dollars. But still magazines hung on, with *Life* and *Look* attracting six to eight million purchasers an issue at almost give-away prices. But finally, as the 1960s ended and the 1970s began, the demise of *Colliers, The Saturday Evening Post, Look* and finally *Life,* institutions all, appeared to confirm the end of the consumer magazine—at least, of the mass circulation magazine.

But again the obituary was premature. Magazines of all varieties have shown strong vital signs. A new category, the city and regional magazine, found a niche as a slick format for local advertisers while providing useful information and occasional solid journalism for a geographically prescribed market. Special interest magazines have flourished, as the very leisure time that was supposed to spell the demise of magazines has enhanced the consumer's wish for detailed information in both editorial and advertising material. Even television has contributed to the desire for certain magazines. For example, the popularity of televised spectator sports has stimulated the sales of magazines that report on those activities. The fast-breaking national and international news that gets cursory television coverage has created opportunities for journals that can provide greater perspective and analysis. This includes not only the newsweeklies (which have gone up 400% in circulation since the advent of television), but also many of the smaller political and intellectual magazines.

In sum, magazines have adapted to a dynamic environment and carved out a niche as a special interest information medium and a special purpose entertainment medium. The success of the magazine is in part accounted for by the specific quality that some had thought spelled its doom: the printed format in an electronic age. But literate societies have shown that the portable, clipable, filable, easily retrievable—and above all affordable—characteristics of magazines (as well as newspapers and books) continue to preserve their place in the media mix.

PURPOSE OF THIS BOOK

In 1974, at the height of the most recent wave of doomsaying about magazines, a study[1] that focused on the trends in special and general interest consumer magazines reported among its findings that:

- Both types of magazines showed strong growth signs in circulation and advertising, but special interest magazines were significantly outperforming general interest ones.

- Improvements in printing and production technology had been particularly helpful to the economics of shorter run magazines.

- Postal rates, while moving up rapidly, would not substantially hurt magazines that could otherwise justify their need to readers and advertisers.

- Magazines were well situated to compete against even newer media, such as video cassettes and disks, or cable TV.

The impetus for the current study was created by the 1974 investigation. After a recession or two and increased media competition, how have magazines fared? The overall answer is clear: they have done well.

---

[1] Benjamin M. Compaine, *Consumer Magazines at the Crossroads: A Study of General and Special Interest Magazines* (White Plains, NY: Knowledge Industry Publications, Inc., 1974).

But many questions arise. Why have magazines succeeded? Are some types of magazines doing better than the industry overall? Are special interest magazines still outperforming general interest magazines? Is the trend away from general interest publications, hinted at in 1974, still valid? Can an entrepreneur without major financial backing still hope to start and succeed with a magazine when well-financed ventures still fail? What has been the impact of rapidly increasing subscription and single-copy rates, and how have publishers weathered the now complete phasing in of higher second class postal rates?

These are only a few of the questions that deserved to be addressed. To answer them, as well as to investigate other issues, this book has been organized to assess the following developments:

- Segments of the industry have moved to a greater emphasis on single-copy at the expense of subscription sales.

- There are economic relationships that suggest that adding circulation can lead to decreased profits as it increases revenue.

- General interest, mass circulation magazines showed renewed vigor since 1973, while special interest magazines continued to make strong gains.

- The tight supply of paper has been more of a nuisance than a hindrance in expanding publications or starting new ones.

- Printing technology in the 1980s will benefit publications with shorter print runs as the lower limit of "long run" decreases.

- An entrepreneur with a solid editorial concept and the willingness to invest sweat equity when cash is short can still succeed in establishing a new magazine.

- Multi-magazine publishing groups have only limited economies of scale as they add publications.

- Consumer magazine publishing remains diversely held and highly competitive for advertising dollars and readers' attention.

This type of analysis can be useful in several ways to publishers, investors, students and others who have an interest in the magazine industry. Most important, unlike studies conducted by those with a vested interest in the industry (such as an advertising agency, a supplier or a participant), it is the product of an unbiased point of view. Readers may therefore use this report to reinforce (or revise) their own opinions, learn of new developments, or simply get an overview of the territory from a source that is not down in the trenches.

Second, studies such as this one try to pull together many existing but far-flung pieces of information. The study thus becomes a useful reference work and can serve as a baseline study for future work.

Finally, this book may help provide some insights or fresh perspective on an industry that, on the one hand is economically and technologically mature, yet on the other hand is vigorous and willing to change.

DEFINITIONS

For the sake of variety, the terms magazine, periodical, publication and journal have been used interchangeably in this study. Although there have been various attempts to define "magazine," the term is used here to refer to a printed and bound medium that appears (or is intended to appear) at regular intervals of four or more times per year. Since this study concerns itself with consumer magazines only, it is further limited to publications that are intended for and available to the general public by subscription and/or through retail outlets for a stated price and meet the U.S. Postal Service requirements for second class mailing privileges. Finally, "consumer magazines" is intended to encompass only those publications that are listed in or are qualified for unpaid listing in Standard Rate & Data Service's *Consumer Magazine and Farm Publication Rates and Data* directory (Skokie, IL, monthly) or for audit by the Audit Bureau of Circulation (Chicago). Thus, *not* included in this definition are business and trade magazines, academic journals and newsletters. Also, although various magazine-like publications such as annuals, semi-annuals and one-shots are also discussed, they are not included in computing statistics on magazine circulation, size of groups and advertising linage.

Special Interest and General Interest

Most people have their own conception of how to define a special interest magazine. As used in this study, the term special interest refers to publications containing "active" information—publications that consumers read to learn about a particular activity, hobby or interest in which they customarily participate, such as skiing, photography, hunting, gardening or model building. Although general interest magazines sometimes contain editorial material that fits this description, they are usually geared to a more passive interest on the part of the reader. "How to Improve Your Tennis Serve" would be a special interest article; "Excitement at the U.S. Open," a general interest piece.

Chapter 6 offers a more complete discussion of how the terms limited audience, mass circulation, general and special interest can be usefully differentiated.

LIMITATIONS

While a strength of this study is its outsider's viewpoint, there is also a related limitation. It will be no surprise to those in the industry to know that publishers of individual magazines are quite reticent to divulge proprietary information such as actual advertising revenue, return rates, acquisition plans or budgets. Accurate circulation information is available through the Audit Bureau of Circulation and sworn postal statements (although the latter can be exaggerated). Public documents, such as annual reports and 10-Ks, can provide useful insights into operations of some publishers on a group basis; line of business report requirements have been extremely beneficial in this regard. The Magazine Publishers Association compiles many needed statistics. But some figures, such as the advertising revenue calculated by the Publishers Information Bureau, are overstated by an amount that can only be approximated.

Some publishers are very cooperative in providing inside information, usually not for direct attribution, but nonetheless helpful. Moreover, compared to some other industries, magazine publishing has a reasonable pool of data, in part thanks to the need of the advertising agencies for information on cost per thousand, readership, product usage by readers and effectiveness of advertising.

However, more could be done. Standard Rate & Data Service has a wealth of information but does little to organize it into such compilations as average cost-per-thousand rates by classification, single-copy and subscription prices, even number of magazines. In its listing of magazine groups, it is woefully incomplete. As one glaring example, Triangle Publications, publisher of *TV Guide,* is not listed as a group owner, since *Seventeen* technically has a separate corporate publisher, Triangle Communications. For all reasonable purposes, however, they are of the same ownership. There are other omissions. The purpose here is not to criticize SR&DS, but to highlight the amount of raw data that are available but sometimes difficult to put in useable form.

2
Size and Structure of the Industry

Periodical publishing (here including business publications) was the fastest growing segment of the print media industry between 1973 and 1980, having increased its value of shipments by 128% compared to 106% for print media in general. Nonetheless, newspapers still accounted for more than half of the shipments of print media, while periodicals account for about one-fourth. Table 2-1 shows these comparisons, as well as growth in the overall economy as measured by the Gross National Product (GNP). Periodical publishing is also shown to have outperformed the economy in general.

However, this rapid rise in revenues since the mid-1970s is in marked contrast to sluggish growth in earlier periods. As seen in Table 2-2 between 1960 and 1970 magazines had a revenue growth just over half that of the GNP. For the total 1970-1980 period, the increase almost matched that of the economy.

Industry employment in 1980 reached 82,100, about 21% higher than

Table 2-1: Value of Industry Shipments in the Print Media Industry, 1973 and 1980
(in billions)

	1973	1980	Percentage Increase
Periodicals	$ 3.9	$ 8.9*	128%
Newspapers	8.9	17.5*	97%
Books	3.1	6.4*	106%
Total	$ 15.9	$ 32.8	106%
GNP	$1,306.6	$2,626.1	101%

*Estimate
Sources: U.S. Bureau of Economic Analysis; *U.S. Industrial Outlook 1979, 1981.*

the 1975 level.[1] Although periodical sales are nearly half as high as those of newspapers, periodicals employ only one-fifth as many workers, in part because most newspapers do their own printing, while periodicals tend to contract printing to independent firms.

Table 2-2: Value of Periodical Industry Shipments Compared to Gross National Product, Selected Years, 1960-1980

Year	GNP (billions)	Industry Value of Shipments (millions)
1960	$ 506.0	$2,133
1965	688.1	2,626
1970	982.4	3,195
1975	1,528.8	4,380
1976	1,706.5	5,044
1977	1,889.6	5,800
1978	2,106.6	6,612
1979	2,413.9	8,052*
1980	2,626.1	8,937*
Percentage increase:		
1960-1970	94%	50%
1970-1980	167	180

*Estimate
Sources: U.S. Bureau of Economic Analysis; *U.S. Industrial Outlook 1965, 1971, 1976, 1981.*

COMPONENTS OF GROWTH

Number of Magazines

The number of periodicals increased by nearly 56% between 1950 and 1980, reaching a record level of 10,873 publications.[2] However, most of these were business, trade, alumni, organization, professional or academic journals. The number of consumer magazines accepting advertising in 1980 was about 1124, reflecting a rise of only 8% since 1970 (although there has been a greater turnover in actual titles).

---

[1]*U.S. Industrial Outlook, 1981,* (Washington, D.C.: U.S. Government Printing Office, 1981), p. 96.
[2]*Ayer Directory of Publications, 1981.* (Bala Cynwyd, Pa.: Ayer Press, 1981), p. vii.

Circulation

As shown in Table 2-3, circulation growth was modest between 1960 and 1970 after dropping from the 1954 level. Average circulation per issue fell substantially from 1954 to 1970, presumably as many new and often limited audience magazines joined the industry.

The trend shifted dramatically in the 1970s. Total circulation per issue shot up 45% between 1970 and 1975 and retreated slightly by 1980. Average circulation per issue was up substantially in 1980 from a decade earlier, but also down from 1975. Circulation per adult, which had hovered near two in the 1960s rose nearly 50%. Not only are more magazines selling a greater number of copies, but consumers are purchasing a greater number of titles.

In recent years, magazine publishers have been concentrating more on "quality" circulation, rather than just increasing circulation numbers. Because of rapidly increasing postal costs and significant increases in

Table 2-3: Consumer Magazine Circulation in the United States, Selected Years, 1954-1980

Year	Number of Magazines	Aggregate Circulation Per Issue (millions)	Average Circulation Per Issue (thousands)	Circulation Per Adult
1954	575	254.5	443	2.36
1960	545	245.0	450	1.98
1965	768	291.9	380	2.18
1970	1009	307.0	304	2.11
1975	924	444.4	481	3.03
1980	1124	425.7	447*	2.57

Percentage increase (decrease):

1960-1965	40.7%	19.1%	(15.6%)	10.1%
1965-1970	31.4	5.2	(20.0)	(3.2)
1970-1975	(8.4)	44.8	58.2	43.6
1975-1980	21.6	(4.2)	(7.1)	(17.9)

*Omits 171 magazines counted in total that do not report circulation.

Source: Number and aggregate circulation from Audit Bureau of Circulation (ABC). ABC derives this figure by adding to its own 400-plus magazine members other consumer titles listed in Standard Rate & Data Services' *Consumer and Farm Publications Rates and Data*. This includes publications of less than quarterly frequency. Circulation per adult calculated from adults 16 years and over, July 1, 1979 from U.S Bureau of the Census, *U.S. Census of Population: 1960 and 1970*, Vol. 1 and Current Population Reports, Series P-25, No. 870 for 1980.

paper and printing costs, a number of publishers have built their distribution pattern increasingly around newsstand sales. The New York Times Co.'s *Family Circle* and CBS' *Woman's Day* have traditionally followed this pattern. *Playboy* depends on single copies for most of its sales. More recently, *People, The Star* and others have built circulation strategies exclusively or largely around the newsstand and the supermarket checkout counter.

In aggressively raising both single-copy and subscription prices, publishers have pushed magazine prices up faster than consumer prices in general during the 1970s. The average subscription cost of general interest magazines in 1970, according to R.R. Bowker Co., was $8.47. This was up 135% to $19.87 by 1980. During the same period, consumer prices rose 78%. Single-copy prices increased commensurately.

Advertising

Advertising revenue in magazines rose faster than total advertising volume in 1976 through 1980, reversing the trend that saw the consumer magazine share of total advertising dollars decrease from 12.7% in 1945 to a low of 5.2% in 1975. Between 1976 and 1980, magazine ad revenue increased 120% to $3.2 billion, while total advertising expenditures for all mass media were up 94%. Table 2-4 and Figure 2-1 compare consumer magazine share with those of competing media. Television, in its infancy in 1950, has experienced the strongest growth, while newspapers, radio and magazines have suffered in market share.

Most of the magazine revenue increases, at least until 1977, came about through higher ad rates per page, as advertising pages stayed relatively constant between 1955 and 1975. Table 2-5, based on reports by those magazines reporting to the Publishers Information Bureau, shows that while actual revenue declined only in 1975, true growth in advertising pages did not become a significant trend until 1976. Even so, magazine advertising revenue in the 1970 to 1980 period lagged slightly behind the growth in the economy.

By factoring out the effects of inflation using the GNP price deflator, real advertising revenue shows a stagnant pattern between 1960 and 1976 that matches that of ad pages. However, 1977 and 1978 did manifest true growth in revenue, but growth in constant dollars inched up 2% in 1979 and actually declined slightly in 1980.

Figure 2-2 compares changes in circulation since 1950 with changes in advertising pages. Use of the index compensates for the difference in the number of magazines used in calculating the two totals. For the entire period, circulation gains ran ahead of advertising page growth, although

Size and Structure   11

Figure 2-1: Percentage of Advertising Expenditure by Medium, 1950 and 1980

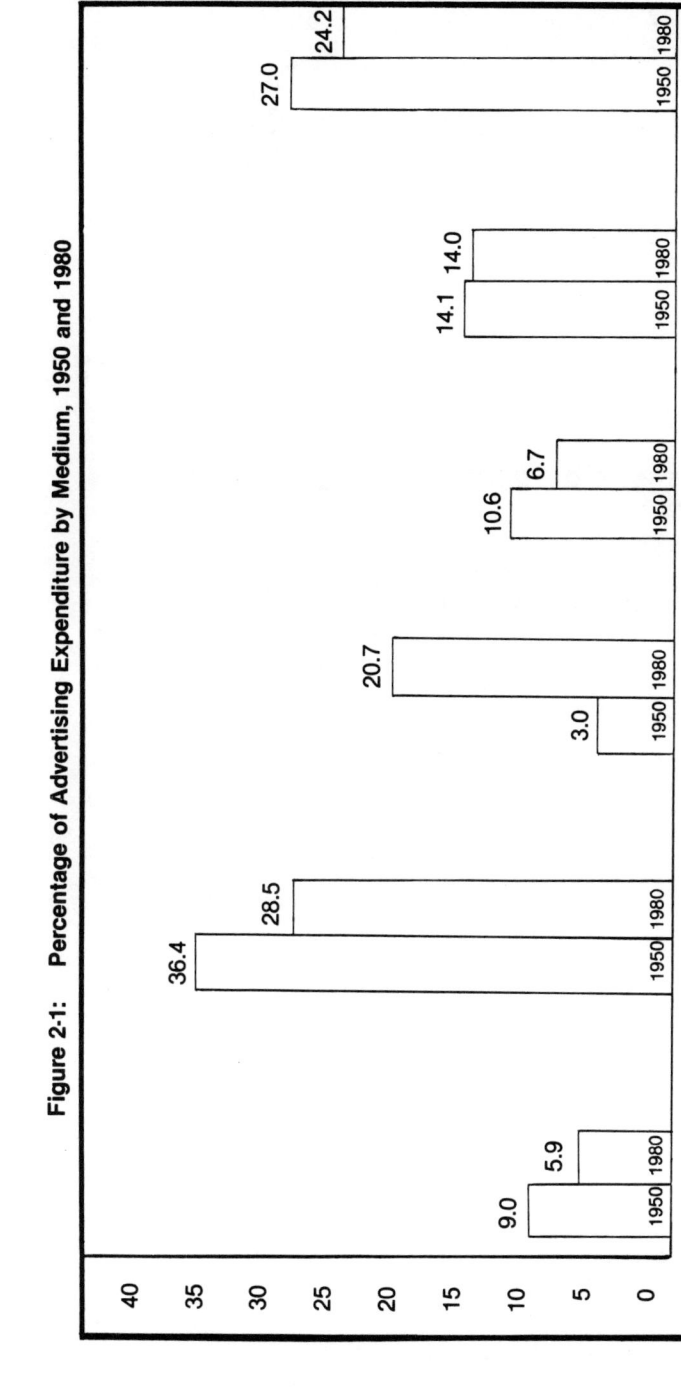

Medium	1950	1980
Magazines	9.0	5.9
Newspapers	36.4	28.5
Television	3.0	20.7
Radio	10.6	6.7
Direct Mail	14.1	14.0
Others	27.0	24.2

Source: Based on Table 2-4.

Table 2-4: Annual Advertising Expenditures, by Medium, Selected Years, 1935-1980
(in millions)

	Total Advertising	Magazines Total	Magazines % of Total Advertising	Newspapers Total	Newspapers % of Total Advertising	Television Total	Television % of Total Advertising
1935	$ 1,690	$ 136	8.0%	$ 762	45.1%	—	—
1945	2,875	365	13.0	921	32.0	—	—
1950	5,710	515	9.0	2,076	36.4	$ 171	3.0%
1955	9,194	729	7.9	3,088	33.6	1,025	11.1
1960	11,932	941	7.9	3,703	30.8	1,590	13.6
1965	15,255	1,199	7.9	4,457	29.0	2,515	16.5
1970	19,600	1,323	6.8	5,745	29.3	3,596	18.3
1971	20,740	1,370	6.6	6,198	29.9	3,534	17.0
1972	23,300	1,440	6.2	7,008	30.1	4,091	17.6
1973	25,080	1,448	5.8	7,595	30.3	4,460	17.8
1974	26,780	1,504	5.6	8,001	29.9	4,851	18.1
1975	28,230	1,465	5.2	8,442	29.9	5,263	18.6
1976	33,720	1,789	5.3	9,910	29.4	6,721	19.9
1977	38,120	2,162	5.7	11,132	29.2	7,612	20.0
1978	43,740	2,595	5.9	12,690	29.0	8,850	20.2
1979	49,520	2,932	5.9	14,493	29.3	10,154	20.5
1980	54,750	3,225	5.9	15,615	28.5	11,330	20.7

Compounded Annual % Change:

	Total Advertising	Magazine Advertising	Newspaper Advertising	Television Advertising
1945-50	14.7%	7.1%	17.7%	—
1950-55	10.0	7.2	8.3	43.1%
1955-60	5.4	5.2	3.7	9.2
1960-65	5.0	5.0	3.8	9.6
1965-70	5.1	2.0	5.2	7.4
1970-75	7.6	2.1	8.0	7.9
1975-80	14.2	17.1	13.1	16.6

Table 2-4 continued

Year	Radio Total	Radio % of Total Advertising	Direct Mail Total	Direct Mail % of Total Advertising	Other Total	Other % of Total Advertising
1935	$ 113	6.7%	$ 282	16.7%	$ 398	23.6%
1945	424	14.7	290	10.1	875	30.4
1950	605	10.6	803	14.1	1,540	27.0
1955	545	5.9	1,299	14.1	2,508	27.3
1960	692	5.8	1,830	15.3	3,176	26.6
1965	917	6.0	2,324	15.2	3,843	25.2
1970	1,308	6.7	2,766	14.1	4,862	24.8
1971	1,445	7.0	3,067	14.8	5,126	24.7
1972	1,612	6.9	3,420	14.7	5,729	24.5
1973	1,690	6.7	3,698	14.7	6,189	24.7
1974	1,837	6.9	3,986	14.9	6,601	24.6
1975	1,980	7.0	4,181	14.8	6,899	24.4
1976	2,330	6.9	4,813	14.3	8,157	24.2
1977	2,634	6.9	5,333	14.0	9,247	24.2
1978	2,955	6.8	6,030	13.8	10,620	24.3
1979	3,277	6.6	6,653	13.4	12,011	24.8
1980	3,690	6.7	7,655	14.0	13,235	24.2

Compounded Annual % Change:	Radio Advertising	Direct Mail Advertising	Other Advertising	GNP
1945-50	7.4%	22.6%	12.0%	6.2%
1950-55	-2.1	10.1	10.2	6.9
1955-60	4.9	7.1	4.8	4.9
1960-65	5.8	4.9	3.9	6.3
1965-70	7.4	3.5	4.8	7.4
1970-75	8.6	8.6	7.2	9.2
1975-80	13.3	12.9	13.9	11.4

Source: Aggregated from annual tabulations prepared by McCann-Erickson and published in *Advertising Age*. GNP from Table 2-2.

Table 2-5: General Magazine Advertising Revenue (in Current and Constant Dollars), Pages and GNP, Selected Years 1929-1980

Year	Number of Magazines	Adv. Revenue (millions)	Adv. Revenue (Constant 1972 $) (millions)	Adv. Pages	Average Rev./Page	GNP (billions)
1929	61	$ 185.7	—	N.A.*	—	$ 103.4
1933	106	92.6	—	N.A.*	—	55.8
1945	97	286.7	—	N.A.*	—	212.3
1950	84	430.6	—	68,321	$ 6,303	286.2
1955	81	622.0	—	76,428	8,138	399.3
1960	79	830.0	$1,208.2	74,861	11,087	506.0
1965	91	1,055.3	1,420.3	80,147	13,167	688.1
1970	89	1,168.7	1,278.7	76,924	15,193	982.4
1971	91	1,235.2	1,286.7	77,008	16,040	982.4
1972	83	1,297.7	1,297.7	82,007	15,824	1,063.4
1973	85	1,309.2	1,237.4	85,665	15,283	1,171.1
1974	93	1,366.3	1,177.8	86,305	15,831	1,306.6
1975	94	1,336.3	1,050.6	80,735	16,552	1,412.9
1976	93	1,622.0	1,211.4	93,253	17,394	1,528.8
1977	96	1,965.4	1,390.9	103,307	19,025	1,889.6
1978	102	2,374.2	1,582.8	115,266	20,597	2,156.1
1979	102	2,671.1	1,614.0	119,832	22,290	2,413.9
1980	102	2,846.1	1,604.7	114,705	24,812	2,626.1
Percentage increase:						
1929-1980	67%	1,433	—	—	—	2,044
1950-1980	21	617	—	70	321	818
1960-1980	29	243	33	53	124	419
1970-1980	15	144	25	49	63	167

* Not Available.
Source: Advertising: Publishers Information Bureau (does not include Sunday supplements); GNP: U.S. Bureau of Economic Analysis.

Figure 2-2: Comparison of Changes in Circulation and Advertising Pages, Selected Years, 1950-1980

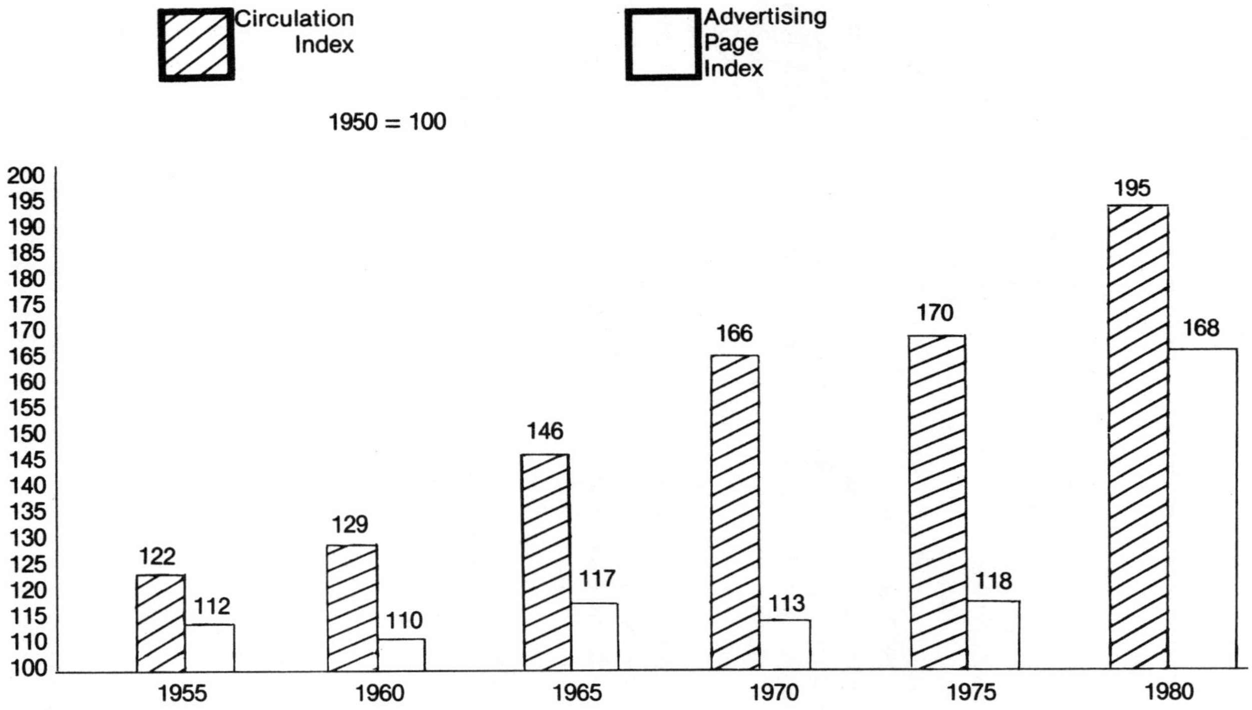

1950 = 100

Year	Circulation Index	Advertising Page Index
1955	122	112
1960	129	110
1965	146	117
1970	166	113
1975	170	118
1980	195	168

Source: Compiled from statistics provided by Magazine Publishers Association. Based on figures from magazines reporting to Publishers Information Bureau (ad. pages) and A.B.C. (circulation).

the strength in advertising after 1975 significantly narrowed the difference.

PROFITABILITY

Despite several strong years of revenue increases, publishers cannot point to improvements in the basic operating margins and returns on investment in consumer magazine publishing. As the president of one group explained, "I'm not saying you should cry for us," because profits have been good enough to encourage publishers to seek additional publications. But the substantial increases in paper, printing and postage costs have absorbed most of the added revenue. For example, a 2 million circulation magazine paid about 84% more for paper in 1978 than in 1973. Second class postage, used to mail subscriber copies, was up 413% between 1971 and 1979.

Nonetheless, the pretax operating profit of a reasonably successful consumer magazine would be between 10% and 12% in a good year. A poor year would see a margin of 6% to 8%. The after tax return on stockholders' equity for magazine publishers is about 16% to 20% in a good year, with isolated examples of higher returns. (In 1978, *The New Yorker,* one of the few publicly owned publishers with most of its revenue from consumer magazines, had an estimated 18% return on equity.) The median return on equity for all printing and publishing companies in the *Fortune 500* was 15.9% in 1980.

Of course, operating margins are also affected by the circulation size of the magazines, since there are real economies of scale in editorial, composition and printing costs (see Chapter 9). A magazine that is part of a group may benefit from supporting services (such as circulation fulfillment, group advertising sales) that can be priced more efficiently than can a single magazine's (see Chapter 8).

ECONOMICS OF MAGAZINE PUBLISHING

Magazine publishing is an easy entry business. It requires little capital equipment, as printing and even typesetting may be handled by outside suppliers. By relying on free-lance writers and an advertising sales force compensated largely by commission, fixed costs can be held to a minimum. It is not unusual for a relatively small circulation bi-monthly to be produced from the publisher's home with one or two full-time employees.

On the other hand, when an established publisher is considering a new title, it may budget millions of dollars for development, producing one or more dummy issues, test marketing and doing extensive subscription mailings.

In this century, magazines have derived the bulk of their revenue from advertising. This was not always the case, as magazines before 1900 tended to depend on circulation revenue, which kept prices high and circulation low. In 1893 Frank Munsey reduced the subscription price of *Munsey's Magazine* from $3.00 to $1.00 and the single-copy price from 25 cents to 10 cents. In so doing, he was pricing his magazine at less than the cost of production, but he saw that this would be more than offset by the large volume of advertising a hefty circulation could attract.

This economic philosophy was the operating model for most consumer magazines until the early 1970s, when the impact of television as well as large increases in postage and paper costs finally caught up with the mass circulation magazines. As recently as 1973, Time Inc. derived 70% of its magazine revenue from advertising, which was a common proportion for many consumer magazines up to that time. However, magazine publishers, following the lead in many cases of special interest magazines, pushed circulation prices up aggressively in the mid-1970s, so that today, advertising is typically providing closer to 55% of operating revenue. In 1980 for example, advertising provided 59% of Time Inc.'s magazine revenues. (See Chapter 3 for a more complete discussion of pricing.)

Table 2-6 shows the percentage of revenue from advertising and circulation and the percentage allocation of expenses to major categories for a single magazine in the mid-1960s and in 1980. Since every magazine is unique, the table is best understood as a relative guide to revenue and cost. It presumes that the magazine has reasonable newsstand sales, but relies primarily on subscriptions. Clearly, a magazine such as *Playboy* or *People* that has primarily single-copy sales would have a somewhat different breakdown. On the other hand, a small circulation special interest magazine might have virtually no single-copy sales and relatively little advertising.

What Table 2-6 does show, however, is the general decline since the 1960s in the proportion of revenue coming from advertising, although it still accounts for the bulk of magazine revenue. Typically, highly specialized small circulation magazines would show a somewhat higher percentage of circulation income (70% or even higher), while a mass audience magazine might have that proportion of advertising.

Although second class postage costs have been the fastest growing in percentage terms over the period, higher subscription revenue and some mailing efficiencies (such as using additional mailing locations) have helped moderate postage expense. Single-copy sales commissions and promotion have become relatively more expensive, reflecting in part the competition for space on the newsstand and at supermarket check-out counters. Retail display allowances are commonplace and some larger magazines have been using other media, including some television, to

18 CONSUMER MAGAZINES

Table 2-6: Operating Revenues and Costs for Consumer Magazines, 1965 and 1980

Revenues and Expenses		1965		1980
Revenue				
Net Advertising		70%		55%
Subscription		23		30
Single Copy		7		15
Total Revenue		100%		100%
Expenses				
Advertising: sales, promotion, research		10%		8%
Circulation and Distribution				
1) Subscription:				
Fulfillment	3		2	
Postage	4		9	
Commissions & promotion	14		12	
	21		23	
2) Single Copy				
Commissions	2		4	
Distribution & other	2		3	
Total Circulation & Distribution	4	25	7	30
Editorial		9		8
Manufacturing and Production				
Paper	20		18	
Print & bind	19	39	17	35
Other Operating				
1st class postage	1		1	
3rd class postage	1		2	
Other	1	3	1	4
Administrative		5		6
Total Expenses		91%		91%
Operating Profit (pretax)		9%		9%

Source: The author's calculations based on data from Magazine Publishers Association.

boost single-copy sales.

Editorial expense, which includes composition, has held steady over the period. Despite the significant increases in the cost for coated paper, relative cost has actually declined. This decrease comes in the face of fatter magazines and increased frequency of some large magazines, such as

Woman's Day and *Family Circle, Fortune, Forbes* and others. Some of the added paper cost has been offset by the move to smaller trim sizes and lighter weight grades.

Overall, a typical magazine might look to a 9% operating profit in an average year, although as noted previously, margins of 10% or 12% would not be unusual.

Editorial/Ad Ratios

The ratio of advertising to editorial linage has remained close to 50-50 over the years, with editorial accounting for as much as 54% in 1970. Table 2-7 summarizes the linage reported by the Russell Hall Co., measuring a selected group of consumer magazines. Overall there has been a decline in editorial content from 55% in 1961 to 48% in 1978.

The ratios vary somewhat by magazine category. In 1978, science and mechanics magazines, for example, had the lowest percentage of editorial, 45%. Shelter, women's fashion, newsweeklies, outdoor and women's magazines are all at 48%-50%. Romance magazines averaged 61% editorial while men's "sophisticates" (e.g., *Playboy*) had the highest proportion of editorial, 67%.

Even within each category there is a wide variation among individual titles, with the leader in the field sometimes having the least editorial and the weakest the most. On the other hand, some publishers work hard at

Table 2-7: Advertising and Editorial Linage Ratios, Selected Publications, Selected Years 1961-1979

Year	Percent Advertising	Percent Editorial
1961	44.6%	55.4%
1966	46.6	53.4
1967	46.7	53.3
1969	47.3	52.7
1970	46.0	54.0
1971	46.8	53.2
1973	49.3	50.7
1975	46.5	53.5
1976	49.3	50.7
1977	51.1	48.9
1978	51.8	48.2
1979	52.4	47.6

Source: Russell Hall Magazine Editorial Reports, as compiled by Magazine Publishers Association.

maintaining a given ad-copy ratio even as advertising increases. The range in 1978 went from 35% editorial (in Condé Nast's *Bride's*) to as much as 76% (in the now defunct *Viva*).

EDITORIAL TRENDS

A 1974 study of the magazine business[3] identified three then-current fads in editorial content: growing seriousness, increasing attention to graphics and design, and the "new journalism" style of writing. Although graphics still receives modest attention (as in the redesign of *Newsweek* in early 1979), there is little to support the continued recognition of the other two trends.

They have, however, been replaced by several other identifiable trends and fads. In the latter category is the pervasive emphasis on gossip and celebrities. Precipitated perhaps by the success of *People*, periodicals of all types have exploited this apparently insatiable desire on the part of consumers. "Personality" covers are among the best newsstand draws. *Ladies' Home Journal* found that its best success is with TV personalities. *People*'s best selling issues featured "Tony Orlando's Breakdown" with his picture on the cover, outperforming another issue featuring "Star Wars" and a picture of android C-3PO. A *People* editor noted, "What we know is that young sells better than old, pretty sells better than ugly, sports figures don't do very well." Although his picture was not on the cover, Jimmy Carter's November 1976 "lust" interview helped *Playboy* to a 92% sale for that issue (compared to an average 80%). *Look* paid big dollars to have rights to the non-news Patty Hearst wedding. Even the newsweeklies have played the gossip/personality game, as with *Newsweek*'s April 1979 cover story featuring California governor Jerry Brown, including a prominent sidebar on his relationship with singer Linda Ronstadt.

A second, though perhaps less obvious trend, is the increased frequency of medical articles, ranging from topics in the news such as Laetrile (an alleged but unproven cancer treatment) to more general self-help features on coping with backaches and maintaining physical fitness.

Both of these trends may be summed up as an overall turning away from the strong political climate that existed after the Watergate investigations of 1973 and 1974. Perhaps most symbolic of this change was the death of *New Times* at the end of 1978. It was designed to go beyond the newsweeklies, to give greater depth to the news. In closing it down when

---

[3]Compaine, p. 48.

it could not keep its audience, founder and publisher George Hirsch blamed in part a declining interest in social issues and "tough investigative reporting." To its credit, it recognized the "personality" fad syndrome in magazines: at one point it ran a cover blurb saying "In this issue: absolutely nothing about Farrah Fawcett-Majors." At the same time, Hirsch was finding new success with *The Runner,* keyed into the "me" trend featuring self-help and how-to type articles.

Editorial Costs

While editorial costs are about 10% of revenue, they actually tend to vary with the size of the publication. Publishers of high quality small circulation magazines know that to attract top writers they must often pay prevailing rates, yet they work from a much lower revenue base than the big magazines. As a result, editorial budgets as a proportion of total revenue are greater for small magazines, as summarized in Table 2-8.

Table 2-8: Editorial Cost as a Percentage of Revenue for Magazines of Varying Size

Total Revenue of Magazine	Average Editorial Cost as % of Total Revenue
Under $500,000	16%
$500,000 – $1 million	13
$1 million – $2 million	12
$2 million – $10 million	8
Over $10 million	6

Source: Knowledge Industry Publications, Inc.

3
Circulation and Distribution

The number of magazines sold in the consumer market is a combination of those sold under prepaid long-term contracts—subscriptions—and those sold by issue at newsstands, chain stores and supermarkets. Managing these two areas of circulation is becoming an increasingly sophisticated part of magazine publishing for two reasons.

First, advertising revenue, which for most magazines is the more substantial and more profitable segment of the revenue stream, is quite dependent on the circulation level. Magazine advertising rates are usually compared on a cost per thousand (CPM) basis: that is, what it costs an advertiser to reach 1000 purchasers of that magazine.

In general, a publisher tries to keep the magazine's CPM competitive with similar types of magazines (although, as will be seen in Chapter 4, what is an acceptable CPM to an advertiser often depends on the perceived audience). Thus, in order to raise advertising revenue while holding CPM constant, a publisher can either sell more ad pages or increase circulation. A higher circulation enables the publisher to raise the page rate, and therefore revenue.

The second reason for added attention to circulation control has been the recognition that circulation itself can be made more profitable (or less costly) by acquiring added sales at the most efficient cost. Computer-aided analysis has shown management that incremental newsstand sales may be very efficient when sales are above a certain break-even level of the draw (the number of copies of an issue shipped out). On the other hand, gaining added circulation through subscriptions can be most profitable when returns on a given promotion surpass the break-even point for that promotion. Though publishers frequently lament the high cost of postage, a subscription mailing that can achieve a 5% return without steep discounts may be quite profitable indeed.

SINGLE-COPY VS. SUBSCRIPTION SALES

In 1973, with the first round of second class postal increases at hand, the word was out that the era of low-cost subscriptions was at an end and that, once again, single-copy sales would dominate. Between 1925 and 1945 single-copy sales had increased 366% while subscription sales edged up only 34%. But after 1945 the trend reversed, as many mass circulation consumer magazines went after higher subscription circulations as a means of holding on to advertisers being tempted away by television. While general interest magazines found security in having large circulation liabilities, most limited audience and special interest magazines, with inherently small circulations, have always relied on subscription sales, thereby avoiding the high cost of printing enough copies to distribute to newsstands.

The general trend is seen in Table 3-1. Although the proportion of single-copy sales has inched up during the 1970s from a low of 29.0% in 1970, the trend has not been dramatic. Between 1978 and 1980, the trend reversed, perhaps reflecting the high postal costs.

Table 3-1: Subscription and Single-Copy Sales of A.B.C. General and Farm Magazines*

Year	Percent Subscription	Percent Single-Copy
1945	48.2%	51.8%
1950	67.9	42.1
1955	60.5	39.5
1960	67.3	32.7
1965	69.1	30.9
1970	71.0	29.0
1971	69.8	30.2
1972	66.7	33.3
1973	65.9	34.1
1974	65.8	34.2
1975	65.5	34.1
1976	64.5	35.5
1977	64.9	35.1
1978	65.5	34.5
1979	66.4	33.6
1980	69.3	30.7

*Excludes comics.
Source: Calculated from Magazine Publishers Association supplied data, second six months A.B.C. audit of each year.

Although industry-wide trends should not be discounted, the needs of individual magazines differ. Some magazines, such as *Playboy,* have been turning increasingly to subscriptions, while others, such as *Woman's Day* and *Family Circle,* were almost exclusively single-copy long before it was "fashionable." The magazine with the largest circulation in the United States, *TV Guide,* derives about 62% of its 18 million weekly circulation from single-copy sales, while the two next largest, *Reader's Digest* and *National Geographic,* are overwhelmingly subscription. Of the 100 largest consumer and farm magazines whose circulation is verified by the Audit Bureau of Circulation (A.B.C.), 23 derive more than half from single-copy sales. The group is dominated by the men's and women's "sophisticated" magazines: *Playboy, Penthouse, Cosmopolitan, Glamour, Mademoiselle,* but the three sensationalist supermarket tabloids are also included. (See Table 3-2.) In fact, a third of

Table 3-2: Largest 100 A.B.C. Magazines with More Than 50% Single-Copy Sales, 1980

Rank	Magazine
1	TV Guide
5	Woman's Day
6	Family Circle
12	National Enquirer
13	Playboy
16	Penthouse
17	The Star
19	Cosmopolitan
21	People
26	Glamour
30	Midnight Globe
37	Seventeen
42	Hustler
49	New Woman
56	US Magazine
57	Vogue
58	Mademoiselle
70	Omni
83	Grit
84	Playgirl
87	Oui
97	Soap Opera Digest
98	Harper's Bazaar

Source: Calculated from figures provided by Magazine Publishers Association. See Table 3-10 for specific percentages.

these single-sales leaders depend on display at the supermarket check-out counters for a considerable bulk of their sales.

Moreover, the assertion that smaller circulation magazines are less dependent on single-copy sales receives some support in that only three of the largest 10 and 14 of the largest 50 are single-copy oriented. Chapter 6, Table 1 indicates that special interest magazines are about 75% subscription, while for a similar index of general interest magazines, subscriptions account for 64% of circulation. Both percentages were changed little from 1973.

Economics of Circulation

Rather than resort to overall generalizations about the advantage of single-copy or subscription sales, many publishers are becoming increasingly watchful of *yield* per issue sold. This is the net revenue after acquisition cost has been taken into account. Publishers have been able to use computers to process the historical data from years of single-copy and circulation results to find the best mix and, more importantly, help decide the most efficient source for added circulation.

Tables 3-3A and 3-4A present a greatly simplified approach to circulation management. The tables compare single-copy and subscription sales profits for a hypothetical magazine with a current circulation of 400,000 to 800,000 in single-copy sales and 400,000 in subscription sales.

Table 3-3A looks at the single-copy figures. Columns one and two show what the estimated sales would be at various draws, while column three shows sales as a percentage of draw at each level. Column four lists

Table 3-3A: Profit Analysis of Single-Copy Sales at Alternative Levels of Draw

Assumptions:
Current single-copy circulation: 400,000
Single-copy price: $1.50/75 cents net

(1) Draw	(2) Sales	(3) Sales as % of Draw	(4) Total Rev. from Sales	(5) Direct Mfg. Cost for Draw	(6) Net Circulation Revenue
500,000	400,000	80%	$300,000	$175,000	$125,000
550,000	429,000	78	321,750	192,500	129,250
600,000	456,000	76	342,000	210,000	132,000*
650,000	474,500	73	355,500	227,500	128,000
700,000	480,000	69	360,000	245,000	115,000
750,000	483,000	64	362,250	262,500	99,250

Table 3-3B: Marginal Analysis

(7) Marginal Draw	(8) Marginal Sales	(9) Sales as % of Marginal Draw	(10) Marginal Revenue	(11) Marginal Cost	(12) Marginal Net Circulation Revenue
—	—	—	—	—	—
50,000	29,000	58%	$21,750	$17,500	$ 4,250
50,000	27,000	54	20,250	17,500	2,750
50,000	18,000	36	13,500	17,500	(4,000)
50,000	6,000	12	4,500	17,500	(13,000)
50,000	3,000	6	2,250	17,500	(15,250)

*Point of approximate revenue maximization.
Source: Knowledge Industry Publications, Inc.

the expected revenue for the publisher, based on a net of 75 cents for a magazine retailing at $1.50. Column five is the total manufacturing (paper, print and bind) expense for the entire draw and column six is the gross profit. Table 3-3B has been added as an alternative approach, showing the marginal percentage of draw, revenue and cost for each addition of 50,000 copies to the draw.

It is evident that *revenue* is maximized at a draw of 750,000 and sales of 483,000. Nonetheless, gross profit reaches its peak with a draw of 600,000 copies and a 76% sale. As seen in columns 10 and 11, beyond that level, marginal cost exceeds marginal revenue, and profit declines. Based on this analysis, if this magazine wished to increase its circulation by single-copy sales, at the current time with the existing cover price and

Table 3-4A: Profit Analysis of Subscription Revenue at Alternative Levels of Acquisition

Assumptions:
Current subscription circulation: 400,000
One-year subscription price: $12.00

(1) New Subscriptions	(2) No. of Pieces Mailed	(3) Return Rate	(4) Total Added Revenue	(5) Promotion Cost	(6) Added Gross Profit (Loss)
20,000	575,000	3.5%	$240,000	$ 115,000	$ 125,000
30,000	937,500	3.2	360,000	188,000	172,000*
40,000	1.6 million	2.5	480,000	320,000	160,000
50,000	2.5 million	2.0	600,000	500,000	100,000
60,000	4.0 million	1.5	720,000	800,000	(80,000)
70,000	7.0 million	1.0	840,000	1,400,000	(560,000)

costs, it would not wish to push past 456,000.[1]

Table 3-4A undertakes a similar approach to subscription acquisition. The key component here is the cost of promotion. The table shows the expense of mailings, the number of pieces mailed, the overall return rate, the new subscriptions acquired (assumed in this example to be all in one year), the revenue the subscriptions produce the first year and the gross margin from the promotion (revenue minus mailing cost). The analysis is taken a step further in Table 3-4B by adding return rates, expense and margin for each incremental group of new subscriptions. In this example, the yield is maximized with the addition of 30,000 subscribers from a mailing costing $188,000, with a gross margin of $172,000. On a marginal basis, trying to add 10,000 subscribers beyond 30,000 produces marginal costs that exceed revenue, as the rate of return on increasing the size of the mailing drops below 1.5%.

Table 3-4B: Marginal Analysis

(7) Marginal No. New Subscriptions	(8) Marginal No. Pieces Mailed	(9) Return Rate	(10) Marginal Revenue	(11) Marginal Cost	(12) Marginal Gross Profit (Loss)
20,000	575,000	3.5%	$240,000	$115,000	$125,000
10,000	362,500	2.8	120,000	73,000	47,000
10,000	662,500	1.5	120,000	132,000	(12,000)
10,000	900,000	1.1	120,000	180,000	(60,000)
10,000	1.5 million	0.7	120,000	300,000	(180,000)
10,000	3.0 million	0.3	120,000	600,000	(480,000)

*Point of approximate revenue maximization.
Source: Knowledge Industry Publications, Inc.

With this information, a publisher is armed to expand circulation intelligently. First, he or she can see that adding circulation, up to about 56,000, would involve the least expense through newsstand sales: a total additional manufacturing cost of $35,000 per issue would produce additional circulation revenue of $42,000. Revenue from advertising page rates based on the larger circulation would then provide the additional revenue from such growth. Second, adding circulation through subscriptions would bring in more cash quickly, but at a greater up-front cost. The question of which is *better* is one, therefore, that does not have a

---

[1] For an analysis of the added effect of increased advertising revenue from higher circulation, see Chapter 4.

uniform answer other than, "It depends." Chief executives at more than one magazine group, Times Mirror and Hearst among them, claim allegiance to a management philosophy that eschews the circulation "rat race" that still exists in many categories. A Times Mirror executive notes that its titles run behind the competition in each category. But by keeping circulation at manageable levels, the company claims it has been able to improve its profit margins. (This analysis is continued in Chapter 4.)

PRICING

Many mass circulation magazines were once nearly given away by subscription; with the steep discounts offered, most were priced below their production cost. As costs rose, publishers allocated a larger share of costs to advertisers. But in the 1970s rapid increases in the cost of manufacturing and distribution (especially paper and postage), combined with a weak advertising position, forced publishers to turn to readers to assume a greater share of the burden. As seen in Table 3-5, the average single-copy price for the 50 leading magazines in advertising revenue more than doubled between 1970 and 1979, about twice the rate of the previous decade. Subscription prices, which had risen at a somewhat faster rate than single copies in the 1960s, again rose faster in the 1970s,

Table 3-5: The Cost of Magazines to the Reader

Year	Average Single-Copy Price	Index 1970 = 100	Average Yearly Subscription Price	Index 1970 = 100	Ratio of Single-Copy to Sub. Price
1960	$ .39	62	$ 4.58	64	8.5%
1965	.46	73	5.32	74	8.6
1970	.63	100	7.16	100	8.8
1971	.63	100	7.38	103	8.5
1972	.64	101	7.57	106	8.5
1973	.68	107	7.72	108	8.8
1974	.81	128	8.98	126	9.0
1975	.87	138	10.14	142	8.6
1976	.98	155	11.52	162	8.5
1977	1.09	173	12.70	178	8.6
1978	1.21	191	14.86	208	8.1
1979	1.33	211	16.30	228	8.2

N.B. Taken from the single-copy and one-year subscription prices reported to the Audit Bureau of Circulation, in effect December 31 of each year, for 50 leading magazines in advertising revenue for that year.
Source: Magazine Publishers Association.

better than doubling on average. As a result, the ratio of single-copy to subscription price stayed near its lowest level in 1979. (The subscription averages are for full-priced, one-year subscriptions. Since many subscriptions are sold at some discount, the actual average might be somewhat lower. Using the full price might understate the true increase, however, since prices for most of the decade were far more likely to be deeply discounted than those toward the end).

Probably to the surprise of many publishers, the higher prices did not have a significant long-term effect on circulation. As the vice president at one group pointed out, readers are conditioned to pay more for everything, and they will continue to pay more for their magazines. "There has been a lessening of the boundary between discretionary and necessary expenditures," which this publisher planned to exploit. Others, however, are not as certain that the pace of increases of the past decade should be maintained. At Condé Nast, the feeling was that "circulation prices will have to level off." And at Hearst, the concern is with yield, rather than cover price *per se.* Times Mirror believes "the bloom is off the rose" regarding continued strong increases.

In many instances, publishers have used higher prices to rid themselves of fringe circulation. Subscribers who could not be renewed after being initially enticed with discounted introductory rates were cut loose by *Esquire, Good Housekeeping* and others. To be sure, some publishers may have used the excuse of planned reduction in circulation to cover up uncontrolled fall-off. But at other times, as when Clay Felker took over *Esquire* (since sold to the 13-30 Corp.), the reduction was announced well in advance and the higher prices were part of a plan to produce a readership of interest to a particular body of advertisers, often with an accompanying higher CPM.

As with most consumer products, it is often difficult to determine the optimum price level for a magazine. To a greater extent than mass market paperback book publishers, magazine publishers have been able to make some use of varied single-copy cover pricing in test cities, while subscription test mailings are an ongoing part of almost all publishers' promotion.

Except for the relative handful of magazines that derive most of their circulation from newsstands, the cover price is often designed as the basis for subscription pricing. Only 46 audited magazines had as many as 300,000 single-copy sales per issue in 1980. In 1977 the average magazine price broke the $1.00 barrier. Magazines such as *Omni, Gentlemen's Quarterly* and *Science Digest* have sold for $2.00 or more for several years, while hundreds of magazines now list prices of $1.50. But for a weekly such as *Time,* single-copy sales are a small part of total circulation and a high cover price makes subscriptions seem like a better bargain.

Moreover, since what readers are buying in a magazine is *perceived* value, the price elasticity for individual titles varies considerably. For example, *Hustler,* as a new magazine, priced itself at $1.50, while *Playboy* and *Penthouse,* ostensibly the competition, were at $1.25. Sales for *Hustler* were strong and continued to move upward even when the price rose to $1.75. On the other hand, the venerable *New Yorker,* in a more mature stage of its life cycle, was hurt on the newsstand when cover price was raised from 25 cents to 35 cents in 1965: sales fell 25%. In 1968, the price went up to 50 cents, and by 1969 newsstand circulation was below 80,000. This fall-off did not affect gross newsstand revenue (160,000 at 25 cents is the same as half that at 50 cents), but it may have affected advertising revenue.

Thus, in pricing magazines, perhaps the first question is the essence of marketing: what is the publication trying to do—sell magazines or sell readers to advertisers? The latter alternative, of course, has long been the operating philosophy of mass circulation magazines, but the new wisdom is that a well-defined audience may be more profitable than just large numbers. (See Chapter 4.)

One member of the magazine publishing community has proposed that periodicals be priced according to a formula, similar to that of book pricing. Warren Styer as president of ABC Leisure Magazines told a gathering of circulation managers that cover prices should be five or six times the production cost, or $1.75 and up for most magazines. "If the higher cost reduces circulation," he continued, "then it means circulation has gone beyond the natural bounds of the readership." Few publishers appear willing to be that aggressive in pricing. More likely, price increases in the 1980s will be tied to the health of the economy and the market strength of individual magazines or categories. Barring a string of double-digit inflationary years, the prices of magazines should not advance as rapidly as they did in the last years of the 1970s.

SINGLE-COPY DISTRIBUTION

Retail sales of consumer periodicals are accomplished through distribution to between 135,000 and 145,000 retail outlets, including supermarkets, convenience stores (e.g., food markets such as 7-11), drugstores and newsstands. A system has developed (very efficient in some aspects) whereby 450 regional wholesalers service the retailers on a weekly basis, while performing many accounting services for the publishers.

Figures 3-1 and 3-2 diagram the basic flow of magazines and receipts. Besides the publisher, the participants are:

32   CONSUMER MAGAZINES

Figure 3-1: Flow of Magazines and Receipts in Single-Copy Distribution

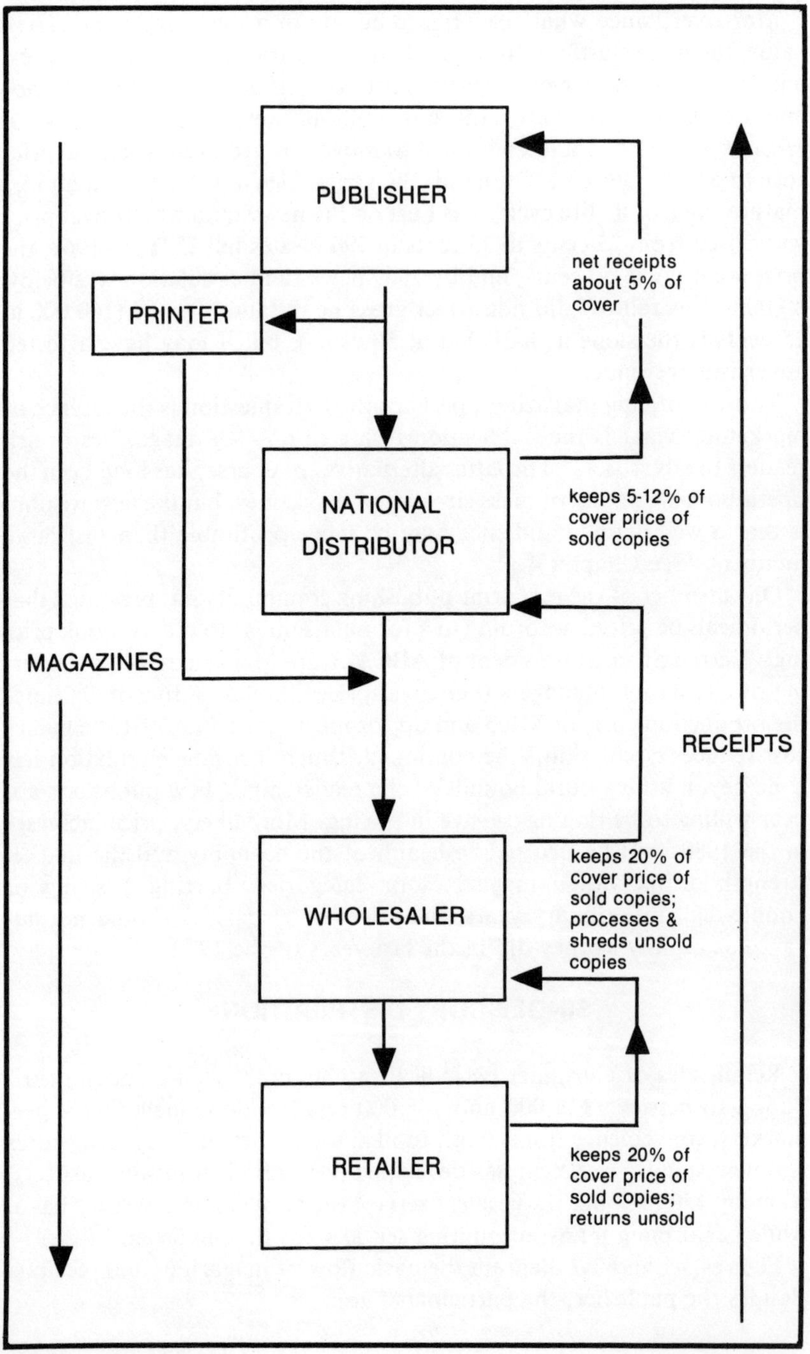

```
                    ┌──────────────┐
                    │              │◄─────────────┐
                    │  PUBLISHER   │              │
                    │              │              │
                    └──────┬───────┘     net receipts
                           │             about 5% of
       ┌──────────┐        │             cover
       │ PRINTER  │◄──┐    │              ▲
       └──────────┘   │    ▼              │
                      │ ┌──────────────┐  │
                      │ │   NATIONAL   │──┘   keeps 5-12% of
                      │ │ DISTRIBUTOR  │      cover price of
                      │ │              │◄──┐  sold copies
                      │ └──────┬───────┘   │
  MAGAZINES           │        │           │
                      └────────┤           │
                               ▼           │             RECEIPTS
                        ┌──────────────┐   │
                        │              │───┘   keeps 20% of
                        │  WHOLESALER  │       cover price of
                        │              │       sold copies;
                        │              │       processes &
                        └──────┬───────┘       shreds unsold
                               │        ◄──┐   copies
                               ▼           │
                        ┌──────────────┐   │
                        │              │───┘   keeps 20% of
                        │   RETAILER   │       cover price of
                        │              │       sold copies;
                        │              │       returns unsold
                        └──────────────┘
```

Source: The author

Figure 3-2: How Wholesalers Streamline Single-Copy Distribution

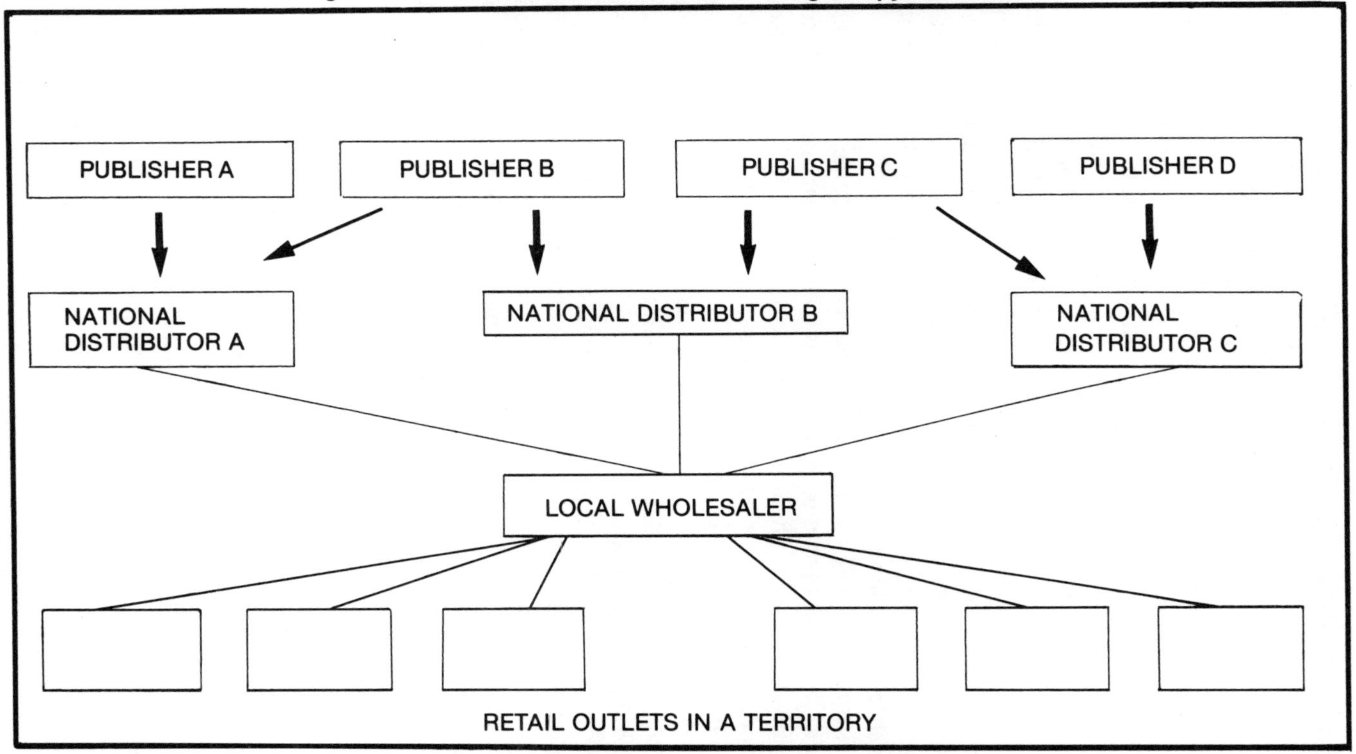

Circulation 33

Source: The author.

The national distributor. Most publishers use the services of a national distributor as an intermediary between themselves and the wholesalers. The distributor serves largely an administrative function and generally does not take physical possession of the magazines. Working with the wholesalers and the publisher, the national distributor plays a major role in establishing the draw, or the number of copies of the magazine that each wholesaler will be sent. This, in turn, establishes the print order for the publisher. The distributor allocates the number of each issue of each title to each of the 500 wholesalers. Magazines are usually sent on a consignment basis to the wholesaler, who is billed for actual copies sold at 60% of the cover price. The national distributor takes a commission of 5% to 12% of the cover price on actual copies sold—the amount is negotiable and depends on the reputation of the publisher, the success of the magazine, the volume of copies of each title handled and the amount of advance the publisher desires.

There are 11 major national distributors of magazines in the United States. Some magazines or groups act as their own national distributors, dealing directly with wholesalers and in some cases with retailers. Among the major national distributors are International Circulation Distributors (ICD), owned by Hearst; Select Magazines, owned by four publishers (Time Inc. and the New York Times Co. withdrew as owners in 1978 and 1979, respectively); Independent News Co.; Curtis Circulation Co.; and Capital Distributing Co.

Wholesalers. Also called independent distributors, there are now about 450 of these businesses around the country. Each operates in a well-defined geographical territory and, through contracts with national distributors or publishers, has a virtual monopoly over periodical (and mass market paperback books) distribution in its area. Using their own fleet of trucks, wholesalers make the rounds of each retail outlet in their area each week, delivering new issues and bringing back outdated ones. By spreading the cost of this delivery network over many different magazines and books, the wholesalers can be very efficient in their coverage and make possible the timely delivery of dated material to the 140,000 retail outlets across the country within a day.

Wholesalers provide weekly statements to retail customers, collect payments for copies sold and credit them for returns, shred unsold copies, then send the publisher or national distributor a summary and a check. Wholesalers thus serve both the retailer and publisher:

- For the publisher, the wholesaler provides rapid retail placement, performs the basic accounting and bookkeeping, and does initial inventorying for each issue. The publisher thus avoids having to deal with tens of thousands of separate customers.

- For the retailer, the wholesaler provides regular deliveries of many publications all at once. The retailer receives a single statement, rather than one from each publisher or even from a dozen national distributors.

Retailers. Estimates of the number of retail outlets for magazines vary from 137,067 (*Folio,* February 1979) to 155,000, including Canada (the *New York Times,* July 27, 1978). According to a compilation by the International Periodical Distributors Association, convenience stores make up the single largest category of retailer (19.5%), while newsstands are only 3.7%. Table 3-6 shows the type and number of outlets. This listing, however, does not tabulate the percentage of magazines sold by each type of outlet, nor does it take into account the breadth of publications carried. Most supermarkets, for example, carry only a dozen or fewer of the major general interest magazines, while drugstores and newsstands are more likely to have a full selection of smaller circulation magazines as well. Special interest and limited audience magazines (see Chapter 6) may be restricted to distribution in perhaps half the total number of outlets.

Table 3-6: Outlets for Consumer Magazines, in the United States, 1978

Type of Outlet	Number	Percent
Total	137,067	100.0%*
Convenience Stores	26,784	19.5
Chain Supermarkets	21,360	15.6
Independent Supermarkets	19,480	14.2
Independent Drugstores	16,045	21.7
Confectionery/Sundry Stores	8,278	6.0
Variety Stores	7,595	5.5
Chain Drugstores	7,539	5.5
Liquor Stores	5,733	4.2
Newsstands	5,027	3.7
Discount Stores	2,804	2.0
Other	16,420	12.0

*May not total to 100% due to rounding.
Source: International Periodical Distributors Association.

Promoting Single-Copy Sales

Few magazines are large enough to support campaigns to promote single-copy sales to the consumer. Most efforts aim at encouraging wholesalers to distribute the publication, and retailers to carry it and give it favorable display. Such promotions are done by direct mail and perhaps an advertisement in a trade publication such as the *CPDA News* (published by the Council for Periodical Distributors Associations). Many magazines offer a retail display allowance (RDA). This is a commission bonus of 10% of the cover price to retailers who apply for the allowance and agree to give the magazine favored positioning. A publisher prefers to have his title displayed on a separate rack or on the first row for a full cover view, rather than buried in the rear with only its title sticking up above the previous row.

In a few cases, mass media advertising has been used to promote sales. Condé Nast's *Self*, launched in 1979, made heavy use of television in spot markets during its introduction. Robert Guccione's *Omni* also used spot TV during its 1978 introduction. Time Inc. makes extensive use of fringe time (early morning, late evening) television, as well as radio, to promote *Time, Discover* and *Money,* although it is primarily seeking subscribers by offering a premium to call a toll-free number to order.

Moreover, all publishers recognize that there may be some residual effect on single-copy sales from the subscription mailings they do. Such promotions indirectly encourage some recipients to buy a few copies on the newsstand or at the supermarket as a sort of "trial purchase," before subscribing. Although there is extensive research on subscriber demographics and on the effectiveness of various mailing pieces and offers, there has been virtually no research on the factors leading individuals to making newsstand purchases.

Levy Cooperative Ad Plan

The Chas. Levy Circulating Co., the country's largest magazine distributor, initiated an innovative cooperative advertising plan with publishers oriented toward single-copy sales in 1978. Levy arranged to promote these publishers' magazines in a four-color full-page advertisement in the Thursday food section of the *Chicago Sun-Times.* Each ad featured six magazines, with a paragraph of copy highlighting the contents of each under a photograph of the cover. In addition, Levy supported the effort by putting display racks with a copy of the ad and the six featured magazines in 300 outlets.

The results have been impressive. The first advertisement displayed *Daytime TV, Rona Barrett's Hollywood, Lady's Circle, New Woman, Vital* and *True Story.* Sales at the stores with the special racks went up 50% for these magazines, while in Chicago generally sales leaped 25% to 30%. The program was expanded to promote 12 magazines over a three-month period, with six titles being featured in an ad every two weeks.

Other titles subsequently joined the program; these include *Life, Bon Appetit, Redbook, Woman's Day, Self, Soap Opera Digest, Apartment Life* and *The Saturday Evening Post*. In its initial stages, each of the magazines experienced increased sales of 3000 to 4000 copies each month. This represented a 17% increase for *Redbook,* but 125% for the smaller *Daytime TV.*

The objective of the Levy program is to make magazine buying a planned purchase, rather than the impulse buy it is generally believed to be. (One estimate is that shoppers at the check-out counter take three seconds to decide whether to purchase a certain periodical.) "When a woman decides on Thursday that she is going to buy a particular brand of cake mix, we think she might be preconditioned to think about buying a magazine," explained Harvey Wasserman of Chas. Levy.

Although the Levy program started operation in October 1978, by mid-1979 there was no evidence that it had been picked up by wholesalers in other areas. It does involve expense on the wholesaler's part, including about $50 for each of the 300 racks. The Chicago ads cost about $10,000 per insertion, with each magazine and Levy contributing one-seventh. Levy estimates that its cost for the first three-month program was $50,000. Nonetheless, the project appears financially rewarding for all parties. If incremental magazine sales bring Levy an average of 20 cents in revenue (the magazines range in price from 49 cents to $1.50), the average monthly increase in sales for the group of 64,000 copies yields $38,400 in gross revenue for the three-month period. Since the initial $50,000 included one-time costs for the racks and other start-up expense, it would appear to be a profitable deal for Levy. For an established magazine like *Ladies' Home Journal,* the added revenue of about $6600 for the three-month period more than covers its share of the advertisements ($4300) and manufacturing costs, while adding inexpensive circulation to sell to advertisers. For a smaller circulation magazine, such as *Daytime TV* the boost in sales may only barely cover advertising cost, but the added circulation can have a significant effect on advertising rates and pages.

Check-Out Counter Clutter

With the revived interest in single-copy sales, the subject of clutter at supermarket check-out counters is on the minds of publishers. About 50% of all single-copy sales comes from supermarkets, and competition for valuable space at the check-out counter has become fierce. The national tabloids, *Woman's Day, Family Circle* and *TV Guide* have been joined by *People* and *Us,* and in some places, the newsweeklies and even *Life.*

In general, supermarkets seek high turnover magazines for the check-out counter. Magazines with a new issue each week therefore get preference over magazines that change less frequently, and those that do not produce the requisite turnover will likely be dropped.

Not all magazines sold in supermarkets, however, are displayed at the check-out counter. The Family Reading Centers, an idea promoted by the wholesalers, places a 16 to 24 foot paperback book and magazine display area in many chain stores. Each has 40 to 50 magazine titles (with some chains banning certain titles); they are reportedly quite profitable for the chains, yielding gross margins of about 28%, well above typical grocery gross margins.

Wholesalers themselves have complaints about the proliferation of newsstand titles. Stan Budner, president of a wholesaler in Wilmington, DE, put much of the blame on "imitator" magazines that ride the coattails of the original. He calculated 162 imitators of *Playboy* and *Penthouse*, 138 car and van magazines and 146 crossword magazines. "Although the coattail riders can make money with a 30% to 35% sale, we need a 60% sale to make a profit," he complained. Budner found that 34 titles out of 2000 produced 50% of his agency's gross profit. It is this explosion of titles, he says, that has driven up the error in posting returns and is causing delays.

Developments in Distribution

Although higher postal and subscription fulfillment costs have encouraged publishers to look to the magazine racks for more sales, many think it is merely the lesser of two evils. Jack Scott, president of Times Mirror Magazines, would just as soon have 100% single-copy sales, but laments that "the newsstand business is not well run. There's no fix on what sales were for three or four months," making it hard to set print runs and paper purchases.

Although widespread use of the Universal Product Code (UPC) may help reduce this problem, there are other criticisms such as one expressed by Ronald Kops, a CBS Publishing vice president: "None of the 15 or so national distributors who take 6% to 8% of the magazine's retail price assumes any financial risk," he reasons. The wholesalers "run monopoly operations and skim 20% of the retail price for transporting the magazines...."

Such complaints have led several companies to establish in-house national distribution services. For example, Time Inc. formed the Time Distribution Service in 1975 to help bolster sales of *People*. After a strong start, circulation of the new periodical had stalled at about 1 million. A field force of nearly 400 part- and full-time employees was sent out to check the racks in the supermarkets, making sure they were being properly serviced and positioned. Circulation then resumed its climb to reach more than 2 million. The field force has since been increased by 30% and services all Time Inc. magazines. In explaining its severance of a long association with its distributors, Select Magazines, the chief of the Time Distribution Service said, "We realized early on that no matter how good a distributor is, if you want something done your way, you've got to do it yourself." The New York Times Co. made a similar move in 1979, withdrawing from its part ownership of Select to use its own Retail Management Marketing Co.

The move of these and other firms, such as Flynt Publications (*Hustler, Chic*), to in-house national distribution has some earmarks of a trend. Some other magazines or groups supplement their dependence on the wholesaling network with a field force. Although Condé Nast believes its distributor, Curtis Circulation Co., has "done a good job," it doubled its field force in 1978. For many publications and groups, however, it is not feasible to consider becoming their own distributors.

There have also been some suggestions that publisher dissatisfaction with the wholesalers might result in them being bypassed more often in favor of direct sales, much as mass market paperback publishers deal increasingly with retailers. This would be particularly ironic in light of the widely acknowledged disarray of distribution in the book industry. To be sure, some publishers already do deal direct to an extent. *Family Circle* and *Woman's Day,* for example, sell 35% to 40% of their copies to the supermarket chains, which then distribute them to their own stores. But even that is a far cry from trying to reach 140,000 outlets. And the independent distributors would not likely be very cooperative should publishers take all the large accounts for themselves and leave them with the small stops.

Anti-Trust Activities

The issue of local wholesaler monopolies and exclusive franchise agreements has not completely escaped the notice of government regulators. ARA Services, a Philadelphia-based vending and catering firm, has assembled a chain of wholesalers, with 22 firms in Milwaukee, Los Angeles and San Francisco, among other cities. However, it has accepted a consent decree from the Federal Trade Commission agreeing not to expand further in this field. In 1979 it also settled a Justice Department suit in connection with wholesalers it had acquired in Kansas City, New Orleans and St. Louis in 1976 without proper FTC approval. ARA paid a

$300,000 civil penalty and had to divest itself of 35% of the business gained in these disputed acquisitions.

Also in 1979, the San Mateo County (CA) district attorney filed suit under state law charging five magazine and book wholesalers in the region with restraint of trade. The suit alleges that the companies created a "virtual monopoly" in the seven-county area with "a price-fixing scheme which forces the public to pay more for magazines."

SUBSCRIPTION CIRCULATION

Although more than half of all magazines are now sold on a single-copy basis, this is more often true of the mass circulation magazines. Most magazines still depend on subscriptions for the bulk of their circulation. As was shown in Table 3-5, subscription rates have been rising even faster than single-copy prices. Some of the newer magazines, such as *Life,* are offering subscriptions at the full single-copy price: the benefit they sell consumers is the convenience of having the magazine delivered to their homes. Some observers of the industry have long questioned why home delivery has been provided at a steep discount, considering this convenience factor.

The answer, of course, is a holdover from Frank Munsey's idea of making the advertiser pay the freight. In the past, having a known level of subscribers was preferred for several reasons:

- Subscriptions were long term and thus could be used as a firm basis for paper and print run orders.

- Because of this known quantity, advertising base rates could be guaranteed with considerable certainty.

- Total circulation could also be fine-tuned to keep circulation growth orderly. If circulation rose too far above the base rate, new subscriptions could be delayed a month, so as not to "give away" too much of a free bonus to advertisers.

- Although new subscriber acquisition might be expensive, renewals could be more profitable at minimal levels (above 50%).

- Delivery through the U.S. Postal Service was subsidized under authorization of Congressional statute in 1879. Single-copy distribution had to pay its own way.

Most of these advantages still hold. What has changed the economics is the five-fold increase in second class postage since 1971, as well as the first and third class rates used for billing and bulk mailings. Furthermore, the substantial increases in paper and printing costs, combined with competition from other media (including direct mail) for advertiser dollars, means that less of the increased costs can be passed on to advertisers and more has to be borne by subscribers. Table 2-6 showed the results.

Publishers thus tend now to pursue subscriptions with greater attention to their existing audience, using mailing lists that provide a population most closely matched to this profile. Computers have aided greatly in the task. One major breakthrough has been in the mailing list industry, where segmentation of lists has been so refined that, as one publishing group president explained, "You can buy a list that has only Catholics with household incomes of over $20,000, with 95% accuracy." The basic units of the lists are ZIP codes. Computer analysis has also provided publishers the wherewithal to track the source of subscriptions: subscription agencies, field sales, specific mailings, bind-in cards, first or other renewal notices, etc. All this aids management in improving the yields in subscription acquisition and in providing analysis such as that in Tables 3-3 and 3-4, only with greater detail.

Some publishers, eyeing long-term trends, have hesitated to cast their magazines' fate with the single-copy strategy because of the energy crunch. Wholesalers, which use a great deal of gasoline in their truck fleets to make deliveries, are affected by both high energy prices and instances of short supply. The result may be that wholesalers will have to cut down on their routes, primarily by first reducing service to the most rural and suburban areas.

On the other hand, the rapidly escalating costs of production and fulfillment have made publishers somewhat concerned about acquiring too great a liability through long-term, fixed revenue subscriptions. Even the value of cash up front and the savings on added subscription promotions do not balance out the uncertainties of paper and postal costs. If these expenses could easily be passed on to the advertisers, they would not be so important. But if advertisers balk at escalating rates, the publisher is stuck with fulfilling long-term subscriptions sold at yesterday's prices.

Subscription Economics

Today, the objective of many consumer magazines is to have subscription revenue pay for all the direct costs of printing and paper, subscription acquisition and fulfillment. This is not always an easy objective to achieve.

Table 3-7 follows the fictional history of a 500,000 piece subscription mailing for *Popular Widget,* a special interest monthly with 350,000 subscriptions, and 50,000 in single-copy sales. With a per copy cover price of $1.25 and a full one-year subscription price of $15.00, the basic introductory subscription discount offer is for $12.00. To keep up circulation, the magazine would have to mail out perhaps 3 or 4 million pieces annually, so the example may be considered just one of several promotions annually.

The cost of the mailing itself may vary considerably, depending on printing and paper expenditure. A four-color broadside piece may drive the price to $350 to $400 per thousand. In the table, a modest two-color brochure, plus letter and return card, is used. The creative/art work is incurred only when a new package is made up.

Based on a 2.5% return (and good payment), the acquisition cost is $13.92 per subscriber, plus entering and billing. Revenue is $12.00. Total acquisition cost is $14.75. The estimated cost of fulfilling those subscriptions is $6.60 for the year, so a total direct cost of $21.35 per subscriber is offset by $12.00 in revenue. These 12,500 subscribers thus resulted in a negative cash flow of $116,875 for the year.

However, the second and subsequent years are different. If 60% of the initial group renews at full price, there is a $51,450 contribution to operations; a 70% third-year renewal (loyal readers by now) yields another $36,015. However, after three years, *Popular Widget* will not have recovered all the expense of the 500,000 piece mailing as well as fulfillment costs. Essentially, subscription sales are at best a break-even operation for consumer magazines of this size. (This example does not take into consideration subscriptions that come in through subscription agents or other sources that substantially reduce the first-year revenue, without affecting fulfillment costs.) Presumably higher postage and paper costs in subsequent years would be met with higher subscription rates.

Postal Rates and Alternative Delivery

Since the Postal Reorganization Act of 1970, magazine publishers (as

Table 3-7: Economics of Subscription Acquisition and Fulfillment

Promotion Mailing per 1000 Pieces		Cost for 500,000 Piece Mailing	
Postage	$104	Mailing	$163,500
Mailing list	35	Creative/art	7,625
Lettershop	18		171,125
Print & paper	170	Business reply postage	
(two color)		for returns	2,875
	$327	Total	$174,000

Table 3-7 continued

First-Year Acquisition Cost
(based on 2.5% return & payment)

Cost per Acquisition	
$174,000 ÷ 12,500 returns	$13.92
Entering Costs per Unit	.40
Billing per Unit	.43
	$14.75
Revenue	
$15.00 regular price with	12.00
$12.00 introductory offer for one year	
Net Loss/acquisition	($ 2.75)*
Less:	
Postage and fulfillment	
$.17/issue x 12	$ 2.04
Print & paper	
$.38/issue x 12	4.56
Total Circulation Loss	($ 9.35) x 12,500 = ($116,875)

Second-Year Cost
(60% renewal rate)

Renewal Mailing Cost per Unit	$ .71
Entering Cost	.40
Billing Cost	.43
	$1.54
Revenue	$15.00
Net gain	$13.46
Less:	
Postage & fulfillment $.17/issue x 12	$ 2.04
Print & paper $.38/issue x 12	4.56
Total Contribution	$ 6.86 x 7500 = $51,450

Third-Year Cost
(70% renewal rate)

Renewal Mailing, Entering, Billing	$ 1.54
Revenue	15.00
	$13.46
Less:	
Postage, print, paper, fulfillment	6.60
Total Contribution	$ 6.86 x 5250 = $36,015
Three-Year Totals	($29,410)

Source: Knowledge Industry Publications, Inc.
*Numbers in ( ) represent losses.

well as direct mail marketers and others) have been fighting a mostly losing battle against rapidly escalating postal rates. Prior to that time, the Postal Service was heavily subsidized out of the general Treasury: 17% to 18% of its total budget. The 1970 law established a quasi-independent Postal Service with a mandate to make operating revenues match expenditures and to make each class of mail pay for itself. In the meantime, federal subsidies were set at a flat rate, rather than a percentage of the postal budget. Moreover, rate increases no longer needed Congressional approval, but could be sanctioned by the Postal Rate Commission. Given the objective of becoming self-sufficient, the Rate Commission has been willing to go along with almost all Postal Service requests for rate increases.

Magazines have naturally been affected by the 150% increase in first class rates between 1971 and 1979. Third class bulk rate, used for vast subscription promotion mailings, has more than doubled. But what affected publishers most dramatically was the 557% increase in the cost of mailing an identical magazine between 1971 and 1979. (See Table 3-8.)

The actual charge for second class postage depends on three variables: the advertising/copy percentages, the distance the issues are being sent and the weight of the magazine; in addition, there is a flat per piece charge of seven cents.

Table 3-8: Cost of Mailing a Magazine, 1971, 1972, 1977, 1979

Date*	Cost (no presort)	Cost (ZIP code presort)
1971	2.3¢	2.3¢
1972	3.48	3.48
1977	7.43	7.43
1979	15.1	13.5
Percentage increase:		
1971-1979	556.5%	487.0%
1977-1979	103.2	81.7

*On or after July 6.
Source: U.S. Postal Service, from rates approved March 10, 1981. Represents 7.6 ounce publication, 60% advertising, to Zone 3 from originating Post Office.

Before the beginning of phased-in rate increases, a 7.6 ounce magazine, 60% advertising and 40% editorial, sent to zone three from the originating post office, cost 2.3 cents. After July 6, 1979, the cost was

15.1 cents. Large circulation magazines can get a discount of 1.6 cents per piece by presorting magazines into five- and three-digit ZIP codes, but only if they occupy one third of a mail sack or weigh at least 20 pounds. Publishers may also do more of the Postal Service's work by sorting to specific carrier routes, earning a further discount. This may be practical for large circulation magazines, but smaller national magazines may not be mailing in sufficient volume to specific ZIP code areas to take significant advantage of the discounts. The impact of the announced nine-digit ZIP code must also be factored into the final rate.

A decision of the Postal Service that split the publishers involved the Red Tag service used by weekly magazines. Traditionally, these time sensitive publications were provided special service to speed them through the system. The Postal Service decided to make such Red Tag service available to *all* magazines, but for a premium. Rates for non-Red Tag service were decreased slightly. This pitted the interests of monthly magazines against the weeklies. Various legal and political barriers delayed the implementation of the rates as scheduled in 1981.

As postal rates have increased, so has the incentive to find other methods of delivery that bypass the Postal Service. As early as the 1950s *The Saturday Evening Post* had experimented with its own delivery routes. But it was not until 1974 that publishers began experimenting in earnest. In that year, *Reader's Digest,* the second largest circulation magazine, began delivering 10,000 copies monthly via private carrier. By the end of 1978 the number was close to 200,000. *Reader's Digest* is committed to alternative delivery: "It is here to stay," declared one executive.

Most magazine publishers felt that until the full rates became effective in July 1979, any effort at private delivery was for the sake of experience, since the Postal Service was still less expensive. Time Inc. experimented with higher priced private delivery in 1978, with about 100,000 copies (2% of subscriptions of *Time*). *Sports Illustrated* was soon added to the experiment. *Newsweek* began similar trials in 1978 with about 30,000 subscribers. On the other hand, Condé Nast claims that none of its attempts at alternative delivery has worked out. "It's very difficult unless you have a large distribution in a limited area," was their finding.

But Meredith Corp.'s *Better Homes and Gardens* found considerable savings in private delivery even before 1979. The magazine said that its private delivery cost in 1978 was 10 cents per copy, compared to 13.6 cents in 1978 and 16.5 cents in 1979 via the Postal Service.

For most publishers of large circulation magazines, however, the break-even for private delivery did not arrive until the 1979 fully phased-in rates became effective.

The private carrier industry is quite young. The National Association of Selective Distributors, Inc., formed in 1977, consists of the early entrants into this field, the largest being southern California's Inland Carriers, Inc. and Sweeney News Service (near Boston). At the beginning of January 1977, the nine member firms served 106 ZIP codes, delivering 174,000 magazines monthly. By June 1979, 13 member firms covered about 450 ZIP codes with 1.2 million copies monthly, encompassing 27 different titles. Altogether, there were more than 40 companies delivering magazines, as well as books and in some cases advertisements. A few daily newspapers have experimented with using their already established carrier networks to deliver magazines as well. *The Louisville Courier-Journal, The Passaic* (NJ) *Herald-News* and *The Boston Globe* are among the papers that have delivered *Time* on a trial basis.

Alternative delivery by private carrier presents added revenue sources for magazine publishers. For example, *Better Homes and Gardens* cooperated in selling local advertising that was tied into national advertising in the magazine. The local ad was delivered with the magazine by private carrier. Part of the added revenue went to the carrier, but the rest went to the publisher, thus reducing the actual cost of delivery from 10 cents to eight cents. There is some doubt if this could be done under Postal Service regulations.

One model of how private carrier delivery would compare to U.S. Postal Service delivery is illustrated in Table 3-9. It assumes that only large volume magazines would be handled by the carrier and that service would be only to the highest density areas. Since private carriers charge exclusively by the piece rather than by weight, heavier magazines save proportionately more than thinner ones. (Those with a higher percentage of advertising also save more, since advertising material is charged at a higher rate than editorial content under Postal Service calculations.) Savings would range from 32% for *Good Housekeeping* to about 9% for *McCall's*. For the group overall, the hypothetical savings would be 24%, or $668.9 million. There may be additional savings in bypassing the mail room and the possibility of new revenue through local advertising inserts.

About 20% of the subscriptions of these magazines in the Washington, D.C. area would still be distributed by the Postal Service. To make the carrier's network economically feasible, however, the model assumes that advertising circulars, books and records would also be distributed, with a volume actually 2.5 times that of the $2.1 million for magazines. Projecting the same model on a national scale, at 1977 prices the private carrier delivery industry would have receipts of about $200 million annually; almost all of this would be lost revenue of the Postal Service. Nationwide, the best estimate is that about 60% of all magazine subscriptions can be privately delivered, with the Post Office handling

Table 3-9: Hypothetical Cost and Savings Using Private Delivery of 13 Magazines in the Washington, D.C. Metropolitan Area

(1) Publication	(2) Washington, D.C., SMSA per Issue Subscription Circulation[a]	(3) Copies Delivered per Month[b] (thousands)	(4) Copies Delivered per Year (thousands)	(5) Copies Privately Delivered per Year[c] (thousands)	(6) Postal Service Rate/Copy[d]	(7) Private Delivery Rate/Copy	(8) Total Cost Postal Serv. (thousands)	(9) Total Cost Private Del. (thousands)	(10) Savings (thousands)
Monthlies:									
Better Homes and Gardens	124,405	124.4	1,492.8	1,194.2	19.9¢	15.0¢	$ 237.6	$ 179.1	$ 58.5
Ebony	52,386	52.4	628.8	503.0	21.2	15.0	106.6	75.5	31.1
Good Housekeeping	56,659	56.7	680.4	544.3	22.0	15.0	119.7	81.6	38.1
Ladies' Home Journal	85,169	85.2	1,022.4	817.9	14.9	12.5	121.9	102.2	19.7
McCall's	95,859	95.9	1,150.8	920.6	16.5	15.0	151.9	138.1	13.8
Reader's Digest	225,467	225.5	2,706.0	2,164.8	11.3	9.0	244.6	194.8	49.8
Redbook	49,922	49.9	598.8	479.0	18.6	15.0	89.1	71.9	17.2
Southern Living	39,608	39.6	475.2	380.2	20.9	15.0	79.5	57.0	22.5
Weeklies:									
Newsweek	72,371	311.2	3,734.4	2,987.5	10.8	8.5	322.6	253.9	68.7
Sports Illustrated	47,726	205.2	2,462.4	1,969.9	12.5	8.5	246.2	167.4	78.8
Time	120,887	519.8	6,237.6	4,990.1	12.2	8.5	608.8	424.2	184.6
TV Guide	69,916	300.6	3,607.2	2,885.8	8.5	7.0	245.3	202.0	43.3
U.S. News & World Report	41,461	178.3	2,139.6	1,711.7	11.0	8.5	188.3	145.5	42.8
Total		2,244.7	26,936.4	21,549.1			$2,762.1	$2,093.2	$668.9

[a] Audit Bureau of Circulation, first six months 1977.
[b] Assumes 4.3 weeks per month.
[c] Assumes private delivery of 80% copies in column 4.
[d] Zones 1 & 2.
Source: Direct testimony of James O. Edwards before Postal Rate Commission (R77-L), October 14, 1977.

Circulation 47

the less efficient small towns and rural routes, as well as the majority of magazines that have a circulation too scattered to make private carrier distribution feasible.

Problems of Private Delivery

There are two possible problems facing private carriers. The first is maintaining a supply of cheap but reliable labor. Clearly, the difference between Postal Service and private delivery charges is largely a reflection of the difference in labor costs. The average postal worker earns more than $20,000 annually. Private carriers, on the other hand, may pay its full-time regional distribution office managers about $15,000 and part-time deliverers the minimum wage, $3.35 hourly in 1981. This low pay also means that it is difficult to attract and hold competent, reliable workers. Moreover, only the Postal Service is, by law, permitted to put mail in mail slots or boxes; thus private carriers must leave magazines in plastic bags on door handles or loose in mail rooms at apartment houses, another obstacle to efficient service. As newspapers have long known, poor delivery service can lose subscribers.

A second problem that publishers and private carriers must face is the response the Postal Service might make to an erosion of its business. United Parcel Service has already skimmed the cream off the parcel business. Current statute gives the Postal Service a monopoly only on first class mail. But a loss of second class revenues (which should be evaluated on an incremental basis, given the vast fixed cost of the postal system) may draw a reaction from the Postal Service. This may result in new services, a Congressional move to reinstitute second class subsidies, or a new statute giving the Postal Service new monopoly powers for other classes of mail. Most publishers would just as soon rely on the mails, other factors being equal. If subsidies are brought back, in recognition of the public service nature of the mails, then the private carriers might find themselves out of favor as quickly as they appeared. Developments in this area, however, depend as much on politics as on economic and marketing decisions.

Advantage for Nonprofit Organizations

The popular image of a nonprofit organization is often that of an impoverished do-gooder. This is sometimes the case. But under the law, not-for-profit organizations need not be unprofitable or worthy. Yet they all share certain benefits from the government. They do not pay income or property taxes. Contributors to them can deduct donations from their income taxes. The major limitation on such organizations is that they cannot distribute earnings to shareholders.

For organizations that publish magazines, these benefits can be a formidable advantage in the competition with for-profit publishers. In most cases, the magazines are genuinely designed for the membership of the organization, such as some of the publications of the Elks, V.F.W. or Boy Scouts. Although these magazines may solicit advertising, their subscription price is generally included in a larger fee for annual membership and the magazine is only one of several tangible benefits for joining.

In other cases, however, the organization actively solicits "membership," with the primary benefit being the publication itself. Two examples are *Smithsonian,* published by Smithsonian Associates, and *National Geographic,* published by the National Geographic Society. Both of these are slick publications that actively seek out general advertising, with rates based on their paid circulation. The organizations do offer some other benefits, but they are mostly window dressing.

Such publications receive sizable government subsidies in one of the largest segments of magazine costs: postal rates. Second class rates are about half those paid by regular businesses, while third class rates, used for solicitation mailings, are 25% lower. Phasing in of higher second class rates has also been extended over a much longer period in the case of nonprofit corporations. Until 1978 the differential, especially in bulk rate, was even greater. In 1976, for example, *National Geographic* mailed about 81 million pieces of third class bulk rate mail at a cost of $3 million. Its competition would have had to pay about $6.2 million. In 1979 *National Geographic* would have paid $4.9 million, compared to $6.8 million for a publisher without nonprofit status.

There are drawbacks to the nonprofit format, such as losing the right to advocate a particular position on pending legislation or to endorse political candidates. Such publications also cannot be sold at a profit for their owners, since the gain would have to stay in the organization. But the top people can pay themselves high salaries and provide other benefits.

Publishers of magazines seeking a profit have a legitimate complaint that such publications as *Smithsonian* or *National Geographic* compete with them for advertising and consumer dollars, as well as limited consumer time. So long as the loophole in the law exists, however, this nonprofit legal framework might be a real alternative for new entrepreneurs. *Ms.* magazine, which started life as a typical for-profit venture, turned itself into a not-for-profit corporation, presumably to take advantage of the lower mailing costs.

LARGEST MAGAZINES

The 100 largest circulation A.B.C. audited magazines account for somewhat more than one half of the per issue aggregate circulation of consumer magazines tabulated in Table 2-3. As seen in Table 3-10, there has been considerable change in position since 1973. Although the two leaders, *TV Guide* and *Reader's Digest,* remain well ahead of the nearest competitors, both *National Geographic* and the tabloid magazine *National Enquirer* have shown substantial growth. The other supermarket-distributed tabloids, *The Star* and *Midnight Globe,* are both newcomers to the list. Also arriving in the top 50 since 1973 are *People, Hustler* and *New Woman. Smithsonian,* the slick socio-cultural magazine, moved from the bottom of the list in 1973 to the 28th spot. The second 50 includes many magazines that did not exist before 1973, among them *Book Digest, Playgirl* and *Us.* Several of the top circulation magazines are listed by the Magazine Publishers Association as consumer magazines. In reality they are association magazines, unavailable on the newsstand. They include *AARP News Bulletin, American Legion,* and *Elks.*

Table 3-10: 100 Largest Circulation A.B.C. Audited Consumer Magazines, 1980

Rank 1963	Rank 1973	Rank 1980		Circulation (thousands)	Percent Single Copy	Percent Subscription
2	1	1	TV Guide	17,982	62%	38%
1	2	2	Reader's Digest	17,899	6	94
13	5	3	National Geographic	10,712	0	100
10	6	4	Better Homes & Gardens	8,053	9	91
9	3	5	Woman's Day	7,748	99	1
5	4	6	Family Circle	7,530	100	0
—	—	7	AARP News Bulletin	6,763	0	100
—	—	8	Modern Maturity	6,749	0	100
3	7	9	McCall's	6,218	12	88
7	8	10	Ladies Home Journal	5,601	17	83
11	10	11	Good Housekeeping	5,291	36	74
—	15	12	National Enquirer	5,051	90	10
22	9	13	Playboy	5,011	67	23
16	12	14	Time	4,359	4	96
12	11	15	Redbook	4,354	19	81
—	14	16	Penthouse	4,331	94	6
—	—	17	The Star	3,509	96	4
23	16	18	Newsweek	2,964	8	92
54	26	19	Cosmopolitan	2,837	97	3
17	17	20	American Legion	2,599	0	100

Circulation 51

Table 3-10 continued

Rank 1963	Rank 1973	Rank 1980		Circulation (thousands)	Percent Single Copy	Percent Subscription
—	—	21	People	2,500	82%	8%
—	—	22	Prevention	2,429	2	98
47	19	23	Sports Illustrated	2,266	4	96
33	21	24	U.S. News & World Report	2,056	4	96
34	25	25	Field & Stream	2,022	8	92
41	30	26	Glamour	1,936	62	38
32	27	27	Popular Science	1,933	14	86
—	100	28	Smithsonian	1,905	0	100
44	32	29	V.F.W Magazine	1,845	0	100
—	—	30	Globe	1,803	98	2
—	49	31	Southern Living	1,783	5	95
39	24	32	Outdoor Life	1,734	11	89
38	29	33	Popular Mechanics	1,677	23	77
28	33	34	Elks Magazine	1,652	0	100
—	44	35	Today's Education	1,652	0	100
38	31	36	Mechanix Illustrated	1,626	13	87
43	35	37	Seventeen	1,553	46	54
21	20	38	Parents	1,516	3	97
36	23	39	Workbasket	1,472	3	97
19	18	40	Boy's Life	1,463	0	100
20	28	41	True Story	1,433	25	75
—	—	42	Hustler	1,421	97	3
63	43	43	Sunset	1,417	9	91
—	—	44	Changing Times	1,408	3	97
—	—	45	Life	1,338	42	58
—	—	46	Organic Gardening	1,336	1	99
58	42	47	Ebony	1,288	18	82
59	55	48	Nation's Business	1,266	0	100
—	—	49	New Woman	1,252	69	31
69	40	50	Sport	1,223	15	85
15	22	51	Farm Journal	1,221	0	100
—	—	52	Bon Appetit	1,190	15	85
—	60	53	Psychology Today	1,171	14	86
40	47	54	House & Garden	1,126	38	62
—	—	55	1,001 Decorating Ideas	1,106	8	92
—	—	56	US Magazine	1,103	67	33
77	86	57	Vogue	1,101	60	40
71	57	58	Mademoiselle	1,097	69	31
76	56	59	'Teen	1,059	29	71
—	—	60	Mother Earth News	1,044	17	83
—	73	61	Family Handyman	1,018	3	97
—	75	62	Golf Digest	1,016	8	92
—	59	63	Discovery	1,005	0	100
—	—	64	Travel & Leisure	957	0	100
68	58	65	Hot Rod	900	37	63

CONSUMER MAGAZINES

Table 3-10 continued

Rank 1963	Rank 1973	Rank 1980		Circulation (thousands)	Percent Single Copy	Percent Subscription
—	—	66	Self	890	47%	53%
52	53	67	House Beautiful	870	34	66
88	78	68	Popular Photography	869	20	80
25	38	69	Junior Scholastic	868	0	100
—	—	70	Omni	858	76	24
31	37	71	Scouting	854	0	100
—	—	72	Yankee	851	10	90
—	—	73	Money	835	13	87
—	—	74	Apartment Life	830	12	88
—	—	75	Decorating & Craft Ideas	829	5	95
87	65	76	Business Week	824	4	96
—	—	77	Michigan Living	815	0	100
—	50	78	Family Health	811	0	100
—	—	79	Book Digest	807	1	99
67	54	80	Co-Ed	802	0	100
26	48	81	Progressive Farmer	800	0	100
—	71	82	Weight Watchers Magazine	793	23	77
53	39	83	Grit	792	57	43
—	—	84	Playgirl	787	80	20
—	81	85	Jet	766	41	59
75	80	86	Motor Trend	754	26	74
—	—	87	Oui	751	82	18
—	91	88	Golf	726	9	91
—	72	89	Car & Driver	721	28	72
99	90	90	Scientific American	713	24	76
—	—	91	Rolling Stone	701	41	59
—	—	92	Eagle	694	0	100
98	79	93	Forbes	694	2	98
—	—	94	Games	691	14	86
30	59	95	Successful Farming	684	0	100
83	84	96	Fortune	676	4	96
—	—	97	Soap Opera Digest	661	66	34
—	—	98	Harper's Bazaar	600	54	46
—	—	99	Workbench	659	6	94
85	88	100	Gourmet	653	26	74
Total - 100 Magazines				228,869	35	65

Source: Magazine Publishers Association tabulation of Audit Bureau of Circulation figures for last half of 1980.

On the other hand, among the missing from 1973 are *American Home,* ranked 13 with 3.4 million circulation (no longer published); *Argosy,* ranked 46, with 1.1 million circulation (publication suspended); *Modern Screen,* 52nd with 906,000 circulation (no longer published); *New Ingenue,* 62nd (no longer published); and *The Saturday Evening Post,* 82nd (lost circulation).

Most of the leading magazines are virtually all single-copy sales (e.g., *Family Circle*) or all subscription (e.g., *National Geographic*). An examination of the list indicates that there are only a handful of magazines that show any true mixture of subscriptions and single-copy: *Good Housekeeping, Playboy, Glamour, Seventeen, Grit, House & Garden, Vogue, Jet* and *Rolling Stone.* Thus, most magazines tend to emphasize one means of distribution over the other, making averages for the "typical" magazine unreliable.

4
Advertising

To most publishers, the business of magazines is that of selling an audience to advertisers. Attracting and holding readers with an editorial product is the essence of magazine publishing. As shown in Chapter 3, circulation revenue alone does not usually support the magazine. It is advertising that carries more than half of the burden and provides the margin for profit.

CPM DIFFERENCES

Chapter 3 also outlined the basic equation for magazine revenue. The advertising page rates for magazines of varying circulation are compared by calculating the cost per thousand (CPM)[1]. Cost per thousand is the great leveler for advertising rates for all media. It is an attempt to look beyond absolute dollar costs to determine the relative cost for reaching a potential audience. Thus, if one magazine has a full-page black-and-white rate of $1250 and another aimed at a similar audience charges $1900, which should the advertiser buy? Naturally, there are many factors, such as the size of the advertising budget, the perceived quality of the two magazines, possible differences in the geographical distribution of their circulation and so on. But all else being nearly equal, CPM can be the telling difference. If the first magazine has a circulation guarantee of 150,000, its CPM is $8.33. The second magazine, assuming a circulation base of 240,000, would therefore be "cheaper" at $7.92. Thus, competing magazines in a particular category (e.g., photography, women's, general audience) must keep their CPMs competitive with the general range of others in the field.

---

[1] CPM is a simple calculation: $\dfrac{\text{page rate}}{\text{base circulation} \div 1000}$

Table 4-1 samples CPMs in several categories. Each CPM figure is based on the guaranteed base rate circulation (which is usually slightly lower than current actual circulation) and the cost of a single insertion of a black-and-white full-page ad. In practice, most advertisers pay lower CPMs, since they receive a large variety of discounts for frequency and volume. Color ads would be higher. But the relationships shown in the table would remain constant.

Table 4-1: Cost per Thousand for Selected Magazines and Categories*

Category/Magazine	Base Rate Circulation (thousands)	Cost of B&W Page	CPM
Photography			
Popular Photography	815	$17,920	$21.99
Modern Photography	600	13,134	21.89
Petersen's Photographic	260	4,160	16.00
American Photography	100	1,700	17.00
Women's			
Woman's Day	8,000	$41,600	$ 5.20
Family Circle	8,350	41,600	4.98
Ladies' Home Journal	6,000	30,670	5.11
Glamour	1,700	10,875	6.40
Good Housekeeping	5,000	31,080	6.22
Playgirl	750	5,888	7.85
Self	300	3,750	12.50
Cosmopolitan	2,150	14,855	6.91
New Woman	900	6,000	6.67
Mademoiselle	800	6,550	8.13
Ms.	500	5,910	11.82
Men's Sophisticates			
Playboy	4,700	$29,540	$ 6.28
Penthouse	4,500	20,700	4.60
Hustler	2,000	9,000	4.50
Gallery	750	3,500	4.67
Newsweeklies			
Time	4,250	$37,665	$ 8.86
Newsweek	2,900	26,600	9.17
U.S. News & World Report	2,000	18,250	9.13
General Interest			
TV Guide	18,300	$51,300	$ 2.80
Reader's Digest	17,750	57,920	3.26

*Based on one-time, nondiscounted rate.
Source: Calculated from circulation and rates reported in *Consumer Magazine and Farm Publication Rates and Data*, Standard Rate & Data Service, September 27, 1978.

Note that the CPMs for special interest photography magazines were the highest of any category included in the table. This is consistent with the general operating principles of such magazines (see Chapter 6). Note, too, that the two more established leaders in the field, *Popular Photography* and *Modern Photography,* may have page rates differing by thousands of dollars, but may charge almost identically per thousand circulation.

General interest magazines aimed at predominately a male or female audience have a different range of CPMs. Among the men's "sophisticate" magazines, as they are now labeled, leader *Playboy* also leads with its ad rates. The newsweeklies also have closely matched rates on a per thousand basis. Their rates tend to be higher than those of the men's and women's magazines, but lower than for the special interest group. Finally, two top circulation magazines, which in many ways must compete with television for general advertisers, offer the lowest CPM rates, although the purchase of a page in either *TV Guide* or *Reader's Digest* is still by far the most expensive in absolute cost.

A magazine does not have total discretion in how it sets its advertising rates. It is easiest for magazines to raise their per page rates when circulation is increasing, thus maintaining a constant CPM. Advertisers and ad agencies have less to grumble about, while the magazine is able to add to revenue. In the absence of circulation increases, advertising revenue can be increased by adding more advertising pages or by upping the page rate through an increase in the CPM. In some cases, publishers must lower their guaranteed circulation, which leaves similar options: reduce the page rate and keep CPM constant or maintain the page rate, meaning a higher and possibly less competitive CPM.

Why would any advertiser spend money in a high CPM magazine? When an advertiser can pay $2.80 per thousand in *TV Guide,* why spend $32.13 per thousand for *Art in America*? The answer is: the quality of the audience. A dealer announcing an auction of art masterpieces would be wasting money chasing after the mass audience of *TV Guide* (even if the dealer did have the $51,000 it costs for a single page). But subscribers to *Art in America* have, by their very act of purchasing the magazine (at $20.00 for six issues), put themselves in a select and highly desirable category for the dealer. With a circulation of 45,000, the magazine reaches a high quality audience of possible customers at a cost of $1425 per page.

Cost per Potential Customer

The better a magazine's audience appears to match the market for a particular product or service, the more an advertiser should be willing to pay for the audience. Similarly, direct mail marketers are willing to pay $250 or more per thousand because they are able to select mailing lists that give them a relatively high percentage of positive responses (often, 3% to 4% is high, but it can be 10% or more in some cases, depending on several factors). The key is the cost per potential customer. The art dealer might actually reach fewer potential customers among *TV Guide*'s 18 million than among *Art in America*'s 45,000. Thus, publishers can offer many advertisers less waste in circulation by providing homogeneous audiences in three ways:

- Special interest magazines. These exist to provide readers with information about a specific topic, such as cooking, skin diving or backpacking. Because the audience is specialized, the magazine can charge a premium over general interest magazine rates.

- Demographics. Some magazines are geared to reach an audience with particular characteristics by sex, age, occupation, income, etc. In some cases, large circulation magazines offer special demographic edition breakouts from the total circulation. Executive *Newsweek,* for example, offers separate advertising pages that are bound only in copies for about 500,000 subscribers with personal incomes of at least $20,000. *Fortune* has a financial edition for subscribers whose business involves money management and who would be potential customers for specialized advertisers, such as high-priced financial newsletters or financial calculators.

The special demographic editions also charge a premium over full-run CPMs. In part this reflects a higher production cost to the publisher. But in large measure it merely reflects the value of added service to the advertiser. A full-page ad in Executive *Newsweek* at $6225 in 1978 was one-fourth the full-run rate, but for only 17% of the base circulation. The CPM for the more defined audience was $12.45 compared to $9.17 for the full run. Such editions are only possible in a subscription magazine, where subscriber information can be obtained.

- Regional editions. Most large circulation magazines also offer a variety of regional editions. Meredith's *Better Homes and Gardens* offers more than 149 separate editions, distributed to specific states and cities. Here again, CPMs are higher than full run, but the lower page cost gives local and regional advertisers the incentive to use a prestigious national magazine. The city and regional magazines (e.g., *Philadelphia, Texas Monthly, Washing-*

tonian) originally developed to provide an upscale audience for local advertisers. But since readers of these magazines have impressive demographics (household incomes over $25,000, college educated, young, etc.), national advertisers have come to use them in place of or in addition to zoned editions of national magazines. A marketing executive at Volvo, for example, said that the company uses city magazines "because our sales are heavily concentrated in a limited number of large metropolitan markets. . . . Our product has a very upscale image associated with the lifestyle of a city magazine reader. . . ." For this reason, city magazines are in competition for these advertisers more with national magazines than with newspapers, which are their competition for strictly local advertisers.

The cost per thousand for the city magazines is relatively high: at $14.33 *Chicago* claimed to be at the bottom of the scale. But these CPMs still might be less than those of a zoned edition of a national magazine. *Cleveland* magazine had a $19.83 CPM, compared to *Time*'s local edition at $24.60 or *Newsweek* at $22.23. Moreover, to offer even more attractive rates, several city magazine networks have been put together. Metro Magazines sells national advertising for 10 city magazines and offers a discount for running an ad in any five.

CPM and Circulation Size

A magazine that expects to appeal to a broad audience and thus to mass marketers tends to have a relatively low CPM. Small circulation magazines must charge proportionately more for their pages not only because they are often offering a more efficient audience but because the economics of publishing dictates many of the same first-copy costs as for a mass audience magazine. Because these fixed costs are a relatively higher percentage of their operating costs, limited print order magazines do not get the economies of scale of their bigger circulation cousins.

Moreover, circulation increases cannot always be passed on to the advertisers in the form of higher page rates, particularly in the case of highly specialized magazines. For example, a magazine about model railroads may depend on many relatively small businesses for a large proportion of its advertising. With a small circulation, even a hefty CPM might mean an effective page rate of $1600, and an advertiser could purchase a page each month with a $20,000 ad budget. If the publisher tried to broaden the magazine's appeal (to other types of model builders, for instance), and the circulation doubled, the original advertisers might not have the resources to pay the additional dollars, even if the CPM remained constant.

The relationship between circulation size and CPM is examined in Table 4-2. In a sample of 57 magazines listed in Standard Rate & Data Service *Consumer Magazine and Farm Publication Rates and Data,* there is a clear inverse relationship between size and CPM. For individual magazines, of course, there is a considerable range, based on such previously discussed factors as competitive category of the magazine and homogeneity of the audience.

Table 4-2: Relationship Between Cost per Thousand and Circulation Size

Circulation Size	No. of Magazines	B&W Page CPM	Range
Under 100,000	13	$14.89	$4.50–$28.37
100,000–249,999	12	12.18	4.86– 22.57
250,000–499,999	8	10.93	2.38– 26.66
500,000–999,999	7	9.77	4.39– 22.89
1 million–2 million	6	7.45	2.50– 11.90
Over 2 million	11	6.99	3.49– 12.69
Total	57		

*Correlation coefficient r = −.76
Source: Calculated from sample of consumer magazines in Standard Rate & Data Service, *Consumer Magazine and Farm Publication Rates and Data,* November 24, 1978.

Rate Trends

After more than a decade of relatively constant CPMs for the leading magazines, page rates and the CPM index took unusually large one-year jumps in 1975 (see Table 4-3). That year saw a national recession and, concurrently, a downturn in both advertising pages and circulation for magazines. To keep revenues up, many publishers responded by raising page rates, hence CPMs. After a year of uncertain recovery in 1976, the boom in magazines was on, as was the resumption of steeper cost increases; publishers responded to the strong market with page rate increments that far outstripped circulation increases. (The 50 leading magazines actually lost some circulation.) The result was a 35% increase in CPMs between 1973 and 1978 and an almost corresponding rise in page rates. In the next two years, CPMs jumped 21%, as circulation of the largest magazines remained constant.

Advertising

Table 4-3: Trends in Magazine Advertising Rates and CPMs Selected Years, 1961-1980

Year	Combined Circulation (millions)	Black & White Page Cost Index (1970 = 100)	Black & White CPM	Black & White CPM Index
1961	129.6	75	$4.03	93
1965	147.1	80	4.05	94
1970	160.8	100	4.33	100
1971	159.1	100	4.35	100
1972	155.7	98	4.36	101
1973	157.0	98	4.33	100
1974	159.0	103	4.49	104
1975	155.7	108	4.85	112
1976	156.8	111	4.94	114
1977	155.1	119	5.32	123
1978	155.0	131	5.86	135
1979	155.0	142	6.37	147
1980	155.0	157	7.09	164

Source: Calculated from data supplied by Magazine Publishers Association for 50 leading magazines in advertising revenue each year. Cost of four-color pages are ±1% of Black & White index.

Magazine Rates Compared to Other Media

One reason—perhaps the main reason—that consumer magazine advertising was so strong in the late 1970s was its cost relative to other mass media, especially television. As shown in Table 4-4, magazine unit prices had the lowest increase of any of the mass media. Network television,

Table 4-4: Media Cost Index, Unit of Advertising, 1970-1981

	1970	1974	1975	1976	1977	1978	1980	1981
Magazines	109	115	122	127	136	150	183	198
Network TV	113	151	160	189	223	250	302	330
Spot TV	105	135	145	181	195	207	255	283
Newspapers	115	140	160	176	192	209	249	274
Network Radio	101	106	112	128	147	165	214	238
Spot Radio	107	119	125	135	146	155	192	211
Outdoor	125	166	178	192	207	221	275	303
Composite	111	136	149	168	185	202	244	268

(1967 = 100)

Source: Reprinted with permission from the September 25, 1978 and November 9, 1981 issues of *Advertising Age*. Copyright 1978 and 1981 by Crain Communications, Inc.

which competes for many of the same advertisers as the large circulation general interest and women's magazines, had increased rates 192% in the period from 1970 to 1981, compared to 68% for all magazines.

Even on a cost per thousand basis, network rates increased at nearly twice the rate of magazines (see Table 4-5). Only radio had a lower CPM rise than magazines. Table 4-6 looks at the share of national advertising revenue of television, magazines and newspapers. While the television share flattened out and the newspaper share declined, the magazine share rose between 1975 and 1980. This coincided with increases of 83% for network television CPMs, 69% for spot TV and 53% for newspapers, compared to 36% for magazines. Thus, when television costs rose substantially, advertisers put any additional advertising dollars into magazines as the closest apparent substitute. Magazines (like newspapers) have the additional advantage over broadcasting of being able to add more space as greater volume demands. Broadcasters are limited to a fixed number of commercial messages and once these are sold out, additional revenue is possible only by rate increases.

Table 4-5: Media Cost Index, Cost per Thousand, 1970-1981

	1970	1974	(1967 = 100) 1975	1976	1977	1978	1980	1981
Magazines	106	113	120	125	132	143	173	185
Network TV	108	120	126	149	174	194	231	252
Spot TV	99	112	119	147	157	166	201	221
Newspapers	115	135	154	169	183	197	235	258
Network Radio	96	94	98	111	127	141	178	197
Spot Radio	102	108	114	122	130	136	164	179
Outdoor	117	142	151	161	173	183	222	242
Composite	109	124	136	152	166	178	212	234

Source: Reprinted with permission from the September 25, 1978 and November 9, 1981 issues of *Advertising Age*. Copyright 1978 and 1981 by Crain Communications, Inc.

Table 4-6: Major Media Shares of National Ad Revenue

Type of Media	1975	1976	1977	1978	1979	1980
Network TV	34.9%	34.4%	36.4%	35.8%	36.8%	36.7%
Spot TV	24.5	25.9	23.2	23.8	23.0	23.4
TV Subtotal	59.4	60.3	59.6	59.6	59.8	60.1
Magazines	22.1	21.6	22.7	23.4	23.5	23.2
Newspapers	18.5	18.1	17.7	17.0	16.7	16.8
Total	100.0%	100.0%	100.0%	100.0%	100.0%	100.0%

Source: Reprinted with permission from the September 25, 1978 and February 16, 1981 issues of *Advertising Age*. Copyright 1978 and 1981 by Crain Communications, Inc.

COMBINING ADVERTISING PAGES AND CIRCULATION

As indicated in the discussion of Tables 3-3 and 3-4 in Chapter 3, marginal revenue from various alternatives for raising circulation is only part of the picture. For as circulation increases, at any constant level of advertising pages and cost per thousand, the price per page can be increased, within limits. Table 4-7 builds on the simplified example of Tables 3-3 and 3-4. It is an incremental analysis, again presuming that this magazine, *Popular Widget*, starts with a base of 400,000 single-copy and 400,000 subscription circulation. In the coming year it is expecting to run 480 pages of advertising at an effective cost per thousand of $8.00 (after various agency, frequency and volume discounts).

Solely on the basis of circulation revenue, it was seen that increasing the draw to 600,000, yielding sales of 456,000, was the optimal level for single-copy sales, while a mailing of nearly 1 million pieces to add 30,000 circulation was most efficient for the subscription strategy. However, Table 4-7 shows that when the effect of a higher page rate is factored in,

Table 4-7: Effect of Increased Circulation on Total Revenue, at Constant CPM and Pages

$8.00 CPM (Net), 480 Ad Pages for Year

From Single Copy Sales

Guaranteed Circulation Base	Average Page Rate	Ad Revenue	Net Circulation Revenue	Total Revenue
400,000	$3200	$1,536,000	$125,000	$1,661,000
429,000	3432	1,647,360	129,250	1,776,610
456,000	3648	1,751,040	132,000	1,883,040
474,500	3796	1,822,080	128,000	1,950,080
480,000	**3840**	**1,843,200**	**115,000**	**1,958,200***
483,000	3864	1,854,720	99,250	1,953,970

From Subscription Promotion

Guaranteed Circulation Base	Average Page Rate	Ad Revenue	Net Subscription Revenue	Total Revenue
420,000	$3360	$1,612,800	$4,925,000	$6,537,800
430,000	3440	1,651,200	4,972,000	6,623,200
440,000	**3520**	**1,689,600**	**4,960,000**	**6,649,600***
450,000	3600	1,728,000	4,900,000	6,628,000
460,000	3680	1,766,400	4,720,000	6,486,400
470,000	3760	1,804,800	4,240,000	6,044,800

*Point of approximate revenue maximization.
Source: Knowledge Industry Publications, Inc.

revenue continues to increase for single-copy sales up to a circulation of 480,000 (which requires a draw of 700,000). Although advertising revenue continues to increase at the next highest base rate, it is offset by a steeper decline in net circulation revenue.

Similarly, for subscription sales, revenue is maximized at the 440,000 circulation base rate when incremental advertising dollars are added in, rather than at 430,000 as previously indicated. In both examples, however, it is clear that even with higher page rates, there is a limit to how much additional circulation costs can be offset by marginal advertising revenue.[2]

LEADING MAGAZINE ADVERTISERS AND CATEGORIES

Mass consumption commodities are the leading products advertised in magazines. Food, toiletries and cosmetics, automobiles, beer and liquor, and tobacco products are among the most advertised goods.

The firms that spent the most money on magazine advertising in 1980 are listed in Table 4-8. They are led by the cigarette manufacturers, banned since the early 1970s from putting their advertising dollars in the favored broadcast media. The top 10 include R.J. Reynolds (1), Philip Morris (2), and American Brands (10). Procter & Gamble, although by far the most prolific spender on advertising overall, stresses television for its many packaged goods, devoting only 6% (though still $37 million) to consumer magazines. Seagram Distillers Co. has dramatically increased its magazine expenditures. Although ranked 30 in total media expenditures, it was 3rd in magazines in 1980.

Although the giant companies listed in Table 4-8 spent the most money, they are not equally important to all magazines. For the most part, these advertisers are trying to reach a mass audience and thus advertise in large circulation, general interest magazines, mostly in the top 50 (see Table 3-10). Some products, such as certain liquors or automobiles, might also be advertised in limited audience "class" or upscale magazines, such as the *New Yorker* or *Harper's*. Except for isolated

---

[2]This example has considered editorial, advertising sales and general overhead as fixed costs. Within a modest circulation range and magazine size, these would not change much. Clearly, as the magazine grew substantially, some adjustments would be made in these areas. The example has also equated actual circulation with the guaranteed base. In most cases, the guaranteed base would be set somewhat lower than current circulation.

Table 4-8: Leading National Magazine Advertisers 1979, 1980

Rank	Advertiser	Expenditures 1980	1979
1	R. J. Reynolds Industries	$118,530,200	$114,869,300
2	Philip Morris Inc.	79,326,700	64,650,800
3	Seagram Co. Ltd.	70,624,500	84,877,100
4	General Motors Corp.	55,478,600	67,551,000
5	Loews Corp.	38,210,100	35,745,100
6	Procter & Gamble	37,162,300	40,640,400
7	Ford Motor Co.	35,918,500	31,042,100
8	Time Inc.	35,611,800	27,243,100
9	American Telephone & Telegraph	34,521,100	25,287,200
10	American Brands	34,233,900	31,399,300
11	General Foods Corp.	34,170,100	41,241,000
12	B.A.T. Industries	32,823,900	36,081,400
13	Sears, Roebuck & Co.	32,057,700	13,819,600
14	CBS	29,833,200	28,532,900
15	Dart & Kraft Inc.	27,538,200	21,428,100
16	RCA Corp.	24,176,800	21,773,200
17	Volkswagen	21,708,600	13,275,300
18	Du Pont	21,701,600	16,615,300
19	Bristol-Myers Co.	18,386,700	19,849,200
20	Johnson & Johnson	18,359,700	15,901,500
21	American Broadcasting Co.	18,030,400	16,174,900
22	Hiram Walker-Consumers Home Ltd.	17,572,400	16,806,600
23	U.S. Government	17,571,000	18,788,300
24	Norton Simon Inc.	17,278,100	14,737,600
25	Heublein Inc.	16,460,200	14,861,600

Source: *Advertising Age*, September 10, 1981, based on data from Leading National Advertisers. Farm publications not included.

products, the highly defined, special interest magazine must depend on advertising more directly related to the editorial content of the magazine, i.e., cameras and related equipment in photography magazines, ski equipment and resorts in skiing magazines, etc. Thus, these publishers have their own leading advertisers and product categories. The 100 largest national advertisers accounted for only 48% of magazine revenue from *all* national advertisers. This contrasts with 62% for television, 49% for radio and 35% for newspapers.

Although consumer magazines enjoy prosperous times between the recessions, not all types of magazine fare equally well. For example, Table 4-9 summarizes the advertising page totals for 1974 to 1978 in some categories that report their totals to *Advertising Age*. Since the number of reporting magazines changes over the years, average pages per reporting magazine as well as absolute totals for all magazines in a category are calculated. Women's, fashion and city/regional magazines are among the groups that have performed the best. Business magazines were also solid gainers: the reason for the slight drop in the average was the addition of five quite small magazines to the *Advertising Age* list during the period. For the five magazines included in both 1974 and 1978, the average number of pages increased 34.8%. On the other hand, movie/romance magazines experienced a nearly steady decline during the period. Automotive magazines, some of which were included in the "other special interest" category until 1975, also showed strong gains from the low year of 1975.

In 1979 and 1980, women's and fashion magazines continued to gain pages. The "home" magazines, such as *Better Homes & Gardens*, increased to 17,959 pages in 1980, a jump of 35% from 1978. Movie and romance magazine pages continued their decline, however. Advertising pages in the automotive magazines fell 18% between 1978 and 1980, reflecting the general difficulties of the automobile industry in those years.

Magazine Networks

Many publishers of special interest magazines have created "networks" in an effort to broaden their advertising bases. They offer a package deal that combines some or all of the group's magazines for a single rate. This gives advertisers of mass consumption products or services the equivalent reach of a mass circulation magazine at a competitive CPM.

Special interest publisher Ziff-Davis, for example, charged a CPM of $29.27 for a one-time four-color page in *Popular Photography*, circulation rate base of 815,000 (1978). Nikon might consider that an acceptable price for reaching an upscale amateur photography buff audience, but Winston cigarettes could reach those people better in other ways. The Ziff-Davis network, however, which includes *Flying, Stereo Review, Car & Driver, Skiing, Cycle* and *Boating* (but not *Modern Bride* and *Psychology Today*), offered a circulation guarantee of 3.6 million and a combined CPM for a four-color page of $14.36. Petersen Publishing Co. and Times Mirror are among the special interest publishers offering magazine combination rates.

It is also common for group publishers to offer additional discounts for running advertisements in several publications. East/West Networks combines many of its in-flight magazines into a single buy. Condé Nast and Hearst also offer "corporate buys." An independent firm, Media Networks, sells packages of regional and local editions of mass circulation magazines, such as *Time, Newsweek, Sports Illustrated* and *U.S.*

Table 4-9: Advertising Pages by Selected Category, 1974-1978

Magazine Category	Pages 1978	Pages 1976	Pages 1974	% Change 1974-1978	Average Pages per Magazine in Each Category 1978	1976	1974	% Change 1974-1978
Women's	20,852	18,791	16,287	28.0%	906.6	783.0	740.3	22.5%
Fashion	6,872	5,466	4,700	46.2	1374.4	1366.5	1175.0	17.0
Home	13,342	11,585	9,954	34.0	580.1	643.6	663.6	-12.6
City/Regional	29,808	18,490	10,370	187.4	876.7	770.4	691.3	26.8
Movie/Romance	9,121	9,367	12,089	-24.6	337.8	360.3	431.8	-21.8
Automotive	13,958	11,596	N.R.	46.5[a]	634.4	504.2	N.R.	39.9[a]
Outdoor & Sports	14,227	11,592	14,321	-0.7	490.6	504.0	447.5	9.6
Business	16,382	9,128	8,952	83.0	1489.3	1304.0	1492.0	-0.2
Newsweeklies	11,363	9,854	11,113	2.2	2840.9	2463.5	2778.3	2.2
Other General Interest[b]	28,255	24,953	21,260	32.9	504.5	366.9	462.2	9.2
Other Special Interest	13,818	11,682	19,377	-28.7	812.8	730.1	807.4	0.7

N.R. not reported separately. Some automotive magazines included in "Other Special Interest."

[a]. 1975-1978.

[b]. Includes monthly, bimonthly, quarterly frequency publications.

Source: Reprinted with permission from *Advertising Age*, 3rd or 4th issue in December each year, except for Business and Newsweeklies, reported in 3rd or 4th issue of January of following year. Copyright by Crain Communications, Inc. General and Special Interest categories calculated by the author.

News & World Report, at rates lower than those an individual advertiser could buy, separately in the same zoned editions of each of these magazines.

EFFECTIVENESS OF MAGAZINE ADVERTISING

Strengths and Weaknesses

Despite the strong attraction that television holds for advertisers of mass consumption goods and services, magazines have improved their market share of advertising dollars since 1975. This is partly because most of the time available for commercials on networks, and many local stations, has been sold, and broadcasters are unable to add more. Also, as was shown in Table 4-4, the cost of television time has increased faster than that of any other mass medium.

Magazines, however, have some inherent advantages that remain attractive to advertisers under any circumstance:

- Magazines are purchased, either by issue or by subscription. It is reasonable to assume that purchasers care enough about the magazine to open it and read it. One criticism of controlled-circulation (free) business publications is that it is hard for advertisers to gauge how much recipients really care about the magazine. The same is true with broadcast media, which are free after the initial outlay for the receiver.

- As with other print media, the magazine reader can control his exposure to both the editorial content and the advertising. Advertisers can provide extensive copy to explain their product or why readers should buy/use it, and the ad can be referred to at the convenience of the reader. Of course, this also means the page can be flipped at will, and the ad ignored.

- Exposure to a single ad in a given issue may be repeated several times. Studies confirm that an average issue is picked up three, four or more times by a single reader. Newspapers have a much shorter life span and are typically gone through only once.

- Advertisers know they get a bonus of pass-along readership. Although CPMs are based on circulation, the total readership per copy is some multiple of actual circulation. (This will be discussed in Chapter 5.)

- Advertisers can use magazines to pinpoint very specific audiences. With the exception of direct mail, no other medium offers advertisers the ability to reach an audience with a high identifiable proportion of potential customers, often at a very minimal cost.

- Magazines are less subject to the supply and demand pressures that have allowed television networks and stations to push up their rates in a period of strong demand. It is relatively easy for a publisher to meet advertiser demand by adding extra pages to meet advertiser needs.

There are also drawbacks to magazine advertising from the advertiser's point of view:

- No print medium can offer the action and realism provided by television and, to a lesser extent, radio. Television can offer demonstrations of products in use and has greater creative flexibility.

- Magazines are generally less timely than other media. *Newsweek* has a national black-and-white page closing three weeks prior to publication. The deadline is five weeks for regional editions, and seven weeks for four-color ads. A monthly, such as Lane Publishing Co.'s *Sunset,* typically requests about two months before issue date, even earlier if there is any composition or art work required. Thus, it is difficult to use magazines to reflect quick changes in marketing strategy, price or competitor challenges.

Consumer Attentiveness to Advertising

One approach to determining a medium's effectiveness is to learn the perceptions of its targets, in this case consumers. Individuals do not always understand what makes them buy a product or change an opinion: it is often thought to be the subtle and long-term effect of many sources, including interpersonal contacts and unsponsored information (e.g., a new report), as well as advertising. Nonetheless, asking consumers to provide their conscious thoughts on the subject is useful to a study of consumer response.

Research has suggested that one of the conditions contributing to the effectiveness of a persuasive message is its source. Another may be its environment. That is, a message from a source that is viewed as being credible and trustworthy is more likely to produce the desired behavior than a message from one that is not. The physical environment of the ad may be related to the consumer's perception of credibility. For example, an ad for a high-priced single lens reflex camera in a photography magazine, surrounded by authoritative copy about the field, may be more effective than an ad for the same camera seen on the TV screen in the middle of a situation comedy.

Three studies conducted by the Opinion Research Corporation for the Magazine Publishers Association confirm that magazines are considered an important source of information and ideas.[3] The 1979 *Study of Media Involvement* found that 55% of all men and 62% of all women prefer magazines to television as an advertising medium, reflecting an increase over the 1975 results. When respondents were divided according to their levels of exposure to magazines and television, 73% of those who fell in the heavy magazine/heavy television category preferred magazines. In addition, respondents in all three studies said that advertising in magazines was more likely to make them buy products than that in television, and that magazine advertising more often kept them posted on new products. Although both media rated about the same in the attentiveness respondents said they give advertising, among upscale men and women, attentiveness to magazines increased and attentiveness to television advertising decreased.

The issue of consumer attentiveness was particularly timely in 1979 because the boom in ad pages had raised the question of "clutter"—having so many ads that individual ones get lost in the shuffle. In addition, consumers are learning increasingly to screen out commercial messages. The issue has been most applicable to television, as the old 60-second commercials give way to twice as many 30-second spots, and, as prices increased further, to 20- and 10-second ones. Although magazines are able to expand their publications and add editorial copy, many magazines have been growing unwieldy and advertisers see their messages getting buried. Thickness and advertiser concern were ingredients in the decision of CBS and the New York Times Co. to increase frequency of their women's supermarket magazines and for Time Inc. to change *Fortune,* sometimes running hundreds of pages as a monthly, into a biweekly.

Advertising Research

The only real test of any advertising effectiveness is whether the con-

---

[3] The studies were done in May 1972, March/April 1975 and January/February 1979. Interviews were conducted with more than 2000 adults, and results published for the 1979 survey included trend information.

sumer does what the advertisement wants him or her to do: buy a product, change an opinion, call a telephone number, etc. Since it is very difficult to isolate the outcome for a given advertisement, substitute criteria of advertising effectiveness are used: the degree to which people remember seeing the ad and what, if anything, they recall from it. Researchers can measure whether either of these two characteristics change under varying conditions, such as number of exposures, length or size of the commercial message, the type of medium used, the degree of color, layout, etc.

A few advertisements are designed to test specific response. They include print ads with coupons, an address to write to for something, a telephone number to call or a special request to make that only readers or viewers would know about ("Say that you saw this in *XYZ* and we'll give you a free gift.") Most of the time, however, large advertisers are left to determine the results of an integrated advertising campaign by its effect on sales in general, leaving them with the lament attributed to merchant John Wanamaker: "I know half of what we spend on advertising is wasted; the only trouble is, I don't know *which* half."

Several studies have attempted to measure advertising effectiveness in magazines, using brand awareness or recall as the measure of effect. The studies took into account the effect of other variables, such as age, household income, education, product utilization, exposure to other brands and other media. Those mentioned here, however, are among those promoted by the magazine industry to show its best side. The following studies are described in order to be suggestive, rather than as an exhaustive review of the research literature.

In one study completed in 1971, three samples of product users were created for each of four brands surveyed. The samples were identical in all measured areas except exposure to the brands' magazine advertising. The level of brand awareness among the sample that had no exposure to the advertising was assigned 100 and served as a control group. As seen in Table 4-10, increased exposure to the magazine ads resulted in added brand awareness, with heavy exposure more effective than light or medium exposure. Although this experiment indicated that increased brand exposure added to awareness, it cannot substantiate a claim that magazines are the best or worst medium, unless the experiment is repeated with other media as the variable.

However, another study, sponsored by advertising agency Kenyon & Eckhardt, did compare four sample groups on unaided brand recall (defined as naming the advertised brand first when asked to name a brand in that product category). One had been unexposed to the product's ad campaign. A second was exposed to magazine ads only, a third to television ads only and the fourth to both TV and magazines. Table

Table 4-10: Brand Awareness as Result of Advertising Exposure

Survey Brand	None	Light/Medium	Heavy
Men:			
gasoline "A"	100	135	156
beer "A"	100	126	206
Women:			
lipstick "A"	100	114	130
shampoo "A"	100	127	136
Average Four Brands	100	126	157

(Exposure to Brand's Magazine Advertising)

Source: "Isolating and Measuring the Effects of Magazine Advertising," Magazine Publishers Association, Inc. (no date).

4-11 summarizes the results. Respondents who had seen both TV and magazine ads had three times the recall as those with no exposure. Television or magazine exposure alone had lesser but about equal effects.

Table 4-11: Brand Awareness in Unaided Recall

Exposure to Ad Campaign	Advertised Brand Named First
Unexposed	7%
Magazines Only	11
Television Only	12
Both Magazines and Television	21

Source: Magazine Publishers Association, prepared by Kenyon & Eckhardt, New York, 1968.

The approximate parity between television and magazines as an advertising medium for mass consumer goods was further validated by five studies involving 7000 interviews in 1969-1970. The studies measured recall within 24 hours of exposure to 26 magazine and 29 television advertisements for 23 different brands. In the five studies, the recall scores ranged from a low of 2% or 3% to a high of 42%. But overall, as summarized in Table 4-12, the averages for both media were quite similar.

Table 4-12: Summary of Five Studies of Advertising Recall

Measure	Magazine Ads	Television Ads
Mean Recall	14%	12%
Median Recall	12	8

Source: Magazine Publishers Association, prepared by Grudin/Appel/Haley, 1969-1970.

The difference in medians, however, shows more variation, indicating a less evenly distributed pattern among the television figures.

The first step to an effective print advertisement is assuring that the reader sees it. A 1978 study by Audits & Surveys for three newsweeklies found that 85% of advertising pages were at least turned to by readers of those issues. This is consistent with a similar finding in a study of the old *Look* magazine in 1959.

Magazine publishers also claimed that specific ads were being read at least as much in 1978 as in 1974, according to scores on the Starch Adnorms report for four-color ads noted by men and women.[4] On a scale of 100 for the base year of 1974, the men rated a 99 in 1978 (the same as in 1976, down from 100 in 1977) and women were up to 101 (from a low of 97 in 1975). These slight differences are within the realm of statistical error.

Finally, there is some evidence that advertising in special interest magazines (those with single-focus, "active" information as defined in Chapter 6) is noted more than advertising in mass circulation magazines, where fewer ads are related to the editorial content of the publication. Table 4-13 has separated those magazines with a Starch Adnorms "associated" score of at least 10% above the average for the entire sample of 63 and those with scores at least 10% below the average. In this case, the highest "associated" score, about one third greater than average, was in the most specialized magazine in the survey, *Hot Rod*. The lowest score, about 29% below average, was for *Signature*, at the time sent free to all Diner's Club card holders. On the whole, magazines that scored above average were special interest ones, such as the three outdoor men's, the shelter and women's magazines. Those that scored the lowest were almost exclusively mass circulation magazines. This would indicate that magazines that promote higher reader involvement, where the advertisements are often an extension of the editorial subject of the magazines, sustain greater reader interest in advertising copy.

The Seagram Case

Magazine advertising people have been very pleased with the decision made in 1977 by Seagram Distillers Co. to double its advertising budget

---

[4]Daniel Starch & Staff, Inc., Adnorms reports on the degree to which individual advertisements in actual magazine issues have been recalled by readers. The results include the percentage of those interviewed who "noted" the ad—remember seeing it; "associated"—can recall one or two ideas presented in the ad; or "read most"—read more than 50% of the ad.

Table 4-13: Advertising Readership Averages of Magazines Above and Below Total Survey Norms* for "Associated" Intensity

"Associated" Percentage of 37 or Above	"Associated" Percentage of 30 or Below
Better Homes and Gardens Home Improvement	Dun's
Business Week	Esquire
Family Circle	Newsweek
Field and Stream	National Geographic (female only)
Family Weekly	Reader's Digest (male only)
Girl Talk	Signature
Glamour	Sunset (male only)
Good Housekeeping	True
Hot Rod	TV Guide (male only)
House Beautiful Home Remodeling	
Ladies' Home Journal	
McCall's	
Outdoor Life	
Parents'	
Sports Afield	

* All-advertisement mean for 63 magazines on one page, four-color ads.
Source: Based on information from Daniel Starch & Staff, Inc., Adnorms, 1973.

to $40 million and put almost all of it into magazines (up from one third in magazines and a third each in newspapers and outdoor billboards). The Seagram case provides a unique opportunity to track actual sales based on advertising in a single medium. (Even when individual firms can track the effects of their own campaigns, they seldom release the information for competitive reasons.)

The new strategy started in August 1977. In March 1978 Seagram made public sales figures covering the first seven months of the campaign. Table 4-14 compares changes in unit sales of Seagram brands with changes in sales for the category of each brand.[5] On the surface, at least, the results for Seagram are impressive. However, what the experience proves mostly is that increased advertising *per se* can help boost sales, and that magazines did at least a competent job. In the absence of control markets, it is not known if sales would have been different if the added money had been put into the other media. On the other hand, Seagram increased its prices during this period. In the absence of specific

---

[5] Figures are for 17 liquor-controlled states (i.e., states where liquor stores are state owned and purchases are made through a central state agency), plus one county.

pricing information from the company and the industry, it is difficult to determine the extent to which this affected unit sales.

Table 4-14: Unit Sales of Seagram's Brands Compared to Total Category, August 1977-January 1978

Seagram's Brand Name	Category	Change for Seagram	Change for Category
Seagram "7"	Blend	+ 4.0%	- 1.3%
Extra Dry Gin	Domestic Bottled Gin	30.0	+ 3.5
V.O.	Canadian-bottled	10.0	2.2
Royal Crown	Premium Canadian	24.0	2.2
Meyer's Jamaica Rum	Imported Rum	30.0	21.2
Glenlivet Scotch	Foreign-bottled Scotch	50.0	4.6

Source: Magazine Publishers Association, *Newsletter of Advertising*, May 1978.

Issues Requiring More Research

Although there are outstanding success stories of advertising accomplishments in all media, there is still room for considerable refinement in advertiser strategy and media mix. First, it is often difficult to judge the incremental impact of increased budgets on advertising effectiveness. For example, could Seagram have been as successful with only a $5 million or $10 million increase instead of the $20 million they did add? Or, would Seagram have done significantly better by adding just a bit more to its $40 million budget?

Second, advertisers, aided by self-serving (though not necessarily inaccurate) studies by the media trade associations are improving their understanding of marketing segmentation. Not all products and services are equally promotable to all potential customers through a single theme in just one or two media. The concept of media imperative, discussed in the next chapter, could be accepted as a serious approach to understanding the role of each medium in the advertising mix.

Third, the subject of frequency, especially in the print media, requires further research. Clearly, repetition has an effect, but is there an optimum number of exposures? How many exposures are possible before a particular ad becomes worn out? Are advertisements better when run in concentrated "flights" or should they be spread out evenly over a less intense time period? Magazine research is behind television in this area.

5
Magazine Audience Research

The advertising research discussed in the previous chapter seeks to learn about the effectiveness of advertising in modifying consumer attitude, opinion and behavior. Magazine audience research differs in that it seeks information on the potential effectiveness of particular magazines as advertising vehicles. Magazine publishers want to learn more about their readership so that they can make a stronger pitch to advertisers, editors are helped by knowing their constituency better, while advertising agencies need the information to convince their clients that the agency is buying the most effective media.

Thus, the stakes are large. Publishers pay $30,000 and up to participate in the major syndicated studies. Agencies pay on a sliding scale based on their annual domestic billings. (A fairly large agency, billing $150-$200 million, would pay about $21,500; a smaller agency, with $50-$75 million in billings, would pay about $9500.) The ability of a magazine to sell advertising may be significantly affected by the results of surveys. Yet there is disagreement in the industry as to the validity, reliability and usefulness of much audience research. This chapter looks at some of the issues and developments in the field.

READERSHIP VS. CIRCULATION

Circulation size of a magazine is concrete and verifiable. Readership—the number of people who actually look at a given issue of a magazine—is more conjectural, although there is no doubt that readership is greater than circulation. The question publishers have tried to answer for advertisers is how much "pass-along" readership they have.

This became an issue when television started to erode magazines' national advertising franchise in the 1950s. A single television set is presumed to be viewed by more than one person; the mass circulation magazines added to this numbers game by selling readership over circulation as a means of competing. Conceptually, the readership idea is sound. However, over the years there has been considerable disagreement on how readership can be accurately measured.

Syndicated Audience Research

Syndicated research surveys are those to which more than one magazine and advertising agency subscribe. Some are conducted on a regular basis and can be purchased by anyone with the money. Thus, they may be considered more objective than are surveys conducted at the behest of the particular magazine or group. Moreover, because the cost is spread over many clients, funds are available for in-depth interviewing of a large number of respondents.

The best-known and one of the oldest research firms is Simmons Market Research Bureau, formed by a merger in 1978 between the two major rivals in the field, the original W.R. Simmons & Associates Research and Axiom Market Research Bureau, an operating unit of the J. Walter Thompson Co. advertising agency.

The two firms had competed tenaciously for support—both financial and professional—from the magazine/advertising community since Axiom challenged Simmons in 1972. Although Axiom's Target Group Index (TGI) did gain an increasing following, especially from the smaller magazines, the company reportedly never did reach a break-even position. Meanwhile, the more established Simmons suffered marginal profits, at best, as well as organizational and field research problems.[1] Conflicting results from the 1974 surveys brought in the Advertising Research Foundation (ARF) to audit each firm's methodology. Although both services used rather extensive samples, numbering as high as 30,000, their basic assumptions and interviewing techniques were different and the ARF found problems with both.

The Simmons method is known as "through the book." Respondents are shown the masthead of each magazine in the survey and asked if they have seen a copy of each magazine in the previous six months. If they have, they are shown a stripped down version of an actual copy and must ascertain that they did indeed see that issue. The Simmons method was initially designed to be useful for studying small groups of large circulation magazines—about 12 at most. But in its 1978-79 version, it had 78 magazines included.

---

[1] W.R. Simmons, who founded the company in 1951, left in 1973 (it had since been sold to others), claiming that the data were unreliable.

Axiom's "recent reading" technique asks respondents to designate from a long list of magazines which ones they have read in the past week (for weeklies) or month. This approach picks up more casual readers than does the "through the book" approach, but drawbacks include the length of the list and the possible confusions from seeing names like *Family Circle, Family Health* and *Family Weekly* juxtaposed in the alphabetical listing. The "recent reading" technique is quicker than the "through the book" method and lends itself to a greater number of items.

Both surveys expect much information from the respondents in the 15,000 households. After the initial questionnaire is administered the surveyor leaves behind a thick book (separate for men and women), with hundreds of questions on product usage—e.g., used last month; yogurt, non-dairy cream substitute, ice cream, ice milk, sherbet; brand of each used most often; approximate number of packages of each used; size of package. Have you personally bought any flatware in the last 12 months? Stainless, silver plate or sterling? Number of place settings? Amount spent, etc. The surveys are collected at a later date, at which time the respondents are brought a gift they choose: an alarm clock or flashlight, for example.

Richard Spicer, who was manager of client service for Axiom, believes that by and large people who agree to participate answer honestly. But only about three quarters of initial interviews are completed and only about half the respondents finish the entire survey. As for accuracy, few are satisfied. Advertising agency media buyers admit that they do not really trust the figures but rationalize that "they are better than nothing." Thus, they continue to be used.

The Simmons Market Research Bureau has not yet quieted the doubters. The methodology for the 1978-79 survey included the old Simmons method for magazines with circulation over 5 million and the Axiom TGI method for smaller magazines. When these plans were announced, at least one research director of a large magazine was "shocked." He added, "How can they do this? They've been fighting tooth and nail with each other over methodology." Said another skeptic, "Putting two bad methods together gives you a service which is twice as bad."

Results, released in late September 1979, did little to build confidence in the firm's approach. In particular, the method of adjustment used to make the results comparable to those of past years has been questioned. Although Frank Stanton, president of the Simmons Market Research Bureau, felt the results do compare, Simmons agreed to make any changes recommended by the Advertising Research Foundation (ARF) in both the 1979 analysis and the 1980 methodology.

ARF, meanwhile, initiated a study in 1979 to test the degree to which audiences reported in previous Simmons studies are comparable to those now being reported using the TGI approach. The study also tested the effect of asking some "recent reading" and "through the book" questions in the same survey. "Unless the industry is confident that the very different techniques . . . produce comparable audience estimates, this mixed method system may misdirect advertising dollars and be harmful to both magazines and advertisers who use them," warned the president of ARF in explaining the need for the study. At a cost of $425,000, the project was financed by 60 advertisers, agencies, publications and research services.

There was some initial concern that the merger would leave the new Simmons with a monopoly in the field. Particular concern was expressed by those magazine executives who believed in the "through the book" method but whose magazines would not be measured by that technique because their circulation was too small. Another criticism of the new approach was the decision to report the audience results of large circulation magazines, i.e., those with under a 15% sampling error, on a current-year basis; but smaller magazines, which suffer from a much higher sampling error (as much as 37% in some cases), will have their results reported as a two- or three-year average. This would presumably compensate for over- and under-reporting in any given year by providing a moving average of greater reliability.

Fears of a syndicated research monopoly have proved groundless, as at least three new services have been created. The first, by W.R. Simmons himself, was to have utilized a different methodology. Simmons' new firm, 3-Sigma, adapted SORTEM (Study of Reader's Total Experience with Magazines), which would be based on a diary left with the respondents to record actual usage, rather than simply recall. However, publications were slow to respond to his proposal and it was at least temporarily shelved.

The second new entrant into the primary audience readership field was Starch/INRA/Hooper, best known for its Adnorms studies of advertising recall (see Chapter 4). Primary audience includes the subscribers, single-copy purchasers and members of their households, as compared to total audience, which includes anyone who has seen the magazine. Starch maintains that since the primary audience is more loyal to the publication, reads more issues and is free to remove cents-off coupons, it is of serious concern to advertisers. The first Starch study concentrated on approximately 45 magazines with the largest circulation. Surveys of about 9000 households were all done by personal interviews.

Finally, the three former top officers of TGI regrouped and formed

Magazine Research Inc. (MRI) and quickly signed up 55 magazines and 15 agencies for its first survey in 1979. Not surprisingly, it was using a modification of the "recent reading" technique for its 30,000 personal interviews.

Thus, the competition to provide numbers for magazines and advertisers continues. With it all, more than one industry source sees ad agencies and their clients returning to more reliable circulation figures, as well as plain creative judgment, as the basis for media purchases.

OTHER TYPES OF READERSHIP STUDIES

Ad Hoc Studies

Magazine publishers or group executives sometimes commission readership or usage studies to learn more about their own audience and how it compares to those of competing magazines. In other cases, several magazines will be brought together by a research firm for an *ad hoc* syndicated study—that is, on a one-time basis, rather than as part of an ongoing program, such as those of Simmons or MRI.

One of the more active firms in the audience research field is Audits & Surveys, Inc. For a time, Audits & Surveys planned to use its Magazine Audience Research Service (MARS) as an annual syndicated service. However, it completed only one year's study for 16 magazines in 1975; instead it mostly does surveys for publishers under contract. It carried out a Time Inc.-sponsored readership study of 10 mass circulation magazines, including the three competing newsweeklies, and *Reader's Digest, TV Guide, Business Week, Woman's Day, Family Circle, Better Homes & Gardens* and *Sports Illustrated*. The study sought basic demographic data on readers of each publication, as well as information on place of reading.

The advantage of this type of study for Time was that it could control the methodology and substance of the survey better than by subscribing to a syndicated service. Because it was limited to 10 magazines, the survey did not suffer the possible variance caused by the more extensive number of magazines used by Simmons.

Newsweek used Audits & Surveys to conduct a more generalized pilot study on magazine audience accumulation patterns and activity, as well as attentiveness patterns for various media. The sample size was too small to have meaningful results for individual magazines, but the study, conducted in the Milwaukee area in 1977, elicited useful information on the rate at which newsweeklies as a group were read after publication date. For example, it showed that 60% of those who read the three major newsweeklies first looked at them within seven days of the publication date, and that primary readers (as defined previously) accumulated faster —75% in seven days, compared to 35% for other readers. Not surprisingly, the study also found that, when compared to television, radio and newspapers, newsweeklies were the most frequently read in the absence of other competing activities, such as eating, doing housework or using other media. Clearly, this information can be used to sell advertisers on the concept of advertising in magazines in general and newsweeklies in particular. Presumably, *Newsweek* would get its share of the added business.

Such surveys do not come cheap, and are certainly in the range of what magazines pay the syndicated services.

Subscriber Surveys

All magazines, but smaller circulation and special interest magazines in particular, conduct their own surveys to learn more about their readers, usually by questionnaires to a sample of their subscribers. In 1978, 356 magazines conducted 1565 readership studies; in 1979, the number increased to 419 magazines undertaking 1767 studies. Many of these are conducted by in-house personnel and are of dubious validity. They may use such primitive methods as binding a card into the magazine and tabulating the returns. But more likely they make at least some pretense to statistical sampling. For the purpose of credibility, surveys intended to be used to sell advertisers may be contracted to respected outside consultants and firms, such as Chilton Research Services, Mark Clements Research or Belden Communications, Inc.

Although professionally compiled research should be more reliable, this is not always so. For example, *Us* put together its own quick reader survey of 500 purchasers of its October 4, 1977 issue, not long after it started publication. In 1978, it hired Simmons to undertake a custom study. The small-sample in-house 1977 survey and the Simmons study did show some significant differences as well as similarities, as seen in Table 5-1.

Somehow, the Simmons people were able to have the percentage of all ages add up to 100% of the sample, without including those under 18 years old, which the in-house survey found to be 8% of the audience. More importantly, the Simmons results indicated that no respondent refused to give his or her income. It would be a rare survey without some such refusals, yet the Simmons income percentages still total a misleading 100%; the in-house study performed more professionally in this regard. Such lapses call into question the entire procedure. Nonetheless,

Table 5-1: Comparison of In-House and Simmons Readership Studies for Us, 1977 and 1978

Category	In-House	Simmons
Male	24.0%	42.9%
Female	76.0	57.1
Under 18 Years Old	8.0	not included
18-24	33.0	37.5
25-34	37.0	38.3
median age	26	28.3
Married	45.0	57.5
Single	43.0	33.6
Other	12.0	8.9
Attended or Graduated from College	61	48.9
Household Income:		
less than $10,000	22.0	15.6
$10,000-14,999	25.0	16.7
15,000-24,999	31.0	31.5
25,000+	17.0	36.2
not responding	5.0	not included
median income	$16,000	$19,840

Source: Based on information in Us.

magazine-sponsored studies of their readers are important for marketing and advertising sales, and are quickly demanded of new publications.

PROFILE OF MAGAZINE BUYERS

A study conducted in 1976 of magazine buyer behavior found that about three quarters of U.S. adults were magazine buyers (i.e., had purchased a magazine in the previous 12 months).[2] More specifically, the sampling found that magazine purchasers could be divided into heavy, medium and light buyers. Heavy buyers accounted for 21% of the sample but 59% of magazines purchased; these people were defined as buying nine or more different magazine titles in a year. Moderate buyers (four to eight different titles) accounted for 30% of purchases and light buyers (one to three titles) only 11% of purchasers.

---

[2] "How and Why People Buy Magazines" (Port Washington, NY: Publishers Clearing House, 1976). The survey was conducted by Lieberman Research Inc. Publishers Clearing House markets subscriptions through multi-magazine direct mail promotions.

Table 5-2 summarizes these findings of the Publishers Clearing House survey. It shows that heavy buyers are younger than lighter and non-buyers and that women make up a disproportionate share of heavy buyers. This last phenomenon is explained further by the finding that while men in the sample selected magazines for themselves, women were the primary decision-makers for magazines read by themselves and the rest of the family. Although somewhat dated by now, there is no reason to expect major shifts to have occurred in these percentages.

The results also indicate that heavy buyers tend to have higher incomes and more education than those who buy fewer magazines. (This is consistent with the findings of many studies that concluded that heavier reading of books, magazines and newspapers is correlated with higher income, education and occupational status.) Furthermore, readers between the ages 18 and 34 were more likely to report an increase in magazine reading over the past five years than were readers in general, and those with some college education were even more likely to have increased their magazine readership. Conversely, those who reported reading fewer

Table 5-2: Demographic Profile of Adult Magazine Buyers and Non-Buyers

	Heavy Buyers	Moderate Buyers	Light Buyers	Non-Buyers
Male	35%	39%	54%	53%
Female	65	61	46	47
	100%	100%	100%	100%
Age:				
18–34	50%	43%	35%	26%
35–49	33	26	23	23
50 & over	17	31	42	51
	100%	100%	100%	100%
Income:				
under $10,000	16%	31%	50%	67%
10,000–19,999	57	44	38	25
20,000 & over	27	25	12	8
	100%	100%	100%	100%
Education:				
less than high school grad.	17%	21%	40%	59%
completed high school	36	39	39	29
attended/completed college	47	40	21	12
	100%	100%	100%	100%

Source: Based on information from "How and Why People Buy Magazines" (Port Washington, NY: Publishers Clearing House, 1976).

magazines than five years ago were in older age groups and lower education categories. In short, magazine readership is concentrated among an upscale population—younger, better educated and in a higher income bracket.

THE MEDIA IMPERATIVE CONCEPT

The recognition that magazine use is not spread evenly among the adult population, and that heavy magazine readers spend less time on television, movies and sports, has been conceptualized in a model of "media imperatives." Labeled by Frank Stanton, president of Simmons Market Research Bureau, and first presented in 1975, it centers on the two competing national media, magazines and television. Based on previous research, it was concluded that the population of television viewers can be arranged along a continuum according to the amount of time spent viewing television. Similarly, the adult population can be categorized by its magazine usage, measured by magazines read. Each continuum is divided into quintiles, and a combination of the two groups produces the matrix shown in Figure 5-1. It recognizes four basic groups: those with high magazine use and light television use—the magazine imperatives; heavy television and light magazine—the television imperatives; heavy in both media—dual imperatives; and light in both media—non-imperatives.

The underlying concept of media imperatives, as promoted by the Magazine Publishers Association and adopted by many publishers in their presentations to ad agencies, is that each individual has a different mix of exposure to these two media. It is this actual exposure that determines the cost efficiency with which an advertiser is reaching its intended audience.

According to the MPA, 30% of the population—the most upscale segment—are magazine imperatives. They are least efficiently addressed by an advertiser using a 100% television ad schedule, since they do only 15% of television viewing. The MPA analysis goes on to show how actual exposure of an advertising message for a mass-consumed product can be enhanced by switching a portion of a fixed ad budget from television to magazines.[3]

---

[3] For a full explanation of the concept and its use and justification, see "Media Imperatives . . . Analytical Tool or Hoax?" *Magazine Newsletter of Research* (New York: Magazine Publishers Association, January 1979). The Television Bureau of Advertising (TvB) has criticized the concept, as summarized in "Who's Winning the War of the Imperatives?" *Media Decisions,* December 1978, pp. 64 ff.

Figure 5-1: The Media Imperative Matrix

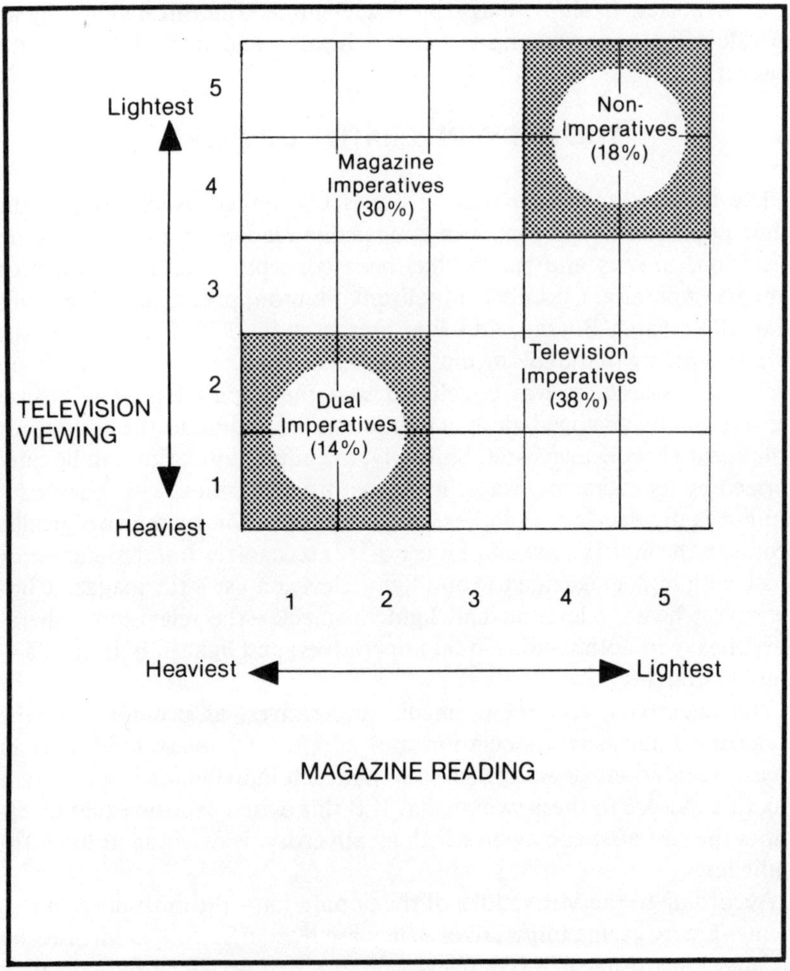
Lightest
5
4
3
2
1
Heaviest
TELEVISION VIEWING
Magazine Imperatives (30%)
Non-Imperatives (18%)
Television Imperatives (38%)
Dual Imperatives (14%)
1
2
3
4
5
Heaviest
Lightest
MAGAZINE READING

Source: Compiled from data in "Media Imperatives ... Analytical Tool or Hoax?" *Magazine Newsletter of Research*, Magazine Publishers Association, January 1979.

The use of the media imperative presentation to ad agencies happened to coincide with the accelerating cost of television time, between 1976 and 1978. Thus, it is hard to ascertain how important the model was in the decision of 75 of the top 100 television advertisers to increase their magazine expenditures an average of 38% in 1977. The increase in magazine share may also owe something to the longer-term impact of a controlled study by General Foods, which compared an all-television advertising schedule to all-magazine or a television-magazine mix for five leading products. The findings of General Foods were largely favorable to increased use of magazines. Although the research was conducted in 1968-69, it is still considered a benchmark study and is widely cited.

The television industry advertising trade association (TvB) called the media imperatives concept a "hoax" and criticized many of its assumptions, even to the extent of putting together a slide show as a rebuttal for advertisers.

Not all advertising agency executives regard the media imperatives concept as something new; in the words of one from Ogilvy and Mather: "Imperatives are a new jargon for things media professionals have been aware of for a long time." However, the media director at Ted Bates, calling the TvB's rebuttal a "hatchet job," was more positive in admitting that the concept connects demographics and magazine readership. "When we draw up media plans, that's what we use."

Whether or not the media imperative concept actually sells more advertising, it is nonetheless a useful tool in helping students of the mass media understand the marketing role of these two mass communication forms. It can also be expanded to encompass other segments of the media and may play a role in establishing new models for how the editorial/information content of the media is used by different groups in the population.

6
How Special Interest and General Interest Magazines Differ

What is a special interest consumer magazine? How can it be recognized as distinct from a general interest consumer magazine? One writer defined special interest magazines as those periodicals dealing with a particular subject matter of interest to a specialized audience, which can be large or small. A *Business Week* article referred to everything from *Skiing* to *TV Guide* as part of what it terms the "special audience" milieu.

On the other hand, when Meredith Corp., publisher of *Better Homes and Gardens, Metropolitan Home* and others, talks about special interest publications, it is referring quite specifically to its annual and semiannual periodicals, such as *Kitchen and Bath Ideas.*

Media Decisions magazine has grouped the likes of *Ebony, Boys' Life, Playboy, Harper's* and *True* under the label of special interest magazines. And Time Inc. went one step further when it referred to *Money* as "the special interest magazine that's of special interest to everyone."

Using conventional designations, there are several dimensions along which interest may be divided:

1) *Sex.* There are "women's" magazines and there are "men's" magazines. Yet even within this division, there is a range from *Ms.* to *Cosmopolitan* to *Modern Bride* to *McCall's* within the women's category and from *Argosy* to *Esquire* to *Playboy* for men. Because there are many dual sex magazines—e.g., *Ski, Gourmet,* or the newsweeklies—gender alone does not provide a very specialized categorization.

2) *Locality.* One of the earliest slices from the mass pie was the regional issue. From that has followed the even more localized city magazine, adding local copy to the local advertising.

3) *Profession.* The business press has taken occupation or business function as the basis for a highly specialized set of magazines. There is a

"general" interest magazine for all MBAs (Master of Business Administration), as well as more specialized publications for international managers, financial managers or marketing managers. Doctors, lawyers, accountants, retail store managers each have their own publications, generally categorized as trade publications, rather than consumer magazines.

4) *Hobbies.* One of the more prevalent divisions, there are magazines for horseback riders, archers, electronics buffs, skiers, amateur photographers and numismatists, to select but a few.

5) *Age.* There are magazines for children, teenagers, college students, those who identify with the youth culture, parents and retired people.

6) *Ethnic background.* While much of the old immigrant ethnic press has disappeared, the black press has grown in keeping with black self-awareness. There are also subdivisions here: *Black Collegian, Essence, Black Sports.*

7) *Income.* Much emphasis is put on the upscale attractiveness of certain magazine audiences. The contention is that advertisers who have quality, prestige goods of high price would want to advertise to an audience able to afford these products. Nonetheless, it is not uncommon these days for truck drivers and plumbers—so-called blue-collar workers—to be making $20,000 a year or more. Working wives have helped push household income in many families past $20,000. Yet discretionary dollars of these families may go into far different goods and services than those of a lawyer or other professional. Thus, "buying" income is not always an accurate guide for many upscale advertisers.

A MATRIX APPROACH TO DEFINING GENERAL AND SPECIAL INTEREST

In 1974 a study of general and special interest consumer magazines defined special interest by dividing magazines into groups according to types of information they provide, and the characteristics of the audience they reach.[1] For the purposes of the study, the first criterion—type of information provided—was divided into two categories: passive and active. "Passive" information is information intended for the reader's entertainment or for his general knowledge. "Active" information, by contrast, is intended for a specific use. An example of "passive" information is an article on the life of Billie Jean King, while "active" information would be a feature on how to cure tennis elbow.

---

[1] Benjamin M. Compaine, *Consumer Magazines at the Crossroads: A Study of General and Special Interest Magazines,* KIP Studies (White Plains, NY: Knowledge Industry Publications, Inc., 1974).

The second difference in magazines, type of audience reached, can be conveniently divided into mass audience and limited audience. Obviously, the editorial content of a magazine might appeal to a vast potential readership or to a very restricted one. A magazine on dulcimer playing could hardly aspire to as large an audience as one on home repairs.

Thus, magazines can be categorized by whether their subject matter is basically active or passive as well as by whether the subject is applicable to a relatively mass or limited audience. The result is the matrix in Figure 6-1, which also includes examples of the specific magazines applicable to each block. For this study, the term "special interest" refers to the types of consumer periodicals that fall under the active information column in the matrix. General interest publications are those that are passive interest (whether mass or limited audience).

However, by nature of the form in which much industry data are accumulated, as well as the economics and logistics of magazine publishing, reference is frequently made instead to "small circulation" and "large circulation" magazines. In these instances, all limited audience and mass audience magazines, respectively, are lumped together without regard for the active/passive differences. In terms of magazine distribution economics, the major distinction is circulation size, in which case *Harper's* has more in common with *Flying* than with *Reader's Digest*.

The Key is Active Information

To really grasp the dynamics of special interest magazine publishing, it is necessary to understand the importance of reader involvement, conveyed by the nature of "active" information.

Special interest magazines deal primarily with high technology, high performance requirements. A person with a casual or spectator interest in sports may read *Sports Illustrated,* but the serious golfer will probably read *Golf* or *Golf Digest* in addition to, or instead of, *Sports Illustrated.* The more serious an individual is about some particular skill-oriented task, the more likely he is to subscribe to a magazine in that field.

The key is that the special interest publications demand high reader involvement—subscribers are participants in the subjects being written about, not just observers. In a special interest magazine, the advertising is usually an extension of the editorial. Contrast the advertisements in a random issue of *Sports Illustrated* with those in an issue of *Wilderness Camping*. In the former, pages promote liqueurs, air conditioners, tires, automobiles or long-distance telephone calling. None has the least thing to do with sports.

The pages of *Wilderness Camping,* on the other hand, have advertise-

92 CONSUMER MAGAZINES

Figure 6-1: Consumer Magazine General-Special Interest Matrix

EDITORIAL ORIENTATION

	Passive (median circ. 668,000)	Active (median circ. 406,000)
Mass Audience median circulation of these examples: 2.1 million	Examples: Reader's Digest TV Guide People Ladies' Home Journal Sports Illustrated Newsweek Playboy Ebony Esquire National Geographic Psychology Today median circ. 3.0 million	Examples: Family Circle Better Homes and Gardens Outdoor Life Apartment Life Glamour Popular Mechanics Sports Afield Popular Science median circ. 1.8 million
Limited Audience median circulation of these examples: 340,000	Examples: Saturday Evening Post Harper's New Yorker Ms. New Republic Ellery Queen Mystery Magazine Philadelphia Forbes Rolling Stone Commentary Modern Romance Gourmet median circ. 478,000	Examples: Golf Digest Trains Popular Photography Flying Yachting Ski Bride's Camping Journal The Magazine Antiques Dirt Bike Magazine Car and Driver High Fidelity Shooting Times Trailer Life median circ. 306,000

Source: Circulation medians derived from first six months, 1977 Audit Bureau Circulation statement.

ments for parkas, sleeping bags, hiking boots, packs and packstoves. These advertisers know that only one type of person picks up this magazine: an activist who buys the needed equipment, regardless of educational level, income, sex, occupation or living quarters. Moreover, the visuals in a special interest magazine, whether as part of the editorial copy or the advertisements, are quite likely to be depicting an activity that the reader will actually be engaged in, as opposed to a picture of Pete Rose diving into second base.

Thus, the special interest magazine is selling a readership of unquestioned homogeneity as related to a specific product or activity; it provides a waiting audience with sought-after information, often provoking intense cover-to-cover reading of editorial and advertising matter alike. The less a magazine focuses on very specific activities or products—say moving from *Guns & Ammo* to the more encompassing *Field and Stream* —the more it moves into a mass audience category, though it may still be activity-oriented.

Limited audience/passive magazines, as noted, share many of the economic and logistical characteristics of the special interest publications. The crucial difference is that these books must rely on demographic data to establish their validity as useful marketing outlets for advertisers and are not as inherently involving as the so-called "nut books."

Using the Matrix

Establishing an acceptable definition of "special interest" is of more than academic importance. First, the concept can help many advertisers to understand how different types of publications are more or less effective for selling their products. Almost any segment of the adult population includes large numbers of cigarette smokers, but how do you best reach the potential customer of a Coleman stove or an auto exhaust system? Second, editors should know the proper orientation of their copy. In some cases, the editor and publisher do what they want and hope an audience finds them. In other instances, as with Time Inc.'s *Money,* the initial editorial concept changed as the interests of the readers became clearer. Third, consumers want to know what to expect from a magazine—more these days than ever as rising subscription rates force readers to weigh more carefully their media choices. Fourth, the publishing logistics of magazines vary by type.

A magazine is one of two things, depending on which side of the newsstand one occupies. For the advertiser and publisher, a consumer magazine is little more than the delivery of a market: a market for skiers, smokers, automobile buyers, handymen, furniture dusters, *ad infinitum.*

A mass circulation magazine must, by its very nature, deliver a generalized market, one that is held together not by any single interest but by some vaguely defined patterns.

For the editor and consumer, a magazine is a source of information: what it was like in Atlanta's ballpark when Aaron hit the 715th home run, why inflation is so high, how to bake chocolate chip cookies, or what's new in ski bindings. The kind of information provided, however, is of two types. Much information in magazines is purely for the edification of the reader. For example, an article in *Ebony* on Roy Wilkins, former head of the NAACP, or a piece in the *Saturday Evening Post* by S.I. Hayakawa on "The Uses of Slang" are read because they are interesting or entertaining. They are not read typically for a concrete purpose or with the intention of acting on the information. Contrast this with information that the reader can utilize or even information that exhorts the reader to act. *Tennis* had Ken Rosewall demonstrating "The Way to Improve Your Backhand," *Popular Photography* told "How to Shoot Pinhole Pictures in Color," *Metropolitan Home* offers "Overnight Guest and No Guest Room—What to Do?" and *Consumer Reports* suggested how to buy room air conditioners.

Almost all publishers could make some legitimate argument for their publication to be included under the special interest rubric. People who are interested in watching television would buy *TV Guide*, for example, while those who don't care much about television would not buy it.

Nonetheless, there are real distinctions among magazines that are reflected in the type of advertising they run, their method of distribution, their pricing of both circulation and advertising, their relative costs of printing, their means of reaching potential readers and other variables. These distinctions cut across the boundaries between general and special interest magazines. For instance, the economics of publishing limited audience magazines tend to have much in common, regardless of editorial orientation.

Other examples include:

- Magazines with small circulations have different alternatives available in terms of single-copy distribution than do high volume magazines.

- Magazines that have homogeneous audiences offer different advertiser incentives than do mass audience magazines.

- Magazines with a single-interest editorial focus are more attractive to certain types of advertisers than others.

- Magazines with high reader identification and involvement have a different equation in subscription pricing than other publications.

- Magazines with small press runs have a different production cost structure than publications with longer runs.

GENERAL AND SPECIAL INTEREST MAGAZINE TRENDS

If general and special interest magazines do indeed have substantially differing characteristics, then it is reasonable to expect some variance in their performance. The 1974 study cited previously did indeed find significant differences between 1963 and 1973 in areas of circulation growth, subscription and single-copy prices and ratios, advertising linage and revenue changes, and cost per thousand calculations. The mechanism for the analysis was two indexes of selected general interest and special interest magazines, each including 12 magazines typical of their genre. An almost identical pair of indexes has been used to update some of the previous findings to 1978. (See Appendix A.)

Circulation and Distribution

Between 1963 and 1973, the general interest magazines in the index increased 55% in circulation, while the special interest magazines grew 88%. As seen in Table 6-1, these special interest magazines continued to outperform general interest magazines by a substantial edge from 1973 to 1978. Five of the general interest magazines showed declines, although some of these may have been planned. Only two of the special interest magazines showed any loss in circulation.

Despite all the activity in single-copy sales, both groups of magazines accelerated their proportion of total subscriptions to total circulation. Between 1963 and 1973, the general interest group maintained a steady 60% subscription to 40% single-copy balance. As also shown in Table 6-1, the same group actually increased its subscription percentage to almost 64% by 1978. Even those magazines in Appendix A that lost circulation tended to take some of the loss on newsstand sales. Special interest magazines, meanwhile, which were only about half subscription in 1963, increased the proportion to two thirds in 1973 and to three fourths in 1978.

The propensity of smaller circulation special interest magazines for subscription sales is consistent with their difficulty in getting much exposure on newsstands, as well as the substantial cost of printing enough extra copies for national distribution. The apparent attraction of subscrip-

Table 6-1: Circulation Changes in General and Special Interest Magazines, 1973 and 1978

Year	General Interest Index	Special Interest Index
	Total Average Circulation Per Issue (thousands)	
1973	74,657	4,320
1978	75,228	5,312
Percent Change	+0.8	+23.0

	Percent Subscription	Percent Single-Copy	Percent Subscription	Percent Single-Copy
1973	60.8%	39.2%	66.3%	33.7%
1978	63.7	36.3	75.0	25.0
Percent Change	+4.8	−7.4	+13.1	−25.8

Source: Knowledge Industry Publications, Inc. analysis from Standard Rate & Data Service *Consumer Magazine and Farm Publication Rates and Data*, May 1979.

Table 6-2: Subscription and Single-Copy Prices for Special and General Interest Magazines, 1973 and 1978

	General Interest Index	Special Interest Index
Subscription Price		
Weeklies		
1973	$12.75	—
1978	22.11	
Percent change	+73.4%	
Monthlies		
1973	$ 6.92	$ 7.83
1978	9.69	12.23
Percent change	+40.0%	+56.2%
Total Group		
1973	$ 9.04	$ 7.83
1978	14.21	12.23
Percent change	+57.2%	+56.2%
Single-Copy Price		
Total Group		
1973	$ .61	$ .96
1978	1.08	1.52
Percent change	+77.0%	+58.3%

Source: Audit Bureau of Circulation statements for second six months 1978.

tion sales to the mass audience magazines—despite all the clamor about higher postal rates and some aggregate statistics that show more magazines than ever being sold on the newsstands—indicates that while a small group of mass circulation magazines has been very successful in exploiting supermarket and convenience store check-out counters, these magazines as a group have still not found this the key to circulation strength.

Not surprisingly, the cost of both groups of magazines has risen substantially. Between 1963 and 1973, general interest magazine subscription prices rose an average 68.0%, close to the 74.4% rate of the special interest periodicals. In the next five years, both groups increased almost identically, about 57% (see Table 6-2). Weekly magazines charged less than twice as much as did monthlies in 1973, but the differential widened by 1978, reflecting significant increases in both second class postage and paper expense.

Monthly special interest magazines have boosted their subscription prices more than have monthly general interest periodicals. This is consistent with the hypothesis that consumers can be expected to pay more for a magazine that is particularly useful to their lifestyle or activities.

Similarly, single-copy prices for special interest publications continued to run well ahead of those for general interest ones in 1978, with increases in the rates about even with the increase in subscription prices. General interest magazines showed somewhat stronger single-copy increments, up 77% over 1973, reversing the 1963-1973 relationship between subscription and single-copy prices.

The more rapid rise in single-copy prices between 1973 and 1978 may be the reason for the greater percentage of subscription sales for the indexed general interest magazines. The ratio of a year's subscription price to single-copy price (buying each issue for a year) is shown in Table 6-3 to have decreased from 53% to 45% for weeklies and from 82% to 64% for monthlies, for a weighted average reduction of from 70% to 56%. Thus, subscriptions become even more attractive for readers of these publications. Special interest magazines have maintained their subscription to single-copy price ratio at about two thirds.

In sum, for the magazines in the two indexes at least, special interest magazines are seen to have enjoyed significantly greater circulation growth during a period generally favorable to all magazines. They remain somewhat more reliant on subscription sales than do general interest publications, although both groups have higher proportions of subscription sales than in 1973. Special interest magazines have higher prices than general publications of comparable frequency, and the differential in subscription prices has grown larger, while it narrowed slightly for

Table 6-3: Subscription Price as Percentage of Single-Copy Price

	General Interest Index	Special Interest Index
1973		
Weeklies	53%	—
Monthlies	82	68
Weighted Average	70%	68%
1978		
Weeklies	45%	—
Monthlies	64[a]	67[b]
Weighted Average	56%	67%

[a] Excludes *Family Circle*, with no subscription price, and *National Geographic*, with no single-copy sales.
[b] Includes less-than-monthly-frequency magazines.
Source: Audit Bureau of Circulation statements, second six months 1978.

single copies. Finally, general interest publications are priced in a way that makes subscriptions much more attractive than single copies in 1978, and general and special interest monthlies now have very similar ratios of subscription to single-copy price.

Advertising

Although advertising revenue for all magazines increased about 80% between 1973 and 1978, the number of advertising pages, based on the weighted average of the magazines tabulated for Table 2-5, was up a more modest 12%. (The number of pages dipped during some years in between, but both 1973 and 1978 were strong years for magazines.) Table 6-4 provides an index similar to that used for circulation. Both general and special interest groups ran 9.3% more pages in 1978 than in 1973. (Even the median increase for the two groups was the same and close to the mean—11.4%.) Among the general interest publications, the weekly magazines performed slightly below average, reporting an 8.7% page increase compared to 10.2% for the monthlies (which include five extra issues of *Family Circle*). Each group had several magazines suffering sizeable losses as well as strong gains.

The similar showing of the two indexes is in marked contrast to the results of the period 1963 to 1973. During that period, special interest magazines had a gain in ad pages of 31%, while general magazines rose only 17%. (Actual revenue for each group had risen the same 136%, however.)

Table 6-4: Ad Pages in Selected General and Special Interest Consumer Magazines, 1973 and 1978

	Pages		
General Interest	1973	1978	Percent Change
New Yorker (W)	3,883	4,061	4.6%
TV Guide (W)	2,533	3,502	38.3
Newsweek (W)	3,239	3,328	2.7
Sports Illustrated (W)	3,021	2,887	-4.4
Harper's (M)	560	391	-30.2
National Geographic (M)	355	400	12.7
Reader's Digest (M)	1,291	1,421	10.1
Mademoiselle (M)	1,494	1,458	-2.4
Ladies' Home Journal (M)	1,060	1,411	33.1
Family Circle (17X)*	1,296	1,705	31.6
Photoplay (M)	596	332	-44.3
Playboy (M)	983	1,295	31.7
TOTAL	20,311	22,191	+9.3%
Weeklies Only	12,676	13,778	+8.7%
Monthlies Only	7,635	8,413	+10.2%
Special Interest			
Golf Digest (M)	788	1,020	29.4
Yachting (M)	1,890	2,185	15.6
Ski (7X)	471	599	27.2
Bride's (B-M)	965	1,071	11.0
Hot Rod (M)	828	637	-23.1
Flying (M)	646	627	-2.9
Gourmet (M)	462	645	39.6
Popular Photography (M)	1,695	1,896	11.9
High Fidelity (M)	731	826	13.0
Guns & Ammo (M)	543	597	9.9
Camping Journal (M)	475	255	-46.3
Popular Mechanics (M)	1,264	1,403	11.0
TOTAL	10,758	11,761	+9.3%
Average for all P.I.B. Magazines	1,008	1,130	+12.1%

*Published monthly in 1973.
Source: 1978 linage as reported to *Advertising Age*, December 18, 1978; January 22, 1979. Used with permisson. Copyright 1978 and 1979 by Crain Communications, Inc. 1973 linage as reported to Publishers Information Bureau.

OTHER FORMS OF SPECIALIZATION

Special Issue Magazines

Publishers of many mass circulation as well as special interest magazines are finding it profitable to spin off special issues of their magazines devoted to a single well-defined activist topic. These include such topics as *House & Garden Kitchen & Baths, Better Homes and Gardens Houseplants, Woman's Day Needlework Ideas, Family Circle Great Ideas One-Dish Meals,* and *Sports Afield Fishing Secrets.* Most of these are annuals, some having started as one-shot publications that did well enough on the newsstand to warrant subsequent editions. If demand is sufficient, frequency may be moved to semiannually and even quarterly. In a few cases, the strength of the idea results in a full-fledged magazine, with subscriptions, bimonthly or monthly frequency and, of course, advertising. These periodicals have several common factors:

- The familiar name of the publication. The special issues are separate publications (although some copy may be rewritten from the basic magazine), but they all use the name of the original publication. They can also be promoted with house ads.

- The built-in distribution network. A magazine with a national distributor and space on the newsstand has a relatively easy time getting another publication with the same name into the distribution stream. The same field force can also check up on its placement.

- Editorial expertise. Editors can dig into their banks of unused stories or can rewrite, expand, redesign or repackage features run in the parent book. A relatively small editorial staff can put the special magazines together. In some cases, it may be just another assignment for the parent magazine's staff.

- Low risk test market for new magazine ideas. Meredith's *Apartment Life* started as a one-shot publication and is now a successful monthly. Hearst's *Colonial Homes* began life as a *House Beautiful* annual before working up to bimonthly status.

- Profit potential. Special issues do not need advertising to make money and are usually 100% newsstand sales, thus requiring no subscription promotion. In addition, the narrow editorial focus attracts serious readers who are willing to pay substantial cover prices—$2.00 is not unusual, although the parent magazine may sell for only $1.25. Thus, the profit margin is much larger.

Some regular advertisers have tended to stay away from these types of special interest publications because there is little information on readers other than what the publisher provides, often from the results of mail-back questionnaires in the publication. However, if the magazine does well enough on the newsstand to warrant subsequent issues, advertisers eventually become more interested. In some cases, advertisers who are too small to use the parent magazine use the specials because of their more focused audiences. Many advertisers also use coupons or special offers in the ads to help measure their effectiveness.

The leading proponents of the special issue magazines are the women's and home magazines, with sports a close third. In 1978 there were at least 90 such publications with circulations of 100,000 or more. *Better Homes and Gardens* alone had 20 different titles, and *Woman's Day* had 24. Table 6-5 covers just a sampling of the many titles.

Specific Topic Regionals

The proliferation of city/regional magazines has continued throughout the 1970s. Most of these publications have been fat with local advertising, but still limited to about 100,000 circulation or less. Ad pages were up nearly 20% in 1978 over the previous year and for the first five months of 1979 were running another 37% above the year-earlier period.

An offshoot of the city/regional magazine has been the introduction of special audience regionals. In Nashville, for example, the publisher had the editorial staff put together two separate annuals that have sold well, thus spreading the overhead and making the entire operation more profitable. Others include local home magazines, such as *Tulsa Home & Garden* and *Dallas-Fort Worth House/Garden,* with typography and covers that look much like their national audience counterparts. There are also regional business magazines, such as *Focus in Philadelphia* and *Crain's Chicago Business.* And now there are regional magazines for women (*Texas Woman*) and spectator sports enthusiasts (*Hockey Northeast* and Newsweek's *Inside Sports*).

These specialized audience regionals presumably meet the circulation and advertising needs of ever-greater readership segmentation. They give advertisers an opportunity to aim not only at locality, but interests as well. *Texas Woman,* for example, which began operation in January 1979, is targeted to those who are career-oriented or involved in civic activities. According to its publisher, the audience does not "have time to

CONSUMER MAGAZINES

Table 6-5: Examples of Special Issue Magazines, 1978

Magazine	Frequency	Circulation	Cover Price
PHOTOGRAPHY			
Popular Photography's Photography Annual	annual	300,000*	$2.50
Popular Photography's How-To Guide	annual	125,000*	2.50
SPORTS			
Ski Magazine's Guide to Cross-Country Skiing	annual	225,000	1.95
Field and Stream Hunting Annual	annual	300,000*	1.50
Outdoor Life's Guide to Fishing the Midwest	annual	150,000*	1.95
Guns Annual Book of Handguns	annual	101,000	2.95
HOME			
House Beautiful's Home Decorating	quarterly	300,000	2.00
House Beautiful's Home Remodeling	semiannual	175,000	2.00
BH&G Building Ideas	quarterly	450,000	2.00
BH&G Kitchen and Bath Ideas	semiannual	450,000	2.00
BH&G Window and Wall Decorating Ideas	annual	400,000	2.00
BH&G How to Buy a Home	annual	450,000	2.00
Good Housekeeping Country Living	semiannual	500,000	1.95
House & Garden Decorating	triannual	300,000	2.00
House & Garden Kitchen & Baths	annual	200,000	2.00
Family Circle Decorating Made Easy	annual	650,000	1.50
Mechanix Illustrated Home Improvements You Can Do	semiannual	300,000	1.35
Sunset Ideas for Improving Your Home	semiannual	225,000	1.95
Woman's Day Apartment Living	annual	300,000	1.25
Woman's Day Kitchen and Bath Guide	annual	300,000	1.35
SEWING, CRAFTS, CHRISTMAS SPECIALS			
American Home Best Products	annual	300,000	N.A.
American Home Crafts Annuals (3 titles)	annual	300,000	N.A.
Sunset Christmas Ideas and Answers	annual	400,000	1.75
BH&G Holiday Crafts	annual	700,000	2.00
BH&G 100's Needlework & Crafts Ideas	semiannual	700,000	2.00
Woman's Day Best Ideas for Christmas	annual	775,000	1.50
Woman's Day Needlework Ideas	semiannual	350,000	1.35
Family Circle Great Ideas, Fashions and Crafts	annual	650,000	1.50
Family Circle Christmas Helps	annual	1,000,000	1.50
Good Housekeeping Needlecraft	semiannual	1,040,000	1.50
Ladies' Home Journal Needle & Craft	semiannual	760,000	1.50
McCall's Needlework & Crafts	quarterly	N.A.	1.50

Table 6-5 continued

Magazine	Frequency	Circulation	Cover Price
BEAUTY, HEALTH			
Good Housekeeping Beauty Book	semiannual	450,000	1.25
Redbook's Be Beautiful	quarterly	600,000	1.50
Vogue's Beauty and Health Guide	annual	400,000	2.50
Woman's Day Hair Style & Beauty Ideas	semiannual	250,000	1.35
Woman's Day 101 Ways to Lose Weight and Stay Healthy	annual	600,000	1.29
Ladies' Home Journal The 1978 Woman	annual	400,000	1.95
Playgirl Health and Beauty Guide	annual		1.95
GARDENING			
BH&G Homegrown Fruits & Vegetables	annual	500,000	2.00
BH&G Houseplants	semiannual	650,000	2.00
House Beautiful Gardening & Outdoor Living	annual	175,000	2.00
House & Garden Gardens	annual	175,000	2.00
Sunset Joy of Gardening	annual	225,000	1.75
Woman's Day 101 Gardening & Outdoor Ideas	annual	250,000	1.35
FOOD, DRINK, ENTERTAINING			
BH&G Outdoor Cooking & Entertaining Ideas	annual	550,000	2.00
House & Garden Wine & Food	semiannual	200,000	2.00
Family Circle Great Ideas One-Dish Meals	annual	700,000	1.50
Woman's Day Great Holiday Baking Ideas	annual	300,000	1.35
Woman's Day Outdoor Entertaining	annual	300,000	1.35
Ladies' Home Journal Guide to Entertaining	annual	400,000	
American Home Beautiful Food	annual	300,000	
Woman's Day Kitchen Appliance Cookbook	annual	300,000	1.35
MISCELLANEOUS			
Woman's Day Today's Woman Money Management for Women	annual	300,000	1.35
Mechanix Illustrated How to Build 20 Boats	annual	200,000	2.50
Playgirl — The First Five Years	one-shot	400,000	2.95

*Copies distributed.
Source: *Media Decisions*, October 1978.

read everything . . . but we feel they will read something that is geared specifically to them and the area they live in.''

The general concept is not unlike the successful approach that has been used by Lane Publishing Co.'s *Sunset,* a home service magazine geared to the lifestyle of western states. Trying to carve out such a specific niche within a city or state may be attractive to advertisers, but beyond the needs of readers. Can the houses and gardens in Indianapolis be so unique and removed from the mainstream that consumers would turn to a local magazine on the subject rather than a national publication?

7
Entrepreneurship and Magazine Publishing

Is there a magazine editor, writer or salaried publisher who does not have visions of owning his or her own magazine? There may be some, but most view magazine publishing as a rewarding, personal business. And despite the six- and seven-figure sums budgeted for some start-up publications, it is still an enterprise that can be undertaken with a bare minimum of venture capital. In magazine publishing, experience has shown time and again that the right idea and the persistence to implement it are far more important to success than a big bankroll and an elaborate business plan.

Magazine publishing is sometimes viewed as a high risk business, but it is not, compared to other small businesses. (The Small Business Administration has estimated that four out of five new businesses do not last beyond five years.) A study of consumer magazines between 1952 and 1977 found that mass interest periodicals had the highest mortality rate among magazines: 40% survive after under 10 years. Fewer than 50% of small special interest magazines survive 10 years. A mass special interest magazine has a 70% chance of surviving.[1]

Although it may seem that we are besieged by new magazines, only a fraction of these are of national or broad appeal. *Folio* estimated that in 1979, 107 consumer magazines were introduced, compared to 115 in 1978 and 165 in 1977. This chapter discusses several approaches to magazine entrepreneurship, the experiences of some new publishers and some of the considerations involved in the decision to start or acquire a new periodical.

---

[1] "New magazines' chances of survival analyzed in study," *Folio*, October 1978.

THE HISTORICAL ROLE OF THE ENTREPRENEUR

A pervasive feature of the magazine industry is the central role of the entrepreneur: the individual with a concept. The history of periodical publishing has proven the role of the idea to be paramount. Money and initial execution are secondary. Hadden and Luce initiated the news summary magazine concept with *Time* and got an edge that *Newsweek* is still trying to overcome. DeWitt Wallace didn't do a mammoth marketing study before launching *Reader's Digest;* he just "felt" that it could sell and used his intuition to guide him. Publishing history is dominated by the names of men, not organizations. It was Edward Bok who made the *Ladies' Home Journal* the largest circulation magazine in the world for a time and Cyrus Curtis who made the *Saturday Evening Post* into the most successful weekly of its time. Curtis could somehow sense a market for a new publication: business associates and advertising people had advised him against starting the *Journal* and later the *Post*.

Theodore Peterson, author of *Magazines in the Twentieth Century,* divides publishers into two rough groups: the "missionaries" and the "merchants." Their behavior is often similar, but their motivation differs. Those in the former group are publishers devoted to their cause, some "secular gospel." Wallace preached optimism; Luce believed in the efficacy of photographs as vehicles for information and education; Harold Ross of the *New Yorker* strived for perfection; and Bernarr Macfadden of *True Story* and *True Romance* used his publications either to promote directly his cause of bringing "health and joy through exercise, diet, and the simple life" or to amass profits to further such ends through his foundation.

Rather than being champions of a cause, the "merchants" regard magazine publishing as strictly a business enterprise to be operated for profit. In this pursuit, they often put out superior publications, such as S.S. McClure's *McClure's Magazine* in its muckraking days. Condé Nast saw a niche for fashion publications catering to luxury-loving readers who would be attracted by a slick, elegant format, and the result was *Vogue, Glamour* and *Mademoiselle*. Wilford Fawcett and George T. Delacorte, Jr. found profits in magazines edited for a lower level of sophistication. Fawcett's *Captain Billy's Whiz Bang* was followed by his version of the confession magazines, then *Mechanix Illustrated,* working on the formula made successful by *Popular Mechanics. Men* copied *Esquire, Spot* followed *Life* and not even Superman was immune from an imitation in Captain Marvel. A more recent merchant is Bob Guccione, whose *Penthouse* is the first serious threat to *Playboy.*

Although it does not have to happen, all too frequently when the entrepreneur passes from the scene, the magazine begins to fade. It is this observation that has led Clay Felker, among others, to postulate the life cycle hypothesis of magazine longevity. "There appears to be an almost inexorable life cycle of American magazines that follows the pattern of humans," wrote Felker, past editor of *Esquire,* in the Spring 1969 issue of *The Antioch Review.* That pattern is "a clamorous youth eager to be noticed; vigorous, productive middle-age marked by an easy-to-define editorial line; and a long, slow decline, in which efforts at revival are sporadic and tragically doomed."

A magazine may survive, but it is usually as a different book, reflecting a new personality, such as *Cosmopolitan* as edited by Helen Gurley Brown. On occasion, however, the original concept can be maintained, or even resurrected, as in *Life* where the Luce format remains viable even at the present time.

This hypothesis strikes a logical note because magazines are so intensely personal. A successful editorial policy is more than just the assembling of data by a committee or an analysis of a market—the failure of the *Saturday Review* under Nicholas Charney and John Veronis demonstrates that. "A key fact about magazines," notes Felker, is that unlike any other mass medium, "one man can influence every idea, every layout, every word that appears in print." Yet a basic problem that faces the successful magazine is that both the publishers and their formulas become obsolete. And a corollary of this hypothesis is that the bigger the book is, the more reluctant it is to change. At the same time, change for its own sake is not necessarily the answer: witness Felker's own unsuccessful revamping of *Esquire.*

Predicting which new titles will fail and which will succeed is an imprecise spin-of-the-wheel. In 1973, about 127 new consumer magazines were announced or made their first appearance. Some of them were well-financed operations, such as George Hirsch's *New Times* or Bob Guccione's *Viva.* Others were obscure and of uncertain origins, like *New Awareness* and *Alaska Geographic.* By 1981, none of these was still a going concern.

In the final analysis, the magazine publishing business is based entirely on the ability to attract and hold readers; if the audience is there, advertisers will be attracted to the magazine. Moreover, the failure of a magazine does not necessarily mean that the editorial premise for it was wrong. Why is it, for example, that there are many well-established and profitable titles that carry a circulation of under 100,000, yet other publications with much larger circulations fold their tents and slip off into the night? Often, those too could make it if they were designed to operate at a lower level—of advertising, editorial expense and circulation.

CHANNELS FOR MAGAZINE START-UPS

As is well known throughout the industry, Time Inc. reportedly spent $25 million and waited for seven years to make *Sports Illustrated* a profitable publication. No story better illustrates the maxim that starting a new publication takes a sound financial base and the perseverance to wait to build circulation and be accepted by advertisers. In publishing circles the current rule of thumb is that it takes at least $5 million and three to five years from the first issue to become profitable. Newsweek, Inc. spent several times that (in two years) for *Inside Sports*.

The widespread acceptance of this figure ignores the type of magazine being started as well as numerous examples of successful magazines that have been introduced with much lower amounts of start-up capital. Moreover, this figure should not be interpreted to mean that the new publisher need have $5 million or anything close to it in the bank before starting. By being willing to gamble, the entrepreneur can start with as little as a few thousand dollars, relying on additional capital from subscriptions paid for in advance, as well as from later investors.

A listing of magazines started in the 1960s and 1970s—both successful and not—gives ample evidence that a big bankroll is not enough to ensure success, and a shoestring budget does not doom a good idea. *Playboy* began in less expensive times but still at the bargain start-up cost of $16,000. More recently, *High Times* had a $25,000 bankroll, *Rolling Stone* all of $6500 and *Mother Earth News* only $1500. *Vegetarian Times,* a slick bimonthly with 32,000 circulation, started with whatever the publisher had left over from his salary as a nurse. *Jazz*, another glossy publication, began with the modest savings accounts of four friends, plus much sweat equity—a substantial but noncash investment. All these publications have been successful.

On the other hand, Triangle Publications, publisher of *TV Guide,* spent millions on introducing *Good Food* in 1974 and it failed to last a year. Harcourt Brace Jovanovich, strong in book publishing and farm publications, spent a reported $4 million and dropped *Human Nature* before its second birthday. McCall's *Your Place,* with plenty of publishing talent and dollars behind it, shut down in under a year; *Politicks and Other Human Interests,* a limited audience tabloid that got considerable trade attention, gave up the fight after running through nearly $1 million in six months.

All else being equal (which rarely is the case), a well-financed venture certainly has a better chance of survival than one struggling from issue to issue. But as one magazine entrepreneur has concluded, money's importance has unfortunately been overemphasized, at least in the start-up phase. Too much money too fast can erode some of the hunger and the urgency that the shoestring operators experience. Paradoxically, the most logical sources of money, the existing magazine publishing groups, are the most reluctant to invest in new magazines themselves. (Time Inc. is a clear exception.) "It's like drilling for oil in Central Park," was the comment of a top ABC Publishing executive.

In general, consumer magazine start-ups follow one of four patterns: a well-financed, carefully planned operation by a publishing group; the natural evolution of a one-shot or annual publication connected with an existing publication; an entrepreneurial but big budget independent start-up; or an under-capitalized entrepreneurial "shoestring" project.

Big Budget Corporate

Daniel Filipacchi, the French publisher of *Paris-Match,* spent $250,000 just to acquire the *Look* logo from Cowles Communications and was reported willing to invest $25 million to revive *Look.* His plan included carrying a staff for as long as a year before the first issue appeared in February 1979. Yet his expectations for the magazine were modest: from newsstand sales of 500,000-600,000 at the start, he hoped to build to 1 million by mid-1980. From the start, however, *Look* was plagued by a lack of editorial identity and an extensive turnover of personnel, from the top on down. Despite Filipacchi's proclaimed desire to keep pouring in dollars to keep the publication alive, and experimenting briefly as a monthly under the management of *Rolling Stone*'s Jan Wenner, the new *Look* was suspended after barely six months.

More typical of a total immersion corporate introduction was that of Time Inc.'s *People* in 1974 and the New York Times Co.'s *Us* in 1977.[2] They involved the development pattern that an operating publisher is likely to implement:

- First, a market niche is sought: What special interest, demographic grouping or other need is not being specifically fulfilled by existing publications (or where does demand seem to be so strong, a second or third publication could be sustained by advertisers)? The size of each potential market is estimated.

- Next, an editorial idea that excites management is expanded into a "treatment"—a definition of the target audience, an explanation

---

[2] *Us* was sold to Peters Publishing Co., an affiliate of Macfadden Group, Inc., in 1980 for approximately $4 million.

of why the magazine would be purchased, what types of advertisers would be attracted. Story topics, sample table of contents and cover possibilities would be described.

- If the idea is still considered sound (and these projects sometimes assume a life of their own if the development executives are not hard-nosed), a budget is determined for the project and a dummy issue is constructed, using a real cover and contents, with advertisements from possible clients pasted in. At this point, a sample rate card might also be drawn up, and the package shown to advertising agencies.

- Up to this point the investment has been relatively modest going, mostly for salaries. The next step, however, requires a decision to put together and print one or more real test issues, and/or begin test mailings of subscription offers, experimenting with various subscription prices, offers and creative packages. Test issues can be done even for a largely newsstand magazine, since it is a sound way to determine public response; test market cities are targeted and the test issues are distributed for sale in those cities. (This was done for *People, Us* and others.)

- If responses to subscription offers or to newsstand sales are satisfactory (some standard by which this can be measured must be established beforehand), a full-scale introduction is made. To abandon a project this far along is no doubt difficult, but a successful publisher (or any business person) knows when to cut losses if the product does not look as if it can be a success.

Of course, not all corporate launchings go through these steps. Triangle Publications, for example, introduced *Panorama* in 1980 without going through the test market stage. (It folded in 1981 after achieving only half its anticipated 200,000 circulation.) Other forms of market research, such as focus groups, might also be used to test editorial ideas, formats and pricing. Such field research could actually be used to develop areas and topics that the new magazine could address.

Among the magazines listed under magazine publisher start-ups in Table 7-1, *Good Food, Human Nature, Geo, Look, New West, Omni, Oui, People, Self, Us* and *Viva* had considerable dollars involved in their start-ups. *Omni,* for example, started with first-issue distribution of 1 million copies—the biggest new introduction since *People.* Subscription promotion alone, on television as well as in other magazines, involved an announced budget of $3 million. It is this type of introduction that makes magazine start-ups seem so expensive.

Corporate Clones

Another way of getting a new title started is to publish a magazine that is a special topic edition of an existing magazine. That's the way *Better Homes and Gardens' Apartment Life,* originally an annual, found enough acceptance in the marketplace to become a quarterly, bimonthly and eventually a monthly. Hearst's *House Beautiful* had enough demand for *Colonial Homes* to make this a regular publication.

In effect, the one-shots can serve as test vehicles with relatively little expense and even less corporate prestige on the line. The titles are usually designed to be all or mostly reader supported, and they command a higher newsstand price than the regular magazine. They may continue as annuals or semiannuals and be profitable at that level. But if they gain in frequency and begin to attract the attention of advertisers, the titles can then proceed to test subscription and alternative newsstand prices.

A one-shot that failed was *Family Circle*'s *Women Who Work,* which was tested in spring 1978. Unlike some other one-shots and annuals, this magazine was started with the intention of becoming a regular title and it solicited advertising from the start. It apparently did not do well, since it disappeared after the test.

Special interest publisher Petersen has started seven of its 12 monthly publications as annuals or quarterlies. Since Petersen had established magazines such as *Motor Trend* and *Hot Rod,* both *4-Wheel & Off-Road* and *Vans & Pickups* were natural offshoots that have since increased their frequencies. Petersen favors this approach because "You've got a better story to tell advertisers." Instead of promising circulation, as in a new magazine, they can show the agencies the results.

An added attraction to publishers is that specials are designed to make money on a per issue basis. A new monthly, however, does not usually expect to be profitable in its first issues.

Not all special titles are intended to become regularly published magazines. Meredith's *Building Ideas,* for example, is a quarterly, which is viewed as its maximum frequency. Once a reader of that magazine builds a house, his or her interest in continuing to receive the publication is about nil. In that case, advertisers are interested in reaching a committed audience, if only temporarily. Loyalty and renewals are not a concern.

Table 7-1: Selected Consumer Magazine Start-Ups Since 1969, by Entrepreneurs and by Publishers

Entrepreneurial Start-Ups	Year
Ambiance	1978
American Photographer	1978
Astronomy	1973
Backpacker	1973
Black Enterprise	1970
Book Digest	1974
Byte	1974
Calendar	1976
Blair & Ketchum's Country Journal	1974
Equus	1977
Essence	1970
Firehouse	1976
Food & Wine	1977
Gambler's World*	1972
Gallery Magazine	1971
Games	1977
Genesis	1972
High Times	1979
Horse, of Course	1971
Hustler	1974
Intellectual Digest*	1970
Kosher Home	1978
L'Officiel/U.S.A.	1970
Mariah	1976
Moneysworth	1970
Mother Earth News	1970
Ms.	1972
New Dawn*	1976
New Harvest	1979
New Times*	1973
Nuestro	1977
On the Sound*	1972
Penthouse	1969
Plants Alive	1972
Playgirl	1973
Quest	1977
Sail	1970
Soap Opera Digest	1975
Vital*	1977
WomanSports*	1973

Table 7-1 continued

Magazine Publisher Start-Ups	Year	Publisher[a]
Americana	1973	American Heritage
Apartment Life	1969	Meredith
Dirt Bike Magazine	1972	Daisy/Hi-Torque
Discover	1980	Time Inc.
Epicure*	1972	CBS
Families	1980	Reader's Digest Association, Inc.
Geo	1979	Gruner & Jahr
Good Food*	1973	Triangle
Human Nature*	1978	Harcourt Brace Jovanovich
Inside Sports	1980	Newsweek, Inc.
Look*	1979	Filipacchi
Money	1972	Time Inc.
Motorboat	1973	United Marine Publishing
New West	1974	New York Magazine
Omni	1978	Penthouse
Oui	1972	Playboy
Outside	1977	Rolling Stone
Panorama*	1980	Triangle
People	1974	Time Inc.
Petersen's Photographic Magazine	1972	Petersen Publishing
Pizzazz*	1977	Cadence
The Runner	1979	MCA
Self	1979	Condé Nast
Us	1977	New York Times Company
Viva*	1973	Penthouse
Your Place*	1978	McCall's
Working Mother	1979	McCall's

Non-Magazine Organization Start-Ups	Year	Publisher
Smithsonian	1970	Smithsonian Institution
Travel & Leisure	1970	American Express Company

*Not being published as of August 1981.

[a.] For identification of ownership affiliation. The legal corporate entity may be different.

Source: Knowledge Industry Publications, Inc.

Entrepreneurial Big Budget

One of the best case studies of an individual raising millions of dollars to start his own magazine was that provided by George Hirsch for his ill-fated *New Times*. Having a good track record from his previous role as publisher of *New York Magazine*, and supported with a business plan spread out on 175 pages, he was able to raise $1.7 million in venture capital from nearly a dozen investors, including such blue chips as American Express Co., Bank of America, Chase Manhattan Bank and several private groups.

It was the apparent foresight of George Hirsch in his original plan for *New Times* that made its success look so certain: he had planned the operation with the clear intent of starting with a modest 100,000 circulation and letting it increase "depending strictly on the economics," with the fifth-year goal of a still-modest 370,000. Ironically, Hirsch reached his goal in four years, but found that once circulation stopped growing, ad agencies became less interested in advertising. At the same time, *New Times* found itself unable to hold its readers any longer. Those initial subscribers who had been acquired with cheap introductory offers, especially those sold by door-to-door and Publishers Clearing House methods, had extremely low conversion (first-time renewal) rates of 11% and less (compared to an overall conversion average of 60% which was slipping to 50% at the end).

Thus, *New Times*, which had won strong positive ratings from 10 out of 12 major ad agency media executives when it opened shop in 1973, found itself with an editorial premise that could not economically maintain an audience—even at the level it had intended to reach. Hirsch pulled the plug in 1978.

Another well-financed start-up was *Games* in 1977, which was purchased the next year by Playboy Enterprises. Publisher Chip Block used an approach more frequently found in the packaged goods industry: he first defined what characteristics his magazine should have, then looked for a subject that would fulfill them. He wanted a magazine that 1) was easy to sell to consumers, primarily by subscription; 2) could generate enough net subscription revenue to cover all operating expenses, so that newsstand and advertising income would be ancillary; 3) was special interest but not aimed at any specific demographic group.

From a list of 40 or so ideas that fit this description, *Games* emerged as the most unique. It involves the reader, who spends much time with each issue, helping to give greater value to the subscription price of $6.00 for six issues. One study showed that readers spend an average of five hours with the magazine and 4.3% respond to difficult reader contests.

With approximately 160 puzzle magazines being published, mostly for newsstand sales, *Games* is differentiated by four-color articles and games on coated stock. (An uncoated stock insert is used for mazes and cross word puzzles.) Its covers are done by first class illustrators. The result has been upscale readership that attracted not only the producers of games and books, but to an even greater extent, advertisers of mass consumer goods, such as cigarettes, liquor, cameras and electronic equipment.

Another type of approach is illustrated by the start-up of *American Photography*. The amateur photography magazine field was apparently well covered by Ziff-Davis' *Popular Photography* and ABC's *Modern Photography*, with *Petersen's Photographic Magazine,* started in 1972, a distant third. But here again, the right idea and enough money to hire some professional consultants to help with pricing, promotion and packaging, as well as a plan for operating at a realistic level, combined for a strong start. *American Photography,* four years in the planning stage, began publication as a monthly in June 1978. Venture capital was raised through Alan Patricof, who specializes in such ventures and was a founder of *New York Magazine.*

The editorial premise of *American Photography* was that the competition concentrates on the technical and mechanical aspects of photography, while the new title is aimed at the creative side. Well over $500,000 was devoted to direct mail solicitation for subscriptions at $12.00 per year. The first mailing of 1 million pieces drew an encouraging 8.5% response (anything above 2% is usually considered a big success). Subsequent mailings of more than 2 million were not as favorable, but the publication had 118,000 subscriptions and a newsstand sale of 40,000 by early 1979. Advertising pages were slower in coming (averaging 18 per issue for 1978), but the owner/publisher, Alan Bennett, was secure enough to tell backers he needed no further capital. In 1980, CBS purchased the magazine and it has continued to grow.

The fact that others have tried and failed to establish a magazine with subject matter aimed at a particular audience does not appear to deter some entrepreneurs from trying the same concept again. For example, *American Stage* was introduced in 1979, although Huntington Hartford (with old A&P money) had not made a go of *Show* and Hefner of *Playboy* had struck out on *Show Business Illustrated. American Stage* also died an early death.

American Stage did have a somewhat different approach. Taking a hint from the success of *Smithsonian* and *National Geographic,* the magazine was not technically sold by subscription, but rather through membership in the newly established American Stage Guild, which also was to offer discounted merchandise and theater tours. The rationale for this, according to the publisher, was to build reader loyalty through auxiliary services as well as the magazine itself.

Having raised at least $1.4 million through the sale of limited partnerships, *American Stage* followed the pattern of other well-financed launchings. It put together a dummy issue and a series of test mailing promotions, starting with a split mailing of 30,000 pieces, a second test with 300,000, then a third with 2.5 million. The start-up goal was 125,000 subscribers and 20,000 single-copy sales. The magazine expected to attract New York retail advertising, given its heavy reader concentration there. This brought it head to head with *New York* and *Cue*, which presumably reached many of the same people.

Another magazine with the earmarks of a sufficiently financed start-up was *Ambiance*, which its organizers claimed would give the Condé Nast and Hearst monopolies a run for their money in the fashion beauty field. It was a slick, 9 x 12 inch 10 issue per year magazine at $2.00 per copy (no subscription discount). A year after first publication in 1978, the book was looking for a buyer, its editor complaining that "it's extremely difficult for an entrepreneur to exist in this market." He added that the dozen financial backers of the magazine "don't know that you don't launch a magazine that does well in a year unless you're Time Inc. or have $15 million behind you.[3] It too disappeared from the scene.

This draws attention to one of the possible differences between a publisher-backed new magazine start-up and one by an independent entrepreneur. The publishing people know—or should know—what they are getting into. When financing is being provided by inexperienced outside individuals, they may be less willing to tolerate the slow period of building up the staying power that is often necessary to convince advertising agencies that the magazine will last.

Of course, this situation need not exist. The entrepreneur should have realistic projections in the business plan and should emphasize to investors that it may take three, four or five years until they start to recover their capital. If anything, the plan should err on the side of conservatism, so that investors do not have their optimistic hopes dashed early on and pull the plug on their commitments to later investments. (Often, backers do not have to put all their promised cash up front, but must provide a commitment to add cash at certain periods as the launching progresses.)

In the case of *Ambiance*, the $2.00 per copy price was set to make the magazine less dependent on advertising, but this also carried risk since

---

[3] "'Ambiance' Hopes Limited Ad Space Fashionable," *Advertising Age,* March 6, 1978, p. 45.

competitors *Vogue* and *Harper's Bazaar* were at $1.50 and $1.25, respectively. The cash flow was also based on obtaining a 300,000 circulation, but the magazine reached only 200,000. At the same time, the entrepreneur vs. corporate publisher difference was highlighted by the publisher's experience with the ad agencies. While the agencies waited to see if *Ambiance* would last, they were much more generous with another start-up, McCall's *Your Place,* "because it's from a major publisher." Ironically, *Your Place,* though thick with advertising, was quickly terminated because it failed to find a sufficient audience.

The most frequent excuse given when a magazine started by an entrepreneur shuts down is "underfinancing," which has been applied to any situation where a business does not have enough capital to meet its bills (regardless of the level at which it started). However, a business is undercapitalized only when its original plan was unrealistic or if the market doesn't respond as expected. Insufficient financing is not an acceptable excuse in a business where the costs and techniques are so well known and planning tools so well established. Insufficient planning, poor management or testing, or going ahead with a poor concept are the real reasons in most cases.

Entrepreneurial Shoestring

Every low budget entrepreneur must be heartened by the thought that DeWitt Wallace started *Reader's Digest* with $5000 and an office rented in the basement of a Greenwich Village speakeasy. The first subscription solicitation was a mimeographed circular that pulled in 1500 readers at $3.00 each. Thirty years later, Hugh Hefner used his bedroom as his office and $7600 to put together his first *Playboy* issue (undated, so it could stay on the newsstand until he had enough money for the next issue).

Are these just examples from a different era, when the world was less complex and competition not so intense? Can their success be matched today with comparable sums? And what about the hundreds, perhaps thousands of others who tried on a shoestring and did not make it, their titles left in the crowded publishers' graveyard?

While the big magazine failures make the trade publication headlines, most of the rest come and go without much of a ripple. But the apparent staying power of some magazines started in the 1970s with little money confirms that magazine publishing is still essentially an easy-entry industry, where even the small publisher has a solid chance of succeeding: large corporations and well-financed promoters have no corner on the idea market. A modicum of know-how and a willingness to work hard to succeed with that idea can succeed where test markets, multi-million subscription piece mailings and slick slide presentations may not.

Paul Obis, a 22-year-old nurse, started *Vegetarian Times* in his spare time as a single-sheet newsletter folded to make four pages. The first issue was composed on a typewriter and distributed free to 300 readers, at a production cost of $17.00. Not a very glamorous start-up, but the word spread and the market found him. In four years, by 1978, the publication had grown to a paid circulation of 32,000 as a 64-page bimonthly. It is printed with a 70-lb. four-color cover. Advertising, virtually nonexistent for the first years, has started to grow substantially. Along the way, renewals have come in at 75%-80% from a dedicated base of readers. Magazine revenue, at $150,000 for 1978, is modest by even magazine publishing standards, but it may still yield a nice return on invested capital.

The entrepreneur's desire to succeed is illustrated by the start-up of *Vegetarian Times*. The owner/editor himself carried home a print order of 1500 copies of a 24-page edition through six miles of city traffic, then addressed, sorted and bundled the issues by hand. As a result, the publishing neophyte learned firsthand about the entire process, from the editorial to production to fulfillment.

Jazz, begun as a quarterly in 1976, survived for two years with no more capital than some magazines-to-be spend on a dummy issue or a direct mail test. In a sense the publisher used a series of dummy issues which generated enough income from circulation and advertising to keep the publication going from issue to issue. The owners did their direct mail testing as they went along.

Both *Vegetarian Times* and *Jazz* made mistakes and learned from them. For example, *Jazz'* founding group of four had envisioned the publication as a subscription-only quarterly of high quality. They learned, however, that the magazine sold best in record and music stores. They started with a $2.50 cover price only to meet postal regulations, but found jazz aficionados willing to pay that much at the newsstand. As a result, about two thirds of the 15,000 circulation are single-copy sales.

As is often the case with low budget start-ups, the founders substitute their own time for capital. *Jazz* did not pay salaries to the four partners, each of whom had particular skills relevant to publishing: an editor at a large city newspaper with production knowledge, an advertising executive, a former business manager of another quarterly and a jazz musician and composer with contacts in the music industry.

HINTS FROM SUCCESSFUL ENTREPRENEURS

Hand-to-mouth financing and sweat equity can take a magazine only so far, however. Both *Vegetarian Times* and *Jazz* have turned to outside sources of funds to help with expansion in size and frequency. In exchange, they will have to give up some of the equity in their ventures. Obis, the founder of *Vegetarian Times,* gave up a majority of his ownership to Associated Business Publications in exchange for the capital to help his magazine grow. But both he and the partners of *Jazz* have discovered that getting financing for an established publication is not only easier than for one that exists only in someone's head, but that the founders are often in a stronger bargaining position. George Hirsch ended up with only a 25% interest in *New Times*, having given away the rest to investors who wanted a substantial return in what is still viewed as a high risk business. In getting past the start-up stage with personal funds, the owner can in effect get more per share of stock and thus retain a greater share of ownership than if the same amount of money had been raised at the very beginning.

Other lessons that these entrepreneurs and others have learned:

- Write for the readers. This makes sense, but is too often forgotten, as publishers write instead for the advertisers. The first need is for loyal, dedicated readers.

- Have a realistic marketing plan. How many people will really want to read the magazine? The numbers may balance nicely at 300,000, but what if, as *Ambiance* found out, only 200,000 people want to buy it? *Family Circle* saw its market for *Women Who Work* as the 35 million working women, but this group has many different segments: successful executives, women in low-level jobs who work to make ends meet for the family, young girls out of high school waiting around to meet the right boy. The actual market must be better defined.

- Keep expenses to a minimum. Does the business really need high-priced Madison Avenue office space to start? Must precious capital be spent for new desks and carpets? Secretarial help is nice, but a circulation assistant can be more useful. Money should be devoted to the quality of the final product, not the surroundings and amenities. William Blair, publisher of *Blair & Ketchum's Country Journal,* found it useful to remember that each $7000 the publishers had to raise by selling stock represented 1% of the firm's total capitalization.

- Find a real niche. Often that means some segment of a larger field, such as jazz, which had previously been considered too specialized for its own publication. But it can also mean a broader market than the competition's: *Equus,* a well financed entrepreneurial launch in 1977, focuses on horses in general, while the other magazines in the field relate to a specific breed, use or region.

- Get into publication incrementally. Although a few of the largest publishers have the wherewithal to establish monthlies and weeklies, a more prudent approach may be that forced upon the shoestring publishers and discovered by some of the general interest publishers: test acceptance and grow with the market. Make adjustments to the business plan as new information comes in on price, renewals, reader surveys and advertiser acceptance. Daniel Filipacchi, with his multi-million dollar commitment to *Look,* had originally planned to publish the magazine on a weekly basis. "If we had stuck to a weekly frequency we would have self-destructed. We were a little too naive and brash. It's hard enough starting up a biweekly," he noted prophetically while *Look* was still in existence.

CORPORATE ENTREPRENEURSHIP

The two words cannot be comfortably juxtaposed: corporate and entre-preneurship. As organizations grow, they invariably become less spontaneous, more bureaucratized. Salaried managers and personally driven entrepreneurs have different incentives; managers tend to be more adverse to risk. The skills required for maintaining an organization are not necessarily the ones needed to create one. The individual who had little to lose in starting up a first magazine becomes less able to gamble when he or she already has an ongoing enterprise.

For these, and perhaps other reasons, many new magazines are eventually purchased by a larger entity, which at one time may have been a small entrepreneurial publishing company itself. The larger firm can often add the talent and capital to make a successful idea a more profitable one.

One of the more significant trends in the late 1970s was the unusual willingness of magazine-owning chains to try start-ups of new magazines in addition to the normal process of acquisition. The high cost of acquiring good magazines made start-ups appear relatively more attractive.[4]

Even so, the established publishers do not have a better track record than the independents. McCall's, having started its first new publication in decades with *Your Place,* did not make it. Cadence, which should know the youth market through its line of Marvel comic books, did not convince advertisers of the worth of *Pizzazz* and killed it in early 1979, less than a year after going national.

Other than the continual development of new titles at Time Inc., perhaps the most significant addition to the magazine lineup from a major publisher was Condé Nast's *Self,* introduced in 1979. Although Condé Nast himself was an entrepreneur, *Self* was the first start-up for the company since *Glamour* in 1939. Within two years it achieved a circulation of 1 million and was still growing.

Apartment Life, an offshoot of Meredith's *Better Homes and Gardens,* never received a big announcement in the trade press because it became a true magazine slowly, starting from a single annual edition in 1969. It illustrates the conservative nature of a large publisher, but also helped establish a pattern for others to follow. (It is now called *Metropolitan Life,* reflecting its intended appeal to city dwellers in general).

Much activity has come from Bob Guccione, who has maintained his entrepreneurial fervor following his success with *Penthouse,* which celebrated its 10th anniversary in 1979. Guccione founded *Viva* for women (1973, suspended in 1979), *Forum* (1968), and most recently *Omni.* He is one of the few true entrepreneurs in magazine publishing today and is willing to spend money to keep his slick periodicals afloat for a decent shot. *Omni* was introduced with a major television ad campaign, a strategy later followed by *Self* and *Inside Sports.*

Although *The Runner* was nominally started by film and entertainment giant MCA, it is more accurately the product of George Hirsch. The special interest magazine was published by New Times Publishing Co., which had been sold to MCA, with Hirsch given the go-ahead to run

---

[4]In 1978, Ziff-Davis estimated (from financial statements) the amount of cash that major magazine acquirers had available for acquisitions: it stopped tabulating at $1.4 billion. In addition to the usual active competition of CBS, Times Mirror, the New York Times Co. and, more lately, ABC, Ziff-Davis had to count the foreign publishers: Gruner & Jahr, Bonnier, Harlequin and Elsevier. (See Chapter 8.)

the operation as he saw fit. *The Runner* was subsequently sold to Ziff-Davis.

The Hearst Corp. has been successful with a stratgegy that mixes the best of corporate know-how with entrepreneurship. First with *Cosmopolitan* and more recently with *Science Digest* it has taken well known but languishing titles and, in effect, given them new bodies—a sort of editorial transplant. The *Cosmo* story has been well documented. *Science Digest* was an old, digest size mostly text periodical with about 200,000 circulation in 1980. In that year Hearst started publishing glossy, full sized magazines with stunning graphics, using the title *Science Digest Special Editions*. The publisher found strong newsstand sales and in 1981 replaced the old *Science Digest* with the new version. In the process, circulation more than doubled and a broader market of both readers and advertisers was brought into the magazine's fold.

By and large the list in Table 7-1 contains very few new magazines from large magazine publishers. CBS has made several unsuccessful attempts. *Epicure* failed to make inroads on *Gourmet* and *Bon Appetit; Popular Gardening Indoors,* tried as a quarterly in 1978, fizzled. ABC, which has been acquiring magazines of all types with its broadcasting profits, claims no interest in starting new titles; Ziff-Davis would also rather acquire—at the right price. Hearst is putting its start-up money for the time being into repositioning faltering existing titles, such as *Science Digest*. Times Mirror, which got into the magazine business solely by acquisition, has been looking at annuals as a means of expansion and considers the current economic outlook a negative factor for introducing new titles. "We'd rather retrench," is the corporate line. The New York Times Co., which never did make *Us* profitable, has also been using the *Family Circle* one-shots and annuals as a testing device. Special interest specialist Petersen did add a new photography magazine in 1972 and, in a departure from form, the religious *Inspiration* in 1978. In September 1979, *Newsweek* began publishing the first start-up in its history, *Inside Sports*. It lost about $12 million in 1980.

Thus, even during a period when magazines were booming and acquisition prices rising, most of the large publishers followed their formula of sticking with what they do best—add money and management to magazines that have proven themselves. Only Time Inc., with its experience and vast resources, appears willing to tackle major new titles on a regular basis. CBS will probably still try. The New York Times Co. also seems to be willing to play entrepreneur. But the thinking of established publishers may be summed up by a response given by former CBS Inc. president John Backe when asked why CBS did not engage in more start-ups: "Bear in mind that the equivalent of starting a new magazine the size of *Road & Track* (565,000 circulation), with all its success, is just about the same as adding another issue of *Woman's Day,* which has a lot less risk."

8
Group Ownership and Competition

COMPETITIVE NATURE OF THE MAGAZINE BUSINESS

Magazine publishing has been a vigorous, highly competitive business primarily because of its economic structure. Since it has traditionally been an easy field to enter, the industry is fragmented, so much so that no one company or group of companies dominates it. *TV Guide* accounts for only 4.6% of the combined per issue sales for 903 consumer magazines. The great diversity of magazine editorial matter, combined with the considerable segmentation of interests within the population, ensures the existence of a large number of differentiated publications.

The great diversity of publishers and publications has its counterpart in a paucity of detailed information about the industry. Publishers are extremely close-mouthed about the economics of their operations: only a small minority report to the Publishers Information Bureau, an industry clearing house for advertising and circulation data. Most small publishing houses and many of the largest are privately owned and therefore need not release any of the details of their operations. Even many publicly owned firms, such as Times Mirror Co. and CBS, lump operating figures of various enterprises together, making an analysis of magazine finances difficult.

CONCENTRATION

The periodical publishing industry shows relatively less concentration of ownership than do large industries overall. Compared to newspaper and book publishing, magazine publishing is somewhat more concentrated at the four- and eight-largest firm level, but the trend from 1947 to 1977 was toward a sizable lessening in concentration for periodicals (see Table 8-1), while newspapers showed a slight increase.

CONSUMER MAGAZINES

Table 8-1: Concentration in the Periodical Publishing Industry, 1947-1977

	1947	1958	1963	1967	1972	1977	Newspapers 1977	Book Publishing 1977
Number of Companies	2106	2246	2562	2430	2451	2860	7821	1650
Value of Shipments (billions)	$1.1	$1.7	$2.3	$3.1	$3.5	$6.1	$13.1	$4.8
Percentage Accounted For By:								
4 largest	34%	31%	28%	24%	26%	22%	19%	17%
8 largest	43	41	42	37	38	35	31	30
20 largest	50	55	59	56	54	52	45	57
50 largest	N.A.	69	73	72	69	67	62	74

N.A. Not Available.
Source: U.S. Bureau of the Census, *Census of Manufacturers*, 1977.

Table 8-1 also indicates that the number of periodical publishing companies went up 25% between 1972 and 1977 and was greater than the previous high measured in 1963.

Many of the largest circulation magazines are independent—that is, published by firms that publish no other magazines. Of the leading magazine publishers in revenue, three (the Reader's Digest Association, Inc., Triangle and the Washington Post Co.) have only two titles.

There were an estimated 80 multiple title publishers of consumer periodicals in 1980, producing 401 titles of quarterly or greater annual frequency. These titles account for 36% of the 1114 periodicals identified by the Audit Bureau of Circulation as consumer magazines that report circulation.[1] It is difficult to measure accurately the proportion of magazines published by multi-title firms, since figures are based on data from Standard Rate & Data Service. (SR&DS itself does not provide the tally.) SR&DS lists only those publishers that accept advertising for their magazines; moreover, its list is incomplete—omitting Triangle, for example, or magazines published by separate corporations or controlled by a single entity (such as *Philadelphia* and *Boston* magazines).

Differences Between Group and Non-Group Magazines

As might reasonably be expected, there are some overall differences between magazines published as part of a group and those that are independent. Table 8-2 summarizes selected characteristics of the two types of ownership. The average circulation of group-owned consumer periodicals is about one and two-thirds times greater than independently owned titles. It would be expected that as an independent magazine becomes larger and more visible, presumably gaining greater revenue and profit potential, it becomes a more promising prospect for either being purchased by a group publisher or forming its own group by acquiring other publications.

Subscription price of both types of magazines are quite similar, reflecting in part the common competition they face for the consumer's magazine budget and price expectations. They also must factor in the same postal rates. Single-copy sales tend to be insignificant for most small magazines and were not calculated here.

On the other hand, basic cost per thousand (CPM) advertising rates are substantially higher for the sample of independent magazines, again

---

[1] This includes 461 A.B.C. audited magazines. The remainder are audited by other agencies, report sworn circulation or guaranteed circulation to advertisers. "United States and Canada Periodical Circulation Study" Audit Bureau of Circulation, December 12, 1980.

Table 8-2: Selected Characteristics of Group-Owned and Independently Published Magazines, 1980

Characteristic	Group-Owned	Non-Group
Average Circulation	669,173	249,567
Subscription Cost	$13.05	$13.25
Cost per thousand (1 time B&W ad)	$14.76	$25.67

Source: Knowledge Industry Publications, Inc. Non-group figures from sample of magazines listed in SR&DS, May 27, 1981. Group-owned from tabulation of actual circulation and subscription prices of all such magazines listed in SR&DS, May 27, 1981. CPM for groups taken from sample of group-owned magazines.

reflecting the tendency of this group to include a greater proportion of small, highly selective special interest magazines with their commensurately higher CPM.

Ownership of Largest Magazines

Table 8-3 lists the 50 leading circulation magazines in 1980 and their parent firms. The top 10 magazines alone account for 22% of the total average per issue circulation of consumer magazines. Of these 10, seven have long been among the leaders. The demise of the old *Life, Look* and the *Saturday Evening Post,* formerly in the top ranks, opened the way for *National Geographic, National Enquirer* and *Good Housekeeping,* the junior members of the top 10.

Although three-fourths of the leading circulation magazines are part of magazine publishing groups, ironically, none of the top three is part of substantial multi-magazine groups. *TV Guide* is controlled by Walter Annenberg's Triangle Publications, which also owns 39th-ranked *Seventeen.* (As previously noted, Triangle is not listed as a multiple magazine owner by Standard Rate & Data Service.) *Reader's Digest* is part of a $1 billion firm that derives a substantial portion of its income from books and other audio-visual media materials, but the company publishes only one small and new other magazine (apart from the many foreign language editions of the *Digest*). *National Geographic* is published by the society and subscribers are technically "members."

Of the remaining top 50, Hearst runs three with 9.8 million circulation; Time Inc. has four with 10.5 million circulation (but mostly weeklies, to Hearst's monthlies); CBS has three with 11.4 million per issue and Charter Co. two, circulating 10.0 million. Times Mirror, Condé Nast and Triangle are the only other firms with more than one publication in the top 50.

Table 8-3: 50 Largest Circulation Consumer Magazines and Their Owners, 1980*

Magazine	Publisher
TV Guide	Triangle Publications, Inc.
Reader's Digest	Reader's Digest Association, Inc.
National Geographic	*National Geographic Society*
Better Homes & Gardens	Meredith Corporation
Woman's Day	CBS, Inc.
Family Circle	New York Times Company
Modern Maturity	The American Association of Retired Persons
McCall's	McCall Publishing Company
Ladies' Home Journal	Charter Company
Good Housekeeping	Hearst Corporation
National Enquirer	*National Enquirer, Inc.*
Playboy	Playboy Enterprises, Inc.
Time	Time Inc.
Redbook	Charter Company
Penthouse	Penthouse International, Ltd.
The Star	World News Corporation
Newsweek	Washington Post Company
Cosmopolitan	Hearst Corporation
American Legion	*The American Legion*
People	Time Inc.
Prevention	Rodale Press
Sports Illustrated	Time Inc.
U.S. News & World Report	*U.S. News & World Report, Inc.*
Field & Stream	CBS, Inc.
Glamour	Condé Nast (Newhouse)
Popular Science	Times Mirror Company
Smithsonian	*Smithsonian Institution National Associates*
V.F.W. Magazine	*Veterans of Foreign Wars of the United States, Inc.*
Globe	*Midnight Publishing Corporation*
Southern Living	Progressive Farmer
Outdoor Life	Times Mirror Company
Popular Mechanics	Hearst Corporation
Elks Magazine	*Benevolent and Protective Order of Elks of the U.S.*
Today's Education	*National Education Association of the U.S.*
Mechanix Illustrated	CBS, Inc.
Seventeen	Triangle Publications, Inc.
Parents (Gruner & Jahr)	Parents' Magazine Enterprises, Inc.
Workbasket	Modern Handicrafts Publications
Boy's Life	Boy Scouts of America
True Story	Macfadden Group, Inc.
Hustler	Flynt Publications
Sunset	Lane Publishing Company
Changing Times	*The Kiplinger Washington Editors, Inc.*
Life	Time Inc.
Organic Gardening	Rodale Press, Inc.
Ebony	Johnson Publishing Company

Table 8-3: continued

Magazine	Publisher
Nation's Business	*Chamber of Commerce of the U.S.*
New Woman	*New Woman, Inc.*
Sport	*Southwest Media, Inc.*
Farm Journal	*Farm Journal, Inc.*

*Non-Group Publishers in italic
Source: Information compiled from Magazine Publishers Association, A.B.C. circulation 2nd six months of 1980. Publishers added from listing in Standard Rate & Data Service, *Consumer Magazine and Farm Publications Rates and Data*, May 27, 1981.

Leading Publishers

By revenue. With its three profitable weeklies, a biweekly and three monthly magazines, Time Inc. is by far the largest magazine publisher in the United States. Table 8-4 identifies the largest publishers by revenue derived from periodical publication. Reader's Digest's revenue does not include foreign edition sales; Triangle's revenue is primarily from *TV*

Table 8-4: Largest Consumer Magazine Publishers in the U.S., by Revenue, 1980

	Revenue from Magazine Publishing[a] (millions)	Number of Domestic Consumer[b] Magazines
1. Time Inc.	$ 747	7
2. Triangle Publications	494	2
3. Hearst Corporation	324	14
4. CBS Inc.	298	10[c]
5. Washington Post Company	262	2
6. Reader's Digest Association, Inc.	214	2
7. Newhouse (Condé Nast)	195	7[c]
8. New York Times Company	192	3[c]
9. Meredith Corporation	167	8
10. Ziff-Davis Publishing Company	165	17
11. Playboy Enterprises Inc.	162	2[c]

[a] All revenues are estimated, except for Time Inc. and Playboy Enterprises, Inc.
[b] Current to October 1981.
[c] Does not include Sunday newspaper supplements.

Sources: Time Inc. and Playboy Enterprises, Inc., as reported in 10-K and annual reports. Others derived from corporate reports or calculated from estimated subscription and advertising revenue. In all cases, estimates reflect net revenue, after discounts, etc.

Guide. The Washington Post Co.'s *Newsweek* includes revenue from the international edition. Ziff-Davis publishes mostly special interest magazines, but has six business periodicals plus annuals as well. The only publisher that would not have been on a similar listing for 1973 is CBS, which acquired Fawcett (*Woman's Day*) and took over that firm's spot in 1977.

By number of magazines. At the end of 1980, there were 76 identifiable firms publishing more than one consumer magazine. Among them they published 310 periodicals. Consumer publishers owned an average of 4.1 periodicals each. The consumer magazines owned by chains averaged a paid circulation of 669,000. Table 8-5 identifies the largest publishers in the consumer area by number of magazines. In addition, broadcasting giant American Broadcasting Companies has moved determinedly into the magazine business in recent years, having purchased *Los Angeles* magazine, several special interest periodicals, two groups of farm publications and controlling interest in business magazine and business publisher Chilton. Hearst is one of the oldest groups, with many long-running titles. *Cosmopolitan* was founded in 1836, *Harper's Bazaar* in 1867.

Table 8-5: Largest Consumer Magazine Publishers, by Number of Magazines Owned, 1980*

	Number of Magazines in Group	Total Annual Circulation (thousands)	Total Average Circulation Per Issue (thousands)
1. Ziff-Davis Publishing Company	17	68,867	6,268
2. Hearst Corporation	14	149,031	12,938
3. Petersen Publishing Company	13	60,503	5,042
4. CBS Inc.	10	186,215	13,569
Scholastic Inc.	10	76,552	6,104
5. Charlton Publications, Inc.	9	27,646	4,087
6. East/West Network, Inc.	8	10,593	882
Laufer Company, Inc.	8	14,580	1,215
Macfadden Group, Inc.	8	59,023	3,611
Meredith Corporation	8	128,829	12,003
Webb Company	8	71,462	9,282
	113	853,301	75,001
Total Consumer Groups 76			
Total Titles for Groups 310			

*Includes groups that publish two or more consumer magazines at least quarterly and report either sworn or A.B.C. audited circulation. Excludes farm publications.
Source: Calculated from Standard Rate & Data Service, *Consumer Magazine and Farm Publications Rates and Data*, May 27, 1981.

There is great diversity among the magazines published by these groups. For example, CBS has a stable of mass circulation and special interest magazines, with an average total circulation per issue of each publication of 13.6 million. East/West Network produces magazines for airlines to put in the seat pockets for free distribution. The total list accounts for 14% of group publishers and 36% of the number of titles published by groups. (The magazines in each group are included in Appendix A. The breadth of magazine coverage is evident by examining the titles for each group.)

By magazine circulation. The most common method for calculating total circulation for all magazines or for any group is to sum up the average circulation for one issue of each magazine. However, since the revenue and the impact of a magazine are based on how many copies it sells annually, it is more valid to factor in frequency per issue, so that a weekly carries 4.3 times the weight as a monthly of the same circulation per issue.

Table 8-6 has ranked the consumer magazine publishers by total copies circulated. By this accounting, Triangle is the largest magazine publisher, but Time Inc., with its group of weeklies, is twice the size of The New York Times Co. It displaced Reader's Digest Association, which was third largest in 1978. CBS' growing stable of periodicals is fifth. (In all cases, foreign editions have been omitted.)

For purposes of comparison, the table also calculates circulation on a straight per issue basis. These 18 magazine publishers produce 136 titles, or 12.1% of the periodicals totaled in Table 2-3. Their combined circulation per issue of 170 million represents 40% of the circulation of the magazines in Table 2-3.

Relative Group Size

Most group publishers are relatively small in aggregate circulation. Of the 76 consumer groups, Table 8-7 shows that 23, or 30%, have aggregate circulation for all their magazines of under 300,000. At the other extreme, only eight group owners have total per issue circulation in excess of 10 million.

THE ATTRACTION OF GROUP PUBLISHING

There is a good reason why most magazines are published by multimagazine groups: a single publication, especially one of limited audience circulation, must carry too great a burden of overhead to make economic sense. The economies of scale are not great in magazine publishing, but

Group Ownership 131

Table 8-6: Largest Consumer Magazine Publishers, by Total Annual Circulation, 1980

	Total Annual Circulation (thousands)[a]	Total Average Circulation Per Issue	Number of Magazines Published[b]
1. Triangle	964,739	19,759	2
2. Time Inc.	538,085	12,464	7
3. New York Times Co.	221,130	10,510	4
4. Reader's Digest Ass'n.	220,329	18,361	2
5. CBS, Inc.	186,215	13,569[c]	10
6. Washington Post Co.	164,795	3,592	2
7. Hearst Corp.	149,031	12,938	14
8. Meredith Corp.	128,829	12,003	8
9. Charter Co.	122,255	10,188	2
10. Newhouse (Condé Nast)	83,072	7,089[c]	7
11. McCall's Publishing	80,703	6,705	2
12. Scholastic Magazines, Inc.	76,552	6,104	10
13. Playboy Enterprises	74,545	6,572	2
14. Webb Co.	71,462	9,283	15
15. Ziff-Davis Co.	68,867	6,287	17
16. Peterson Publishing Co.	60,503	5,042	13
17. Times Mirror Co.	59,633	5,501	6
18. Macfadden Group, Inc.	59,023	3,611	8
TOTALS	3,329,768	169,598	136

[a] Average circulation per issue x frequency.
[b] Includes those owned in October 1981, started, but recent start-ups or investitures after 1981 may not be in circulation totals.
[c] Does not include *Family Weekly* or *Parade*.
Source: Calculated from Standard Rate & Data Service, *Consumer Magazine and Farm Publication Rates and Data*, May 27, 1981.

Table 8-7: Circulation Size of Consumer Magazine Groups, 1980*

Total per Issue Circulation:	Number	Percent	Cumulative Percent
Under 300,000	23	30%	30%
300,000 to 999,999	17	22	55
1 million to 3 million	12	16	71
3 million to 10 million	13	17	85
Over 10 million	8	11	96
Not reported (or unpaid)	3	4	100
	76	100%	

*Excludes nine groups consisting of solely farm publications.
Source: Calculated from circulation reported in Standard Rate & Data Service, *Consumer Magazine Farm Publication Rates and Data*, May 27, 1981.

the natural limits to the size of the consumer and business special interest periodicals make acquisitions and start-ups a necessity if a company wishes to keep growing. Once a periodical reaches a saturation point, ad revenue growth becomes limited to cost per thousand increases or total pages. Consider *New York* magazine, for example. From a start-up circulation of 50,000 in 1968, circulation grew rapidly to 171,000 by 1969, 292,000 in 1971, 342,000 in 1973 and 391,000 in 1978. The rate of circulation growth was 35% from 1969 to 1970, 26% the next year, 10% in 1972 and 6% in 1973. Between 1973 and 1978, circulation grew an average of 2.7% annually. So after some heady growth, *New York* logically turned to the outside for further revenue increases, first by its acquisition of the *Village Voice* and then through the *New West* start-up. Eventually it bought out its closest rival, *Cue*. Yet few notable economies can result from having these three publications under the same corporate banner. Indeed, *New West* was eventually sold to another fledgling group.

Group publishers do gain some synergistic advantages in a few areas over one-magazine publishers:

- A publisher of several established magazines has greater leverage in getting distribution and may be able to negotiate a more favorable deal with a national distributor.

- Bulk acquisition of paper may be slightly less expensive and easier to obtain for a large user.

- Printing contracts can be negotiated for all publications, giving their owners somewhat more leverage with printers.

- Subscription fulfillment contracts for a small circulation book can be combined with those of other books for a more economical rate.

- In-house circulation staffs can be centralized.

- A good publishing group can provide corporate research and management expertise.

On the other hand, most magazine publishing costs vary little from independent to group status. For instance, editorial staffs for each publication are generally strictly segregated, often because of the disparate subject matter of the books. Similarly, advertising staffs are separate, although regional offices can be combined in a single facility and many groups of small magazines sell insertions on a package basis. (Macfadden

Women's Group, for example, sells for all eight magazines in combination.) Postage on subscription mailings is strictly per unit, so mailing costs are also figured separately for each title.

Management approaches vary among multiple magazine publishers. ABC, for example, believes in operating each newly acquired publication or group autonomously. "Synergy is overrated in magazine publishing," states a top ABC publishing executive. More typical, however, is CBS Publishing, which centralizes printing contracts, paper purchases and typesetting, as well as marketing and fulfillment.

Since economies of scale are modest, the quest for a chain lies in the fact that magazine publishing is an industry with good, but small, profit margins. Time Inc., for example, had a 12% pretax profit for magazine publishing operations in 1978. In its heyday (1974), *Playboy* had earnings before taxes of 21%. (By 1978 it was barely 10%). The *New Yorker* magazine, the only major publicly owned firm with income almost exclusively from a single magazine, had a pretax profit of 11% in 1978. Although the magazine industry as a whole reports 3% to 6% pretax earnings, there are many profitable magazines making 15% pretax, according to an official of an acquisitions-minded firm.

Acquisitions

While starting a new magazine has a certain excitement, buying an existing one is quicker, easier and not necessarily more expensive. The key is buying at the right price—profitable titles either are not for sale or are only available at a high price.

"What you're buying is good will," notes an analyst at one of the most highly regarded special interest publication groups. This firm looks for a 30% to 50% return on its investment—and never less than 25%. It expects to achieve this by doing with the property what the seller is not doing, and that's more than just cutting costs. It may mean, for example, adjusting a price or a CPM that is too low. The New York Times paid $8 million for *Family Circle* and claims that the investment was paid for in two years. Ziff-Davis calculated a similar payback on *Psychology Today*.

Table 8-8 identifies some of the major acquisitions in the 1970s.

As in any make-or-buy decision, there are cost tradeoffs in acquiring or starting a book. The first question is, "Do we want a title in this marketplace?" If yes, then the field of available publications can be scouted. The cost of acquiring available books must be compared to the cost of starting fresh. An important factor in the equation is management time. The cost of the management time used in developing a new publication would usually be far greater than in acquiring an existing book.

Table 8-8: Selected Consumer Magazine Acquisitions by Major Publishers

Publisher	Consumer Magazines
American Broadcasting Companies	Los Angeles (1977)* Modern Photography (1976) High Fidelity (1976)
CBS	American Photographer (1980) Sea (1973) Woman's Day (1977) Audio (1979) Family Weekly (1980)
Charter Publishing Company	Ladies' Home Journal (1977) Redbook (1977) Sport (1977) (Sold, 1980) American Home (1977; suspended 1977) WomanSports (1977; suspended 1977)
Condé Nast	Gentlemen's Quarterly (1979)
Davis Publications	Analog (1979)
Dow Jones	Book Digest (1978)
Gruner & Jahr AG	Parents (1978) Young Miss (1978)
Macfadden Group, Inc.	Us (1980)
New York Times Company	Family Circle (1969) Tennis (1972) Golf Digest (1969)
Petersen Publishing	True (1974; suspended 1976)
Playboy	Games (1978)
13-30 Corporation	Esquire (1979)
Times Mirror	Ski (1972) Golf (1972) Popular Science (1970) Outdoor Life (1970) Sporting News (1978)
Ziff-Davis	Psychology Today (1973) Intellectual Digest (1973; suspended 1974) Sport Driver (1977) Backpacker (1979) The Runner (1980)

Source: Knowledge Industry Publications, Inc.
*(Date acquired)

In many ways it is surprising that a giant like CBS would even bother with books like *Pickup, Van & 4WD* or *Sea,* both of which were purchased. *Sea* was a 55,000 circulation book for boating enthusiasts in the West in 1973. CBS claimed then that it was "very profitable," with its 1400 ad pages in 1973. By 1978 it was national, with 177,000 circulation, while *Pickup, Van & 4WD,* which was of similar size and just starting to make money in 1973, had a 211,000 circulation in 1978. Since just about the same amount of time and investigation is needed to buy a publication that has a potential of 100,000 circulation as one of 500,000 circulation, the usual scenario would be for the smaller groups or independents to take over the limited audience magazines while the bigger companies use their earnings to buy magazines with more substantial cash flows. But clearly potential for growth must be a major factor in the decision.

Rather than invest in start-ups or purchases, several publishers have chosen to revamp their existing publications or "clone" them through special issues that may be developed into ongoing magazines (as discussed in Chapter 6).

The Continuing Trend Toward Groups

One firm publishing several magazines is not an innovation. Curtis, Condé Nast, Hearst, Time, Fawcett and Macfadden are among the many that have long been group publishers. The increased desirability of special interest publications, however, makes multi-magazine houses all the more necessary for the future. When giant CBS decided to get into the magazine business, it did not launch or buy up mass circulation magazines but chose to accumulate a stable of smaller special interest books. With the exception of *Field and Stream,* none of them until *Woman's Day* was significant by itself, but as a group they provided substantial revenue and potentially strong profits. The New York Times Co. purchased *Family Circle, Tennis* and *Golf Digest* before undertaking its first start-up, *Us.* Time Inc., accustomed to circulation figures in the millions, has added *Money,* with its modest potential to its house. *People* and the new *Life* have circulation ambitions more in keeping with Time Inc.'s tradition.

ABC got into the magazine business by acquiring *High Fidelity* and *Modern Photography,* and has expanded its presence in the industry through the purchase of additional limited audience consumer (as well as farm and business) magazines.

With the re-emergence of *Life,* the success of *People* and the staying power of *Us,* it may seem that mass circulation magazines are making a comeback. But even at 2 or 3 million circulation, these are a shadow of the 8 and 9 million of the old mass circulation periodicals. And these popular magazines tend to get the publicity, while the scores of small business and special interest magazines, independent and group owned, make up the bulk of the industry.

With the risk still high and the entry cost great, new mass circulation books will be a rarity in the field. Most publishers will thus have to rely on good margins from relatively small revenues from several publications for company or division viability.

INTERNATIONAL PUBLISHING

Foreign Publishers in the U.S.

The strength of many foreign currencies vis-à-vis the dollar in the late 1970s was one reason for increased interest on the part of foreign publishers in entering the U.S. market. European publishers see the U.S. as a vast market, with a far greater potential for a title than in their home bases. Although foreign publishers have purchased some going magazines, they have also committed funds to the start-up of new publications. Among the ventures:

- Gruner & Jahr, Germany's largest publisher (*Stern, Brigitte*), set up a U.S. subsidiary to publish *Geo,* a slick picture magazine not unlike *National Geographic.* In April 1978, the company purchased Parents' Magazine Enterprises, publisher of the 1.6 million circulation monthly *Parents',* as well as *Children's Digest, Humpty Dumpty* and others. Gruner & Jahr is itself 75% owned by German publishing giant Bertelsmann Gütersloh, which directly owns a majority interest in leading U.S. mass market paperback publisher Bantam Books. *Geo,* however, did not catch on with either enough readers or advertisers to satisfy the publisher. It was sold in 1981 to Knapp Publications, which publishes *Bon Appetit* and *Architectural Digest.*

- Daniel Filipacchi tried to revive *Look,* killed by Cowles Communications in 1971. Aiming at a 1 million circulation biweekly, he fell far short of his goal and suspended publication before the end of 1979. Filipacchi had previously acquired Popular Publications, Inc., a group that includes *Argosy, Camera 35* and *Railroad.* His French publishing base includes *Paris-Match* (which sells nearly 800,000 weekly) and the sex-oriented *Lui.*

- Britain's Associated Newspapers Group, Ltd., the owner of 45 publications, has bought a minority interest in the *Soho Weekly News* (a competitor of New York's *Village Voice*) and financed Clay Felker in his brief take-over of *Esquire* in 1977.

- Sweden's Bonnier Magazine group acquired an interest in the venerable *Esquire* when its 50%-owned U.S. partner, 13-30 Corporation, purchased a majority interest from Associated. Bonnier has since sold out its interest to 13-30.

- *The Economist,* Britain's respected financial weekly, is seeking expanded circulation in the U.S. with added coverage of U.S. events and beefed-up U.S. editorial operations. It now prints the U.S. edition locally.

- Harlequin Enterprises, the Canadian publisher best known for its romance novels, has started a magazine publishing venture in the U.S. Its first step in that direction was the acquisition of the Laufer Company, which publishes *Tiger Beat* and associated periodicals for teenagers and a series of Rona Barrett gossip magazines. Total group circulation is about 1.2 million.

So far the presence of the foreign publishers is rather small. Their interest in the market can only add to the competition for the acquisition of existing publications, driving prices higher. But their willingness to start new ventures can also add to the diversity of magazines for the consumer. And, if they follow the form of most publishers, profits will be kept in the U.S. to add further publications.

U.S. Ventures Abroad

U.S. publishers have also been active in other parts of the world. *Reader's Digest* publishes 39 international editions in 15 languages. (*Canadian Reader's Digest* is a separate entity.) Each is locally edited under general supervision from U.S. headquarters. These international editions have a combined circulation of about 11.7 million.

Hearst has long been involved in overseas publishing, directly and through licensing of its titles to local publishers. *Mechanica Popular* is a Latin America look-alike of *Popular Mechanics.* Hearst also owns Great Britain's National Magazine Co., which publishes British versions of some Hearst titles, as well as magazines unique to its own markets.

Condé Nast is also active in international publishing, with both licensing and foreign subsidiaries. *Vogue's* British, Italian and French editions, for example, are owned, while the Australian edition is published under license. Condé Nast, like Hearst, also publishes titles overseas that do not have U.S. counterparts.

Time and *Newsweek* both have extensive international editions that are substantially different editorially from the domestic editions. *Newsweek* has Atlantic and Pacific overseas editions with further geographic subdivisions, while *Time* has these as well as Canadian and Latin American editions. All are printed in English. *Time* has overseas sales of about 1 million copies per issue, while *Newsweek,* without a Canadian edition, has a circulation of about half that.

Family Circle sold off its Australian edition published in partnership with Meredith's *Better Homes and Gardens*. Taking advantage of the proliferation of supermarkets in Japan, however, it entered into an agreement with the Blue Chip Stamp Co. of Japan for a Japanese edition.

Thus, as foreign publishers look to the U.S. as an expansion market, U.S. publishers continue to use their editorial formulas to tap an increasingly literate market throughout the world.

UNIQUENESS OF MAGAZINES AND COMPETITION

Magazines are like no other medium. They do not essentially compete with one another, since the essence of almost every title is to create a monopoly for itself with a distinct audience. *Ski* and *Skiing* magazines do battle for the same audience, but are not in direct competition with *House Beautiful* or *Teen*. Magazines are perhaps the best example of monopolistic competition—many similar products, but each one perceived as being different enough from the others to create its own unique market. The distinction may be by geography (*Philadelphia, Southern Living*), specialized content (*Popular Photography*), demographics (*Town & Country, Modern Romances, Seventeen*), intellectual level (*Marvel* comics, *New Yorker*), generalized content (*People, TV Guide, Better Homes and Gardens*) or other designations.

Although it may be argued that newspapers do not compete with one another in different cities, daily newspapers all tend to provide the same function for a single mass audience each day. While a fire in Cincinnati and a budget hearing in San Jose are reported only locally, any given paper across the country on a given day will have much the same national and international news, similar types of local stories and advertising. Few magazines have such overlapping content.

It is for this reason, perhaps, that group ownership of magazines is seldom raised when discussion turns to media concentration. It is not easy to support the hypothesis that the purchase by ABC of Chilton's *Going Places* gave that magazine an unfair advantage over other magazines. Nor should the fact that Times Mirror publishes *Popular Science* and *Outdoor Life* have any impact on the free flow of ideas through these or other magazines.

9
Production, Paper and Printing

During the late 1970s magazine paper, mostly No. 5 coated ground wood, was in tight supply, but not to the point of disrupting print schedules or discouraging new ventures or expansion. By the early 1980s, the supply problem had eased, although prices remained high. Composition, meanwhile, has been shifting slowly to in-house phototypesetting; the decreasing cost of sophisticated systems has made it possible for even small magazine groups and publishers to justify purchasing their own equipment. In printing, the trend continues toward offset as letterpress facilities are retired, although there has also been an increasing use of gravure presses. This chapter summarizes developments in paper supply and usage, printing technology and overall production expense for magazines.

PAPER

Users and suppliers of paper have been walking a precarious tightrope. Paper manufacturers, recalling the flat demand between 1966 and 1972, have been wary of adding too much capacity, afraid of being stuck with underutilized mills that cost a minimum of $150 million to build. With a three-year lead time for completion, the tight supply of one year could become a glut if the magazine sales slow down.

Wood product and paper manufacturers have recovered from the depths of 1970 and 1971, when profit margins and returns dropped to unacceptable levels. As seen in Table 9-1, median return on stockholders' equity, though traditionally below the median for the largest industrial firms, remained stable at almost 13% from 1978 to 1980. The median return on sales, on the other hand, remained above the *Fortune* 500 industrial median. The largest paper products based company is International Paper Co., with 1980 sales in excess of $5 billion and net income of

140 CONSUMER MAGAZINES

Table 9-1: Selected Profit Criteria for Paper Product Manufacturers in *Fortune* 500, Selected Years, 1971-1980

	1980	1978	1975	1971
Median Return on Stockholders' Equity:				
paper, fiber and wood products	12.8%	12.9%	10.8%	5.6%
all industries	14.4	14.3	11.6	9.1
Median Return on Sales:				
paper, fiber and wood products	5.0	5.3	5.6	2.8
all industries	4.8	4.8	3.9	3.8

Source: Calculated from *Fortune* 500, annual.

$314 million. Other firms among the leading suppliers of coated magazine paper, listed in Table 9-2, include St. Regis Paper, Champion International and Crown Zellerbach. Union Camp had the strongest profit ratios.

In 1978 U.S. mills produced about 2.4 million tons of coated ground wood stock, much but not all of it the No. 5 grade preferred by most magazine publishers. The shortfall in supply that year was an estimated 350,000 tons. About half of this was met by imports, mainly from West Germany and Finland. After steep customs and shipping charges were added, however, the imported paper cost about $1000 per ton, compared to about $650 per domestically produced ton.

Another strategy for coping with short term shortfalls has been to sub-

Table 9-2: Selected Measures of Profitability for Leading Paper Manufacturers, 1980

Company	Sales (millions)	Net Income (millions)	Return on Stockholders' Equity	Return on Sales
International Paper	$5,043	$314	11.1%	6.2%
Champion International	3,753	147	8.4	3.9
Crown Zellerbach	3,070	97	8.2	3.2
Boise Cascade	3,019	149	11.6	4.9
St. Regis Paper	2,714	170	12.7	6.3
Union Camp	1,575	165	16.5	10.5
Westvaco	1,410	88	14.0	6.2
Great Northern Nekoosa	1,373	99	14.4	7.2
Industry Median			12.8	5.0

Source: Calculated from *Fortune*, May 4, 1981.

stitute other paper grades, mostly supercalendered uncoated paper, which also must be imported, but at a cost of 10% to 20% less than coated. Supercalendering is a process of putting a very smooth finish on paper without coating. It is of acceptable quality when run on a rotogravure press. Some publishers have switched to uncoated paper for sections with text and black and white photographs, advertisements and classifieds.

In 1979 the tight supply was on the verge of becoming a true crisis. St. Regis Paper faced a long strike at its Bucksport (ME) mill which produces 15% of the supply of No. 5 coated, while a nearby International Paper Co. plant, which accounts for another 13%, also went on strike. With publisher supplies down to 30 to 60 days at the time, plans were being laid by many publishers to cut back on print runs, eliminate some demographic editions and cut down on the number of pages. As it turned out, the walkouts were settled quickly and the normal tightness was all that had to be coped with. However, the situation did emphasize the delicate equilibrium between paper supply and demand.

Despite the short supplies, not many publishers complained of having to postpone new projects or expansion of existing publications. Most large publishers maintain long-term contracts with the mills which take into account their future needs. If the suppliers cannot fulfill this contractual commitment from their own production, they sometimes import paper themselves and absorb the difference in price. At the other extreme, short-run magazines, which depend on their printers to acquire paper, require such a small proportion of total supply that there is rarely a problem. To illustrate the difference: *Family Circle* uses about 80,000 to 85,000 tons per year; a 300,000 circulation monthly that weighs seven ounces per copy would use under 1000 tons; a 35,000 bimonthly could get by on about 46 tons.

A temporary shortage can delay plans. In 1979, CBS' *Woman's Day* put off expansion to a 16th issue, attributing the delay to the paper shortage as well as a sluggish economy. *Playboy* also complained of being chronically short of paper, with 60,000 tons under contract vs. a need for 70,000 tons, the difference coming from the spot market.

But at Hearst, although it acknowledged the "worst paper situation since World War II," the concern was generally less with supply than with price. Hearst, like any other subscription-based publisher, contracts for delivery of future issues of subscriptions based on expected costs. If these change substantially on short notice, it must fulfill its liability without getting more money from the subscriber. Times Mirror, relying on St. Regis for 90% of its paper, was more than a little concerned when the workers shut the plant there in 1979, but otherwise has not found supply a factor in making decisions on new publications or expansion. Condé Nast has had to "scrounge" for some paper, but this did not inhibit the firm from starting *Self,* which needed about 1600 tons annually at its mid-1979 size.

Cost

The cost of No. 5 coated paper doubled between 1973 when it was about $290 per ton, and 1979. Although much of the increase can be allocated to higher costs for labor, pulp and plant, the role of energy is becoming more dominant. Whereas in 1972 energy costs accounted for only 6% of the value of shipments of paper products, by 1976 this had risen to 10%. With another 100% increase in oil prices by 1980, in a tight market manufacturers pass that cost right along to customers. Paper makers, however, are looking for ways to reduce their dependence on purchased energy: the industry is now among the top four manufacturing industries in the purchase of energy. A shift has been taking place toward concentration on self-generation of power, using by-products from the paper making process, such as bark, for fuel. Nonetheless, No. 5 coated stock prices hit $745 a ton in 1981.[1]

Capacity

Supplies of magazine paper improved in the early 1980s as total capacity for production of coated ground wood paper (about two thirds of which will be used by magazines) increased by about 535,000 tons—or 22%—between 1978 and 1982. The increased capacity resulted from a combination of adjustments to existing machinery, addition of machines to existing plants and addition of some new plants. The supply should easily outstrip the growth in magazines. Among the manufacturers with additions were Consolidated Paper—115,000 tons; Crown Zellerbach—50,000 tons; Great Northern Nekoosa—45,000 tons; Krueger—70,000 tons; Fraser—80,000 tons; and Boise Cascade—160,000 tons.

PRINTING

Magazine printing costs, which barely changed from 1963 to 1973, increased between 22% and 34% from 1973 to 1979. Higher costs have been felt mostly by the smaller circulation magazines, while magazines with mid-range print runs of between 1 million and 2 million faced lower rises.

[1]*Paper Trade Journal,* August 31, 1981.

Continued Change in Types of Presses

The traditional letterpress has given way increasingly to the newer web offset and rotogravure presses. The letterpress was designed to use the stereotype plates that came through the hot metal typesetting process. With that technology virtually phased out in favor of cold type, the remaining letterpress machines have been adapted to use lightweight plastic plates. But printers have found that offset is more economical for short runs, while gravure, long favored for extended print orders, is becoming more efficient for ever-shorter runs, eliminating the need for the letterpress.

In 1970, letterpress held about 39% of the commercial printing market. By 1980 it was down to 21% and in 1990 it is expected that it will account for no more than 5% of printing. For example, Dayton Press planned to eliminate all its letterpress operations by 1984.

In the meantime, however, magazines that can economically use letterpress (runs of between 800,000 and 2 million) are enjoying some price breaks because those presses that are around are underused, so their time is attractively priced. Letterpress also offers some advantages over offset, such as greater flexibility for making page changes in various demographic or area editions. The new offset and gravure presses often have a single press plate that prints 16 pages; thus, changing one or two pages requires a new plate for all 16. In contrast, each letterpress plate is separate. Letterpress can also use lighter weight paper than can offset. Nonetheless, the competition from the other two types of presses has doomed the letterpress.

Offset still has the shortest set-up time and lowest cost of any of the other methods, especially for relatively short runs. It is ideal for getting the pages on and off the presses most quickly and is well-suited to four-color reproduction. Because of its short run capability, it can be used to print many different limited-run signatures for demographic editions wrapped around a common editorial section that may be printed by gravure. It is even suitable for weeklies with large circulations. *Time,* for example, is printed by offset at several locations around the country so the copies can be mailed closer to the final destinations. Offset presses, however, are responsible for more paper waste than letterpresses because of their adjustment needs; they also require paper of 36 pound or heavier weight, compared to 32 pound or less for letterpress.

The major development in magazine printing in recent years has been the increased use of rotogravure, a process that requires the etching of copper cylinders as the printing surface. Until recently the process was too expensive for press runs of less than 2.5 million. But improved etching processes, including the use of computer-controlled laser etching, has brought the minimum quantity down to 1.0 to 1.5 million (or to 700,000, according to one printing firm officer). It is generally believed that by the middle of the 1980s, gravure will be cost efficient for print runs of 300,000 to 400,000 copies.

Gravure will pick up most of the magazine printing now done by letterpress. With only 9% of the market in 1970, it had about 15% in 1980 and an estimated 25% by 1990. Offset will handle most of the rest. In 1990, most large consumer magazines will have at least their full-run pages printed by gravure, while offset will print split-run pages and the smaller circulation magazines.

Publishers and printers also see gravure as a way of containing paper costs. Not only does this process work well with lighter weights of paper than does offset, but it can print acceptable quality color on both newsprint and supercalendered paper, both less expensive than coated stock. This is because the gravure process works by literally sucking the paper into the etched wells of the plate. This produces a heavy impression, even if the paper is not very smooth. The amount of ink can also be regulated by changing the depth of the etching, to account for different types of paper.

Gravure printing in the U.S. has been the province of the largest magazine printers. These include Arcata National, World Color Press, W.F. Hall, R.R. Donnelley, Meredith and Meredith/Burda (a joint venture for gravure printing), Brown, Providence and Krueger. There were approximately 130 gravure presses in the United States in 1981 devoted to magazines and catalogs.

COST OF PRODUCTION

The cost of typesetting and printing 2 million copies of a 168-page issue was about $645,000 in 1979; the cost for each copy was about 32 cents. This per copy cost was 56% higher than in 1973. However, the increase was less than that for a 100,000 or 300,000 circulation magazine, because the larger circulation magazine can be printed by letterpress, which printers are running at relatively bargain rates. Offset printed magazines suffered through a roughly 70% increase, including a 108% jump in the cost for paper.

Table 9-3 compares average production costs for these three different circulation magazines. Whereas paper accounted for only 45% to 50% of total production cost in 1963, by 1979 paper was 58% to 64% of the total cost. Moreover, comparing 1963 to 1973 costs also brings a different perspective to the differences between the large and smaller publica-

Table 9-3: Production Costs for Different Size Magazines

	\multicolumn{3}{c	}{Circulation}						
	\multicolumn{3}{c	}{100,000}	\multicolumn{3}{c	}{300,000}	\multicolumn{3}{c	}{2,000,000}
	1963	1973	1979	1963	1973	1979	1963	1973	1979
Pages*	80	80	80	144	144	144	168	168	168
Composition (per issue)	$1680	$2400	$3120	$3024	$4320	$5620	$3578	$9358	$12,540
Printing & Bindery	.069	.070	.094	.101	.098	.131	.082	.094	.114
Paper	.056	.063	.131	.088	.105	.219	.082	.109	.202
Total Print, Bindery, Paper	.125	.133	.225	.189	.203	.350	.164	.203	.316
Printing Process		Offset			Offset			Letterpress	
Percentage Increase	1963-1979	1973-1979		1963-1979	1973-1979		1963-1979	1973-1979	
Composition	86%	30%		86%	30%		162%	34%	
Paper	134	108		149	109		146	85	
Print & Bind	36	34		29	34		39	21	
Total Print, Bind & Paper	80	69		85	72		93	56	

*Plus cover.
Source: Knowledge Industry Publications, Inc.

tions. The development and improvement of the web offset press in that period helped keep printing and binding costs virtually unchanged for the two smaller size magazines, so that total cost was up only 6% to 8%. On the other hand, the letterpress made no productivity improvements, and magazines paid 24% more by the end of the same period. Thus, looking back over the longer run, from 1963 to 1979, the smaller publications faced an 80%-85% increase while the larger publication paid 93% more.

The switch to rotogravure should help the large circulation magazines slow future increases in printing costs. But with paper now a greater proportion of the total than ever before, much of what happens to production expense depends on its costs. Some printers are also reporting that their labor costs are going up even faster than those for paper and ink. The rise may be partially balanced by further improvements in technology, however. Technological advances include computer-controlled etching for gravure and further automation for web offset, such as the growing use of central consoles for monitoring and controlling color density, ink fountains and color registration.

Changes in Trim Size

In the early 1970s, many of the large format magazines, such as *McCall's* and *Fortune,* reduced their size from 632 or 680 lines (about 11x13 inches) to the standard 420 or 429-line size (about 8½x11 inches). This was partly a response to already rising paper and postage rates, but was even more the result of the requirements of the new offset and gravure presses, which were not being built to handle the larger dimensions. Press size also explains why many of the digest size 224-line magazines such as *Popular Science* increased to standard size: no one was making presses that could handle digest size, either. Advertisers also favored the movement, since it meant fewer mechanicals to prepare.

Some large magazines did persist in the old format. But in 1977, more of the holdouts made the switch: *Better Homes and Gardens, Harper's Bazaar, House Beautiful, House & Garden, Town & Country* and *Vogue. Life,* however, found some unused capacity and recreated its former size (almost) as one of the last oversize magazines.

10
Outlook and Conclusions

The overall outlook for consumer magazines over the decade of the 1980s is encouraging. Magazines have proven their resilience in the face of changing life-styles and competition. They have demonstrated enough value to support rapid increases in costs to advertisers and consumers. Although magazines have defied development by formula, there is abundant evidence that many opportunities remain for new—and still unconceived—editorial approaches to new audiences. Magazines can be profitable, are able to attract capital and continue to interest the largest media conglomerates, as well as ambitious entrepreneurs.

Nonetheless, there are still many unknowns, some that will affect the short-term fortunes of publishers, others that will carry weight over the longer haul. These variables include developing technologies, political influences, demographic changes, the general health of the U.S. economy and the energy crisis.

NEW MEDIA TECHNOLOGIES

Having survived the challenge of television, magazines may next face an enhancement of this medium as a challenge, in the form of video cassettes and discs for the home market. By mid-1981, there were about 3 million homes with video-cassette recorders, out of a total of 80 million homes with television. The rate of sales of the machines was increasing, however, to the rate of about 1.8-2.0 million units annually. The video disc player was still in its infancy, with perhaps 100,000 units of all manufacturers in homes.

Between the two technologies, however, millions of homes will soon have an opportunity to provide their own desired video programming. This can be accomplished either by recording the special interest programming finding its way increasingly onto the cable network, or by purchasing or renting prerecorded cassettes and discs.

As in previous eras when new media seemed to threaten the information franchise of magazines, these new video formats are assumed to compete with magazines because they can provide similar types of information: e.g., tips on skiing techniques, cooking lessons, sports highlights or odd decorating ideas. Certainly the video format does have advantages in such areas over the visual limitations inherent in print.

Even so, magazine publishers have not been very concerned about competition from new technology as a *replacement* for magazines for at least two sound reasons:

- Expense to the consumer. The cassette machines, which can also record off the air, are selling for about $1000, with some models discounted to perhaps $700. Prerecorded tapes, however, sell for $29.95 and up, a rather formidable investment compared to a magazine. Video disc players, now selling for $500-$750, may eventually be as low as $450 for the stripped down RCA model. Discs may sell for as little as $7.95 for a one-hour length. But even at this price, the cost of the machine plus discs is steep compared to the print alternative. There have been some attempts at a rental market, but while this might be appropriate for feature-length movies, it would not serve for the usual magazine subject matter, which does not lend itself to a single three-day viewing; with rented cassettes or discs, consumers also lack the advantage of later reference or clipping a particular article.

- Little incentive for advertisers. Neither video cassette nor discs would provide the needed format for advertisers. It is possible to construct a scenario whereby a video version of a magazine has editorial segments interspersed with commercials, but could a video version of *Playboy* really have 40 or 50 interruptions of 15 or 30 seconds each? Paging through advertising in print magazines is reader controlled; it is not likely that viewers would stand for so many fixed-exposure interruptions on a disc (though "fast forward" remote control could help speed through such advertisements). Sponsored discs and cassettes would be one way of reducing their cost to the consumer, but the usage pattern makes the video format an unlikely substitute for the printed magazine.

Opportunities for Publishers

On the other hand, there will undoubtedly be some market for magazine-like programming on disc and tape. Besides pure entertainment topics, there is the potential for special interest programming that is a natural outgrowth of magazine editorial expertise. These programs would be produced more as a supplement to the basic magazine, in much the same way annuals or one-shots are now published. One type of special interest programming, the "how-to" material, particularly lends itself to video presentation. Such programs might include gardening advice, home repair instruction, yoga, tennis or golf lessons, cooking, etc. If these features could be produced at reasonable cost, perhaps subsidized by two or three advertisers, they might find a market for which magazine publishers have a natural head start.

A few publishers have already explored this area. Playboy has established a separate unit to develop video programming. Time Inc. is well positioned with Time-Life Films along with its Home Box Office and cable involvement. Reader's Digest has been mentioned as looking into the video area. Newhouse, Hearst, ABC and CBS are among the consumer magazine publishers with plans announced by 1981 to participate in production for the new video market.

But on the whole, special interest publishers tend to regard video programming as someone else's bailiwick, despite their obvious expertise in subject matter. Most publishers would probably agree with the strategy that is accepted at Ziff-Davis: when the time is right, it will buy a small company that is already knowledgeable about the field.

A similar philosophy is no doubt at work in extending the programming opportunities for the voracious appetite of the cable television industry to fill its many channels. Here, too, special interest topics would be particularly applicable. Cable had already reached 20 million households by 1981. It also lends itself more readily to conventional sponsorship by advertisers. In fact, the same special interest programs can be developed and produced for cable distribution, then repackaged for tape and/or disc marketing. It has been estimated that when the number of home video units reaches 5 million, the market for a special interest topic such as tennis or golf would be about 100,000 households with an additional 100,000 for each increment of 5 million such units.[1]

OTHER ANCILLARY ENTERPRISES

The tentative nature of magazine publishers' ventures into video programming is linked to the different technology, since many publishers

---

[1] For a more complete analysis of the video market, see *Publishing/Programming Opportunities in Consumer Video* (White Plains, New York: Knowledge Industry Publications, Inc., 1978).

have long been involved in other magazine-related publishing areas. These include:

- annuals and one-time editions associated with magazine titles, as already discussed in Chapter 8;

- book publishing;

- book clubs, offering books published by other companies;

- merchandise, such as T-shirts, key chains, building plans, fruitcakes;

Of all consumer magazine publishers, Time Inc. is the most active in these adjacent fields, with its Time-Life Books (sold mostly by mail order), its special issues of *Life* before its re-establishment as a monthly and its Time-Life Films, most of which are made for television or educational markets. It also owns Book-of-the-Month Club and Little, Brown Publishers.

Newsweek Inc. cut back on its own mail order book publishing ventures, which now account for under 1% of Washington Post Co. revenue. Newsweek does maintain its condensed book program, however. Reader's Digest also uses its extensive mail order capability to promote not only its condensed book club, but its many one-shot volumes, such as *Do It Yourself.*

Hearst, CBS, Times Mirror, Playboy, and the New York Times Co. are among the magazine publishers with book publishing divisions. But for the most part, there is little connection between the magazine and book operations in these projects, other than the use of common mailing lists and house ads. On the other hand, several publishers integrate book and magazine operations much more closely. Lane Magazine & Book Co. whose best known publication is *Sunset Magazine,* publishes softcover travel guidebooks, hobby and crafts books, and building and remodeling books sold through hardware, hobby and craft outlets. The company sells more than 6 million books annually.

Other examples include Meredith, with its long-running *Better Homes and Gardens New Cook Book* and other titles on hobbies, crafts and cooking. Most of its sales are by mail order. Petersen Publishing also gets many of its book ideas from editorial material already on hand through its magazines, producing books on automotive, photographic, sports and hobby topics. Books are sold to its own subscribers, as well as by direct mail and to retail outlets appropriate to the topic (such as photography stores).

Book clubs also can make use of magazine mailing lists and house ads, but otherwise have little editorial or marketing overlap with the periodicals. Playboy has featured books that it expects to be attractive to its largely male readership. Other publishers have tried promoting book clubs that go beyond the interest of their magazine subscribers. These include Time's Book-of-the-Month Club and *Psychology Today*'s club, which offers general trade book selections as well as titles more closely allied to the magazine's subject matter.

Such ancillary enterprises can be very expensive to start up and often must survive on their own as separate profit centers. For example, Playboy has expanded its book publishing activities, including a series of romance paperback books aimed at a female audience. This draws on very little of what the magazine itself either produces or has expertise in marketing.

The types of spin-off activities need not be limited to publishing. Petersen has established an art gallery devoted to "Americana," Western and sports-related art. The retail operation is supplemented by catalogs promoted through house ads. Meredith has initiated a franchised real estate service, licensing the use of the Better Homes and Gardens trademark in what it sees as a natural offshoot of the magazine's home-oriented service reputation.

THE POLITICAL DIFFICULTIES OF MAGAZINES

In the distant past, magazine publishers were thought to be relatively influential in the political arena. Indeed, the special subsidized postal privileges won by magazines in 1879 were a monument to the emergence of such influence. In subsequent years, the muckraking of the old *McClure's* and its turn-of-the-century counterparts and the high visibility of Hearst and later Luce reinforced the image of magazines as important opinion makers. But today, magazine publishers make no pretense of viewing opinion formation in political matters as their primary (or even major) role.

Thus, when Congress had to consider the extent of future postal subsidies for second class mailers, the magazine industry lost at every turn, with the only concession being an extension of the phasing-in period from five to eight years.

In the absence of an effective lobbying effort, publishers should not expect to see any change in the trend toward continually higher mailing expense. This weakness can lead to a further potential problem in switching to alternative carriers.

A Caution Sign for Private Delivery Alternatives

Private delivery of magazines still represents a minuscule portion of all home-delivered magazine copies. Publishers are using private carriers in part as a "lesson" to the Postal Service. The message is that if the Postal Service does not respond to the publishers' desire for lower rates, they will just take this business elsewhere. The assumption is that the high fixed cost of the Postal Service makes the loss of second class revenue undesirable, since there would not be a commensurate drop in expense.

However, experts in the postal field are willing to take issue with this assumption, believing that there would be real savings for the Postal Service—that in fact the present second class revenue still does not cover the handling cost. Moreover, by building up the National Association of Selective Distributors, the trade group representing the private carriers, the publishers are actually creating a lobby that has a vested interest in *opposing* holding the line on second class rates. In the long run, should the publishers increase their use of private carriers to the point of weakening the Postal Service's second class business, magazine publishers will be at the mercy of private business to deliver its product.

More to the point, the private carriers must work within the same labor intensive economic structure as the Postal Service. The primary reason that the private alternative is now less expensive is that private carriers are paying much lower wages. This has produced a situation in which labor turnover is high and service inefficient. *The Wall Street Journal* reported in 1978 that its personnel turnover was more than 100% annually. To stabilize this work force requires paying more competitive wages. Moreover, as the private carriers get larger, they become a more conspicuous target for union organizing. This increases the likelihood of having to pay the higher wages that originally made the Postal Service uncompetitive. Thus, publishers may be faced with being dependent on private carriers with little or no cost advantage. Moreover, those same suppliers could be expected to vigorously oppose new efforts to increase postal subsidies.

DEMOGRAPHIC TRENDS AFFECTING MAGAZINES

As was seen in Chapter 5, heavier-than-average magazine readership has been strongly linked to higher education, income and occupational status, as well as to younger adult ages (18-44). The demographic trends in the U.S. are for the most part favorable to publishers' interests. By 1985, adults 18 to 44 years old will increase 22% in number from 1975 and will account for 58.4% of the population, compared to 55.2% in

1975. At the same time, the 65-and-over group, the least-active magazine reading age, will grow by 20% and the 45-64 group will stay virtually level. However, although 18-44 year olds have been more likely to read magazines and least likely to watch television, many who will now be entering this age category grew up with television. Past studies have measured TV usage among large groups of adults who were introduced to that medium after other media usage patterns had been established. Thus, those entering their 20s and 30s in the 1980s may have patterns more favorable to television than in previous generations.

The percentage of adults who attended or graduated from college will also continue to increase through the 1980s. Whereas 26.3% of adults were college educated in 1975, 31.2% will be in this category by 1985.

Other variables also are favorable to greater readership: white collar occupations will increase faster than service, blue collar and other occupations; there will be more families with household income of $25,000 and over (in constant 1975 dollars); and the percentage of women in the work force will continue to grow.

SENSITIVITY TO THE ECONOMY

The advertising industry in general is quite sensitive to overall economic conditions. During recessionary periods in particular, advertisers cut back across the board on expenditures in all media. In 1960-61, for example, total advertising expenditures fell about 1%, with cutbacks in newspapers and magazines of about 2% and even a slight decline for television. Growth in expenditures flattened again in 1970, in 1975 and again in 1981. As was seen in Table 2-5, magazine advertising pages dropped significantly in 1970 and 1975, although some increases in rates cushioned revenues. Circulation growth also is slowed during such economic downturns.

As described in Chapter 8, even during boom periods, not every magazine, new or existing, could expect to get its share of advertising pages. But a no-growth period will do even more to (once again) shake out some marginal publications. This might include those just hanging on, or some older magazines in trouble. Some magazines may have to depend on special help to survive. *Harper's*, on the verge of being shut down, was bailed out by the McArthur Foundation in 1980. Not many independent publishers could count on such largess.

CONCLUSIONS OF THIS STUDY

If 1979 was the high water mark of several years of impressive magazine performance, it was also the end of a decade that saw consumer magazines reach low ebb with the disappearance, temporarily at least, of two institutions in the industry: *Life* and *Look*. If the 1970s provided any lesson about the industry, it is that making sweeping generalizations about a diverse industry (e.g., that magazines are dying) based on a few isolated, though highly visible, examples is a foolhardy exercise.

More specifically, this study finds evidence to substantiate the following conclusions:

- There is a firm place in the media mix for consumer magazines. Consumers have shown a willingness to pay substantially higher prices, an indicator of appreciation of value received. Advertisers have greatly expanded their commitment to magazines, not only by spending more dollars to keep pace with costs, but by buying more space. This indicates satisfaction that magazines are a reasonably effective medium, even if some advertisers would just as soon put some of that money in television if time were available.

- Many publishers still operate in the time worn ways of the past, accepting at face value certain maxims concerning the absolute advantage of single-copy sales or the benefit of selling subscriptions to boost advertising rates. But more often, publishing executives are learning to appreciate both the art and science of management, quantifying those areas that lend themselves to such modern applications and reducing to a minimum those areas in which the "art" is central (e.g., editorial themes, layout and design, etc.). Optimizing yield from circulation and advertising, balancing newsstand and subscription sales, determining print orders, selecting mailing points and revising mailing lists are just a few of the areas lending themselves to such quantification. In the last analysis, however, it is still the guiding editorial idea and the follow-through that sustain a magazine—the rest can only help the right concept succeed and be more profitable.

- As far as the reader is concerned, the final product will not change very much in physical form over the next decade. But there will be a continuing evolution in production techniques. Photocomposition and CRT typesetters are already a fact. Offset printing will continue to take business from the aging letterpress, and rotogravure presses will help control costs for magazines of increasingly lower print runs. The ability of these presses to use lighter and less expensive papers without significant sacrifice in print quality, along with increased capacity of paper makers to produce coated groundwoods, will take some of the pressure off paper prices.

- Multi-magazine publishers are an integral part of the industry. The inherent limitations of circulation growth for most publications encourage a successful publisher to seek expansion through start-up or acquisition of additional publications. The amount of synergy in group publishing may be overrated, but there are certain economies in fulfillment, printing and paper contracts and management support. Established group publishers, which may not be very successful in starting up new publications, may nonetheless offer independent magazines or small group publishers the capital and management talent to bring additional growth.

- Starting a new consumer magazine is not as risky as it is sometimes thought to be. Moreover, large publishers, though better able to start an ambitious large circulation monthly or weekly, do not have a better track record in successful start-ups generally than do entrepreneurs. Numerous case studies show that a combination of a solid editorial idea, perseverance and dedication by the owners can go a long way toward overcoming a paucity of seed capital. As shown by the examples of *Your Place* and *New Times,* the ability to attract and hold readers is even more important than convincing advertising agencies to buy space: that will come if the audience is in hand.

- Magazines, like most advertiser-supported mass media, are sensitive to the business cycle. In the 1976-1979 period consumer magazines were able to outperform the overall economy and increase their market share of advertising dollars. But the outlook cannot be encouraging when a general economic slowdown is likely. Beyond that, magazine publishers should expect growth, but at a modest level. It is likely that cable television, as it approaches access to a third of households, will begin to drain small, albeit incremental, amounts of dollars away from mass circulation and even some special interest magazines as sponsors experiment with cable programming.

- Magazine publishers have tended to view programming for video as outside their bailiwicks. Nonetheless, magazines have the editorial expertise that is the essence of video programming designed for limited audiences and marketed via video cassette, disc or cable. These media should not be any immediate threat to magazines. They could even provide the same type of ancillary income as have one-shot and annual publications, books and similar ventures that have grown out of magazines' editorial or marketing expertise.

To the surprise of no one in publishing, the key to successful magazines is the providing of information that an accessible audience needs or wants. Individual titles come and go, with life cycles ranging from months to decades. Those publications that are relevant to the times, that deliver an audience to an advertiser at an economical price, will flourish. Those that prove to be amorphous or redundant will not. And given the tenacious hold that the magazine format has maintained over the years in the face of newer mass media, there is every reason to believe that coming forms, including at-home access to computer-stored data and various video formats, will only enhance the place of a printed magazine in the media mix.

11
Profiles of Selected Consumer Magazine Publishers

AMERICAN BROADCASTING COMPANIES, INC.

Consumer Magazines

High Fidelity
Modern Photography
Los Angeles
Schwann Record & Tape Guide

ABC has not been one of the major magazine publishers and has been in the business for only a few years. But with its recent success in broadcasting generating greater profits and cash, the company has been actively broadening its participation in this area, exclusively by acquisition.

The publishing division itself was formed only in 1977. Earlier purchases had included the Schwann guides in 1976 and *High Fidelity* and *Modern Photography*. In October 1977 it purchased CHC Corporation, which included *Los Angeles* magazine. ABC has also acquired Miller Publishing Co. and Hitchcock Publishing Co., the former a publisher of farm magazines and the other a publisher of scientific and engineering trade magazines.

A large segment of publishing division revenues are attributable to Word Inc., a major religious book and recorded music publisher. Its sales were $30 million in 1977.

In 1979, ABC completed its largest acquisition, adding Chilton Co., which publishes trade magazines and books, including *Iron Age, Motor Age, Commercial Car Journal* and 16 others, as well as *Tennis U.S.A.* and *Going Places,* both small consumer magazines. Chilton also owns a direct marketing division, a printing company and a paper mill. Its sales in 1978 were $72.4 million, with net income of $3.3 million. ABC outbid at least 17 suitors for Chilton, paying $51 million for the outstanding stock, or about 15 times 1978 earnings per share. The addition about doubled the revenue of the publishing division.

ABC Publishing has an explicit strategy for its acquisition candidates. It looks exclusively at operations that have a specialized niche for its publications. Thus, it is not particularly interested in more consumer magazines: trade magazines are a better value and don't compete with television. In addition to those already mentioned, it has purchased a publisher of legal service publications in the insurance, hotel and environmental law fields and a publisher of real estate listing directories and computer-based information on properties.

Moreover, unlike some other group publishers, ABC executives profess little or no interest in integrating their acquisitions under a centralized management. Each is run as a separate operating unit, making its own arrangements for printing, production, fulfillment and distribution, etc. Chilton has apparently continued in this mode. With the rapid pace of expansion, it may be that creating a structure to fit the diverse parts would not have much success anyway.

ABC's bold bid for Chilton—outgunning competition from CBS, Macmillan and Dun & Bradstreet, as well as the oil-rich Thomson Organization—epitomizes its determination to make publishing a principal focus of corporate growth. It is generating masses of cash, from profits bolstered by its seemingly firm grip as the most watched television network, as well as depreciation and amortization of good will. Its long-term debt at the end of 1978 was only a fourth of total capitalization. Cash and marketable securities totaled $251 million at that time, helping to explain the ability to make large cash acquisitions.

With far more nonconsumer magazines and information companies available than consumer publications, it is likely that ABC will continue to emphasize trade, farm and similar publications, as well as specialized book publishers, in its growth strategy. But should consumer properties that meet its requirements become available, ABC can be expected to be at the top of the pile of suitors. What ABC Publishing will *not* be doing is starting magazines or picking up companies that need new management and a turnaround. ABC is buying management and earnings and feels no need to modify that philosophy.

CBS INC.

Consumer Magazines

Woman's Day
Field & Stream
Mechanix Illustrated
Road & Track
World Tennis
Audio
Cycle World
Pickup, Van & 4WD*
American Photographer
Family Weekly

The consumer publishing division is part of the publishing group which includes primarily textbook and trade publisher Holt, Rinehart & Winston, textbook publisher W.B. Saunders Co. and BFA Educational Media. Total division revenues accounted for about 50% of total publishing group revenues.

The operating philosophy of the consumer publishing group contrasts markedly with that of ABC. Although both groups have grown by acquisition, unlike ABC, CBS tends to integrate new publications into the group, centralizing many of the production functions and adding its managerial imprint.

CBS Consumer Publishing, which now includes Popular Library and Fawcett mass market paperback books as well as magazines, took a major leap with the acquisition of Fawcett in 1977. The deal brought *Woman's Day,* with its 8 million circulation per issue into the CBS camp. The remainder of the group is aimed primarily at a male audience and consists of special interest titles.

All of CBS' present magazine line-up were acquisitions, although it has been attempting to bring out a few titles of its own. One project was reported to be a sports magazine. But *Newsweek* first introduced *Inside Sports.* CBS almost purchased the ailing *Sport* magazine from Charter Publishing Co. in 1980, but the deal fell through.

Since its acquisition of *Woman's Day,* CBS has more than doubled its newsstand price, which had been $.25 at the time of the takeover, fre-

---

*CBS sold this publication in January 1982.

quency has been increased from monthly to 15 times annually, but CBS is taking a more cautious approach than *Family Circle* in moving to a true every-three-weeks rate. Nonetheless, advertising pages have increased with the added frequency, from 1445 in 1976, before the CBS takeover, to 1607 in 1980 (but down from 1732 for 14 issues in 1977).

Field & Stream is the leading outdoor magazine in circulation (2 million) and advertising revenue. *Mechanix Illustrated,* acquired with Fawcett, set a record for its circulation in 1978, at 1.7 million.

CBS also has a group it calls "special interest," all involving active participant editorial matter. Of these, the largest is *Road & Track,* which has 600,000 circulation, but continues to trail rival Ziff-Davis' *Car & Driver. Pickup, Van & 4WD* was successfully nurtured from a small circulation (under 50,000) magazine to a more substantial size (265,000 in 1980), but CBS sold this publication in January 1982.

CBS expects magazines to continue to be very competitive advertising vehicles in the immediate future, but does not expect growth to keep pace with that of the second half of the 1970s. It believes that the aggressive pricing of broadcasters has made magazine advertising all the more cost effective; thus, magazines' market share of advertising will be maintained, regardless of the level of the economy.

To this end, CBS can be expected to stay in the acquisitions game, although to date it has not been willing to pay the large dollar amounts being bid for successful publications, the Fawcett acquisition notwithstanding. (Fawcett included not only the mass market paperback line, which had about 9% of the market, compared to 2% for CBS' existing Popular Library imprint, but included a strong balance sheet which convinced CBS brass that it could quickly recoup a large chunk of its investment with little risk.)

CBS did have a small development group busy on start-ups. Work proceeded slowly and cautiously and several ideas that have reportedly reached the dummy make-up stage were discarded. One, called "Parks," produced marginal results in a market test. CBS has never proven that it has the entrepreneurial talent to produce a successful start-up, so it is difficult to predict how any impending venture would come out.

Indeed, unlike other magazine publishers that have had to rejuvenate old publications, CBS is still relatively new in the business. It has demonstrated an ability to bring along a small magazine up to its potential, as well as to improve its larger acquisitions (although it has generally relied on the existing management of the acquired firm, such as at Fawcett, adding the financial resources of CBS). In this respect it has yet to be tested.

CBS looks to be in magazines for the long haul and, since the addition of Fawcett, has become one of the leading participants in the industry. It will continue to be a visible and tough competitor.

CHARTER PUBLISHING COMPANY

Consumer Magazines

Ladies' Home Journal
Redbook

The Charter Company is primarily an integrated oil refiner and marketer, with still small but expanding holdings in insurance, real estate and communications. Nearly 90% of its revenue was from the Charter Oil Co.

The communications group is known as Chartcom and encompasses a printing operation—the Dayton Press—five radio stations, a subscription fulfillment house and a direct mail operation in addition to the three consumer and one trade (*Discount Merchandiser*) publications. Charter Publishing Co. includes just the magazines. The nucleus of the magazine group was the acquisition of Downe Communications, Inc. in 1977 and with it, the *Ladies' Home Journal,* at 6 million monthly circulation, the sixth largest consumer magazine in the U.S. Ad pages for the magazine fell to 1218 in 1980, down from 1349 in 1979. *Redbook*, which may be viewed as a competitor of *Ladies' Home Journal,* also showed a decline in ad pages in 1980.

Charter initially purchased a minority interest in Downe and reported the financial results as an equity holding until September 1977, when it increased its ownership to 56% and consolidated its new property. In 1978, the remaining outstanding stock was acquired. Downe's direct mail and broadcasting facilities came along in the deal.

Charter Publishing, however, was a newly created management organization. To date, the management team has acted mostly to consolidate operations, folding the long-suffering *American Home* into *Redbook* (keeping the name alive with special publications) and killing off *WomanSports* altogether. *Sport* was sold to Southwest Media, Inc. in 1981. Management has been somewhat disappointed at the relatively few economies of scale it found possible when the company was finally put together. Nonetheless, a small after-tax profit in 1978 represents a significant turnaround from the immediately preceding years. Overall, publishing operations accounted for about $165 million—or 48%—of Chartcom's 1978 revenue.

In *Ladies' Home Journal* and *Redbook,* Charter has two mature but well established magazines. The former in particular has a loyal readership, and both periodicals are known quantities for advertisers.

Despite the stated strategy of diversification mapped out by the parent company, Charter is still firmly grounded in its petroleum base and in 1979 committed itself further by taking over operations of Carey Oil Co., which some analysts saw as overextending Charter's capital resources. In any event, Charter's balance sheet does not provide a picture of unrestrained cash for acquisitions of further major magazines, nor does the publishing operation appear to have the depth to attempt any new magazines of its own. The publishing group will likely continue to create its own identity as a magazine publisher. Its best hope for acquisition capital may be in proceeds from the sale of Dayton Press, which is a drain on Chartcom's performance. However, the presence of Charter Co. in the consumer magazine business should add competitive strength vis-à-vis the more established players.

CONDÉ NAST PUBLICATIONS, INC.
(Subsidiary of Newhouse)

Consumer Magazines

Vogue
House & Garden
Mademoiselle
Glamour
Bride's
Self
Street & Smith annuals
Gentlemen's Quarterly

Condé Nast Publications was acquired by the Newhouse media empire in 1957. At the time, it was a money-losing operation which has been turned around in part through the dumping of a printing subsidiary and a subscription fulfillment service. The operation today specializes in women's magazines, although it acquired *Gentlemen's Quarterly* from Esquire in 1978. Condé Nast also publishes through subsidiaries in Britain, France and Italy, including such titles as *L'Uomo* and *Hommes Vogue,* both for men.

Prior to 1979, the last magazine the firm started itself was *Glamour,* in 1939. Forty years later, *Self* was introduced as a service-oriented women's magazine. The magazine has been well received by both its audience and advertisers, despite some mid stream adjustments in its editorial approach. Circulation passed 1 million in 1981.

As have several other publishers, Condé Nast executives have been fine-tuning the subscription/single-copy sales ratio for optimum balance. In the cases of *House & Garden, Glamour* and *Mademoiselle,* this has meant planned reductions in subscription sales; *Vogue* added three times as many newsstand purchasers as subscribers. Of the four, only *House & Garden* ended up with less circulation in 1978 than in 1974. *Bride's*, sold only by single-copy, is leading its competitor, Ziff-Davis' *Modern Bride,* in sales.

Advertising pages have also been rising. *Vogue,* up more than 54% in circulation between 1974 and 1978, increased advertising pages by 76% in the period. *House & Garden, Glamour* and *Mademoiselle* all had page increases of 20% to 27%. As a result of such gains, circulation revenue as a percentage of total revenue still hovers at about 30%, in contrast to other publishers who have gotten closer to a 50%-50% split.

Although Newhouse is credited with some progressive management that has helped the company grow, Condé Nast is seldom in the front ranks of publishing initiators. It has relatively few one-shot magazines, although it has assembled some attractive, high-priced coffee table books associated with its fashion names for publication by conventional book publishers. It has experimented with some alternative delivery of magazines, but found that none worked out and plans to stick with the Postal Service. While increased costs have been passed along to the reader, management believes current prices will have to level off soon. With magazines priced at $1.50 and higher, it becomes difficult to raise prices in the small increments possible at lower cover prices.

Condé Nast controls foreign subsidiaries that publish editions of its U.S. magazines, but with separate editorial material. The volume of advertising in Europe has been described as "unbelievable." *Italian Vogue,* for example, is a thick large format publication with a surfeit of color pages. Despite a steep price of about $5.00, it sells about 45,000 copies per issue and runs an astounding 4000 advertising pages annually (compared to 2350 pages for U.S. *Vogue*).

Condé Nast magazines have always been somewhat specialized. Television programming has rarely featured the type of material covered in its magazines; moreover, advertisers of products appropriate to Condé Nast publications tend to find television too expensive for the intended audience. Thus, the company has developed a comfortable niche for its fashion/women's magazines that *Gentlemen's Quarterly* also fits nicely. In fact, management itself is rather surprised at some of its successes, especially the increased interest in these kinds of magazines. "In 1968 you wouldn't believe that *Vogue* could have 1 million circulation," admitted one top level officer.

The willingness to start a new magazine is significant. Although designed for the women's audience the company knows well, *Self* is not a fashion magazine. Rather, it was conceived to fill a gap, offering a new angle for the active, young women who would tend not to read fashion publications but who were not being reached by other women's magazines. Condé Nast has also made extensive use of television promotion to launch the publication.

THE HEARST CORPORATION

Consumer Magazines

Connoisseur
Cosmopolitan
Cosmopolitan Living
Country Living
Good Housekeeping
Harper's Bazaar
House Beautiful
Motor
Motor Boating & Sailing
Popular Mechanics
Science Digest
Sports Afield
Town & Country

Hearst is a low-profile, privately held media conglomerate with substantial broadcasting and newspaper as well as magazine holdings. Its magazine operations include 14 consumer magazines, trade publications (it acquired United Technical Publications in 1980) and Avon Books, one of the leading mass market paperback book publishers. It has acquired Arbor House, a hardcover trade book publisher. In addition to the consumer magazines published in the U.S., Hearst has an active British subsidiary, National Magazine Co., Ltd., which publishes a similar number of magazines, including British versions of *Cosmopolitan* and *Good Housekeeping*. Hearst also owns one of the major national distributors, International Circulation Distributors, which represents dozens of magazines besides Hearst's own.

Hearst magazines have fared much better than its newspapers, which have lost much in size and stature since the heyday of William Randolph Hearst. But Hearst magazines have enjoyed considerable longevity and stability in an industry of constant flux. Hearst Corp. has never been entrepreneurial. Hearst himself started his magazine group by purchasing *Motor,* and growth by acquisition has been the pattern ever since. The company still operates under the Hearst philosophy: "Find out what your readers want and give it to them. And give it to them regularly."

Thus, the firm's magazines do change, as needed. *Cosmopolitan* today is a far cry from the fiction-oriented publication it was for most of its existence (although before Hearst purchased it in 1905, *Cosmo* was a prominent journal of foreign and domestic affairs). As *Cosmopolitan* was completely made over by Helen Gurley Brown, John Mack Carter has rejuvenated *Good Housekeeping*. A comparable make-over was completed in 1981 for the moribund *Science Digest*. This is what Hearst management refers to as "reacquiring our own properties," spending money on such redesigns rather than assuming the large subscription liabilities (and possible legal hassles) in buying magazines. Hearst has also used the spinoff as an approach to a new publication, having moved *House Beautiful's Colonial Homes* from an annual to a bimonthly.

Hearst magazines are very profit-oriented and as such pay sharp attention to costs and revenues. Rather than engage in circulation contests, they have concentrated on effective yield as the key to optimum circulation levels from subscription and single-copy sources. Magazine executives are seeking to achieve "state of the art" management, while recognizing that there is still a need for considerable judgment that cannot be quantified.

The success of Hearst Corporation's magazine operations has been in marked contrast to its retrenched newspapers. Although contribution to corporate profit might leave room for improvement, the group is essentially well-managed and integrated. The strategy of "reacquisition" appears to have been successful and makes sense with so many titles in a dynamic market.

Hearst has developed a cadre of solid top management talent, which should help solidify recent gains and keep the group on a growth track. In past recessions, Hearst magazines have suffered less than the overall industry, owing to the special interest nature of most of its publications.

Although Hearst has moved out in recent years with several newspaper, trade magazine and book acquisitions, a similar move to add a consumer magazine is unlikely, barring an unusual opportunity. Hearst may introduce some new titles in the U.S. that have proven successful in the British market.

MEREDITH CORPORATION

Consumer Magazines

Better Homes and Gardens
Metropolitan Home
Sail

Better Homes and Gardens is the fourth largest circulation consumer magazine in the country, although circulation growth was only about 6% between 1973 and 1980. Advertising pages, on the other hand, have moved up strongly, nearly 50% greater in 1978 than in 1973 and more than twice that of the recent low reached in 1975. Among monthly magazines, only *Reader's Digest* had higher gross advertising revenue.

Besides BH&G, Meredith has successfully built *Metropolitan Home* from an annual spin-off to a monthly with more than 860,000 circulation. Meredith also publishes *Successful Farming* and 19 annual to quarterly special topic issues of BH&G. It has also branched out into community and daily newspapers. Meredith's book publishing activities have also grown steadily, providing almost 20% of corporate revenues in 1978. Book sales, which had been primarily mail order, have been further enhanced by expanded retail sales: the *Better Homes and Gardens Family Medical Guide* sold 70,000 through this channel in 1978. All of Meredith's books are internally produced and carry the BH&G name.

Meredith is one of the very few magazine publishers that still has an active printing capacity. The company's long-term commitment to the printing business is seen in the completion of a $23 million investment in new printing presses in Des Moines, replacing some of the aging letterpresses with six new web offset presses and two rotogravure presses. The operation prints outside publications in addition to Meredith's own magazines.

Still, at the heart of Meredith is BH&G. Not only do its books and special topic publications draw on its name and good will, but a new operation, a franchised real estate service, draws on the magazine's name for its viability. *Better Homes and Gardens* is, in fact, an impressive operation. Besides the national edition of the monthly, there are about 150 regional and demographic editions, providing a logistical nightmare, but maximum flexibility for advertisers. Individual issues have logged more than $10 million in gross advertising revenue. The magazine accounted for more than 80% of Meredith's magazine revenue. The company also has been one of the leaders in exploring alternative delivery services.

Isolated in Des Moines from the hectic pace of New York, Meredith has kept BH&G in the top ranks of consumer magazines. It has been conservative in the addition of new major publications, preferring to expand its special topic collection, all built on the BH&G audience and editorial expertise. Magazine growth has kept pace with overall company growth (despite expansion in broadcasting), and it appears that BH&G will continue to get its appropriate share of attention and resources to maintain the magazine's eminence in the field.

Nonetheless, Meredith has shown itself willing to broaden its base, especially with its newspaper purchases. It is working to improve these properties, having in one case increased the frequency of an acquired newspaper from twice weekly to daily.

Like its centerpiece magazine, other Meredith operations have a positive reputation. The company has invested in original quality programming for its five television stations, for example. And it is looking for new ways to make profitable use of its most valuable asset, the BH&G name, in such areas as insurance and merchandise to be sold in homes.

THE NEW YORK TIMES COMPANY

Consumer Magazines

Family Circle
Golf Digest
Tennis
New York Times Magazine

The Times Company has performed relatively well with the magazines it has acquired. *Family Circle* has been moving toward an every-three-week publication frequency with greater determination than rival *Woman's Day*. *Family Circle* took the lead in advertising pages in 1979 after closing the gap in 1978, then fell behind again in 1980. *Golf Digest* and *Tennis* are the leading consumer magazines in their fields. *Golf*'s circulation has been growing by 5% annually in a sport that is growing by only 3% a year.

Us, on the other hand, has had trouble shaking its *People* clone image. Circulation inched up past 1 million in 1980. Having reached break-even on operations, at best, The New York Times Company sold *Us* to the Macfadden Group, Inc. interests in 1980.

Family Circle is the jewel of the magazine operation, contributing almost 60% of the profit of the magazines. It is 100% newsstand distributed in 85,000 outlets, primarily supermarket checkout counters. In 1978 it was published 14 times, then increased to 17 times in 1979. This was done to lessen the advertising clutter that the thick monthly was facing, as well as to bolster the turnover in the precious magazine racks at the check-out counters. Circulation growth has leveled off. Cover price, meanwhile, has been raised from 45 cents in 1977 to 65 cents in 1981.

Unlike most magazines, *Family Circle* distributes a substantial portion of its issues without using wholesalers. About 35% of the total is shipped directly to supermarket distribution centers, from which they are sent to individual stores. In 1979 *Family Circle* abandoned its part ownership of

Select Magazines, which had been the magazine's national distributor. The Times Co. set up its own distribution operation, which could be more readily cost justified with the greater frequency of *Family Circle* as well as the need to push *Us* every other week.

To a degree even less than in other magazine groups, the Times Company's operation is not integrated. The special interest sports publications are run from their original Norwalk, CT, offices, while *Family Circle* remains in New York. The move to set up its own distribution organization stopped short of establishing a true national distributor, since many accounting functions will still be handled by an outside firm.

At one time, the magazine operation included a group of medical trade publications that came with the Cowles Communication acquisition in 1971. But they were never terribly profitable and were sold after causing some conflicts with editorial freedom of the *Times* newspaper.

The magazine division would not seem to be in the position to acquire new magazines in need of turnaround, or to start any new publications. One attempt at another title, *Women Who Work,* was abandoned after a brief trial.

PETERSEN PUBLISHING COMPANY

Consumer Magazines

Motor Trend
Hot Rod
Car Craft
Motorcyclist
Guns & Ammo
Hunting
Skin Diver
Photographic
4-Wheel & Off-Road
'Teen
Lakeland Boating
Rudder
Sea and Pacific Skipper

Since its founding in 1948, Petersen's strength has been in its automotive-theme special interest magazines. The company has been likened to Ziff-Davis, but Petersen is actually a very different company in both style and content. Like Ziff-Davis, its magazines are oriented to a primarily male audience, but each firm has one title for the female audience. Petersen's editorial thrust, however, is more toward the blue-collar audience. *Hot Rod,* which Petersen started in 1948, still leads its field, with renewed circulation growth after years of stagnation.

Petersen has also been more active in start-ups than most group publishers. In addition to *Hot Rod*, it started *Wheels Afield* (since folded into *Motor Trend*), *Photographic, Hunting* and *Inspiration,* the latter a religious, dual audience title begun in 1978. Petersen has also grown through acquisitions, but it fared poorly during a brief period of trying to turn around the moribund *True* in 1974.

Petersen also has an active book division, playing on its special interest strengths in the automotive, hunting and photographic markets. The company offers dozens of soft cover books and annuals such as *The Complete Book of Pickups & Vans* or *Guns & Ammo Annual.*

As an offshoot of personal interests of Robert Petersen, the company has also established the Petersen Gallery, specializing in art with Western and sporting themes. Petersen has also tried its hand at film and television commercial production.

On the one hand, Petersen's magazines are well positioned to take advantage of the specialized audience and advertiser benefits associated with active interest consumer magazines. On the other hand, the long term energy crunch and the resulting change in automotive performance standards (smaller engines, less power) may erode the "macho" car market associated with several of the firm's mainstay magazines. Advertising pages for *Motor Trend, Car Craft* and *Hot Rod,* were down substantially in 1980 from 1978 levels, while circulation gains have been modest at best. Some of the smaller magazines have produced better results, with *Guns & Ammo* performing best in circulation since 1973 and *Photographic* in advertising (up 93% in 1980, although the 1973 base period was only its second year of publication).

Petersen remains something of an enigma in the consumer magazine publishing field, rarely venturing out to compete for acquisitions, and willing to undertake start-ups in categories that already have established publications. It has made moves indicating an interest in substantial diversification and keeps a relatively low profile in Los Angeles, off the established publishing track.

PLAYBOY ENTERPRISES, INC.

Consumer Magazines

Playboy
Games

Playboy Enterprises' magazines shook off about five years of no growth and declining profits in 1978. In that year the flagship magazine, which had reached $87 million in revenue in 1973 and then languished at about that level, made a strong turnaround. Among Playboy's many ventures, only its casinos managed to make strides during the 1973 to 1978 period, and they were sold in 1981.

For many years, *Playboy* was the unchallengeable men's magazine, with a pretax profit margin that reached an astounding 25% in 1973. But strong competition from *Penthouse, Gallery* and others finally brought the real world to the land of the bunny hutch. Even adding some competition from within, in the form of *Oui,* only proved to be a holding action. *Oui* was itself sold in 1981.

In the meantime, grandiose plans for Playboy resorts, records and books went nowhere, as several resorts had to be sold off. The book publishing operation, which includes general trade titles for the Playboy Press imprint, Wyden Books and Seaview Books, accounted for a $3.1 million write-down in 1978. Playboy's record business was turned over to CBS Records in 1978.

Playboy Enterprises has been reducing the proportion of its business derived from magazines, but this still remains the largest segment of its operations and *Playboy* is the centerpiece around which the rest of the business revolves. Advertising page totals had two bad years, 1975 and 1976, before heading back up. But in the meantime, circulation has fallen from more than 7 million in 1975 to under 5 million in 1978, thus reducing revenue despite increases in cover prices. As a result, the magazine has reformulated its editorial product, balancing out sexual appeal with service, lifestyle and nonfiction entertainment. Circulation gains were nominal but enough to top 5 million monthly in 1980.

At the same time, the company explored new types of magazines, using a unique approach: for a time it provided venture capital to independent entrepreneurs, with the intent of purchasing those magazines that proved to be successful. This was the formula used for *Games*, which has since been purchased, and for its first try, *The International Review of Food & Wine,* which did not do as well. This approach minimized financial exposure, tied up relatively little management time and allowed entrepreneurs to do what they do best—create new products. In purchasing only those that are proven, Playboy reduced uncertainty but did not have to get into bidding wars with other acquisition-minded publishers. Not much has happened since the *Games* acquisition in 1978.

Playboy recognizes that its clear-cut domination of the men's sex cum literary magazine category has ended, after 20 years almost alone in the field it virtually created. As a result, it is looking to other areas that are really separate from its base. The Playboy Press, the book club and newer imprints encompass titles of general audience (including women) interest. Its television/theatrical film productions are also seeking a profile that is not based on the Playboy image. The company has also announced formation of a unit to produce video cassettes for the home market, as well as programming for the cable market in a joint venture called Escapade.

READER'S DIGEST ASSOCIATION, INC.

Consumer Magazines

Reader's Digest
Families

Reader's Digest was for a long time the only magazine published by a company that has failed in trying to branch out into cable television, feature films and magazine publishing abroad (except for foreign editions of *Reader's Digest*). On the other hand, this one successful magazine is read by an estimated 100 million people monthly in 15 languages in 39 editions. Its circulation per issue is surpassed in the U.S. only by *TV Guide*.

Moreover, *Reader's Digest* commands a significant per thousand premium of 52 cents over *TV Guide,* which helped it lead all other monthlies in gross advertising revenue.

Subscriptions make up the bulk of *Reader's Digest*'s circulation, which has led the magazine to quote its subscription price at cost "plus postage," so that postage rate increases can be passed along explicitly. The *Digest* has an extremely loyal readership, with a 70% renewal rate, compared to an average 55% for other major subscription-oriented magazines. It also has an unusually high median age for its readers—46 years—but along with that comes a relatively high median income of more than $17,000, (in 1978).

The Reader's Digest Association derives about a third of its revenue and income from the magazine, about equally divided between domestic and foreign editions. Another third of the revenue is from its hardcover book sales. These started with the condensed book club, which sells about 12.5 million volumes annually, but also includes extensive mail order books oriented to the home and family. The rest of its revenue comes from a variety of operations, including records, audio tapes and equipment and mail order items. One of the firm's greatest assets, its massive mailing list, is tapped to sell much of this material, often using "sweepstakes" giveaways as an enticement. Reader's Digest has one of the most sophisticated mail solicitation operations anywhere.

In 1980 the company surprised many observers by purchasing Source Telecomputing Corp., one of the first firms to provide an electronic text service for the consumer market. This puts Reader's Digest in the forefront of the information "revolution."

Reader's Digest Association is a very private company, with all voting control still in the hands of the founding family. Over the years, there have been frequent rumors about possible new magazines coming from Pleasantville, covering such topics as health, do-it-yourself or sports. *Families* finally got the go ahead in 1980.

TIME INC.

Consumer Magazines

Time
Life
People
Fortune
Money
Sports Illustrated
Discover

Time Inc. must be rated the consummate magazine publishing company in the United States. It is certainly the largest in revenue. The demise of *Life* in 1972 seemed like a major blow, because *Life* was almost an institution. But Time used its freed-up resources and the lesson learned to start *People* which became profitable 18 months after its introduction. *Money,* though a far less ambitious monthly, showed that Time was willing to take some smaller bites. *Fortune,* meanwhile, had about achieved the status of a coffee table book. Its long lead time and monthly frequency made it woefully out-of-date in the business world and its long articles made it difficult to read. Its many pages of advertising also made it difficult to lift. In turning *Fortune* into a biweekly, Time took something of a risk in tampering with a proven formula. Articles were shortened and the increased frequency and shorter production schedule permitted greater timeliness. Advertisers responded by boosting ad pages 31% and revenue 43% in the first year.

Time Inc. is one of the few entrepreneurial publishing giants: all of its magazines were started by the company and it has never had a failure except for the temporary demise of *Life* (although Luce had to carry *Sports Illustrated* for seven years before it made money). It has a separate magazine development group that researches and test markets new possible titles. *People* and *Money* are both products of this process.

As recently as 1973, 70% of Time Inc.'s magazine revenue came from advertising sales. Despite strong increases in revenue from this source, circulation price increases have reduced the advertising share to 60%. Among Time Inc. magazines, *Time* is by far the largest. Indeed, it is first among all magazines. Next is *Sports Illustrated,* followed by *People* and *Fortune.*

From its magazine base, Time Inc. has been expanding rapidly in other media and related areas. With the acquisition of Inland Container Corp. in 1978, forest products became Time's largest segment. Forest products include building materials, paper, timberlands and construction.

Following magazines, books are the third largest segment of the company. Besides the well established Time-Life Books, specializing in continuity series sold primarily by mail, the firm includes Book-of-the-Month Club, having acquired the original major trade book club late in 1977. Little Brown, part of Time since 1968, is a leading trade publisher, as well as a producer of professional books and college textbooks.

Time Inc.'s fastest growing sector is video. Its pretax profit margin is the highest for the company. Much of its growth was through the acquisition of American Television and Communications Corp., the largest cable television system operator in the U.S. Home Box Office was also improving penetration, having passed 7 million subscribers during 1981. Time-Life Films, long active in educational films, has become increasingly busy with original productions for the television market and has made a stab at the developing home video cassette market. Time did withdraw from a venture into Hollywood film-making.

One of Time Inc.'s most controversial and high-risk acquisitions was that of the *Washington Star,* the weak and money-losing afternoon paper in the shadow of the *Washington Post.* The *Star* had been losing circulation for years, although it was once the leading paper in the capital. This was the firm's first venture into daily newspapers, although it has owned a chain of weekly papers in the Chicago suburbs. Time gambled that the 11 unions at the *Star* would take seriously its threat to shut the paper if they did not accept new contracts that permitted Time some added flexibility and lower costs. Having made its case, Time got its contracts, committed $60 million to improving the paper and halted the circulation slide. It also purchased Universal Press Syndicate, which distributed the popular Doonesbury comic strip, and got much attention by switching it from the *Post* to the *Star.* The paper also added a morning edition, a step consistent with the trend of other large city afternoon dailies. With it all, Time executives saw no significant improvement and closed the *Star,* amid much publicity, in 1981.

Time Inc. is a class operation. In an age when businesses often cut their losses as soon as a product seems to be losing money, Time has shown a willingness to stick with ideas it believes in (the *Star* notwithstanding). It also has the resources to carry such efforts. It could be argued that supporting *Sports Illustrated* for seven years was an ego trip for Harry Luce, but supporting Home Box Office, with no Luce around, was purely a long-range business decision.

Magazines are still the largest single segment of the company's business, but the growth in this area has been slightly slower than that of total revenue. As a result, magazines now account for only a quarter of the business down from a third in 1978. Moreover, top management includes a growing cadre of executives from the forest products acquisitions and the successful video division. This could have strategic implications for new publishing ventures.

In general, however, Time Inc. can still be looked to as a leader in the development of new magazine titles, as well as continued expansion in other media forms. What the company could improve on is the *integration* of the different media formats, although it is probably ahead of other media conglomerates in this as well. Magazines, video, books and film are merely different ways of displaying content and Time Inc., so far along in assembling the different formats under a single corporate entity, is better positioned than anyone in the media business to create a true information industry conglomerate in operations as well as organization. It would not be surprising to find the publishing and video groups collaborating on a new magazine for cable and pay television subscribers.

THE TIMES MIRROR COMPANY

Consumer Magazines

Popular Science
Outdoor Life
Golf
Ski
Homeowners How To
The Sporting News

Times Mirror is such a large media conglomerate that its magazine operation, with nearly $100 million in sales, is reported in financial statements as part of "other operations," along with television stations and one of the country's largest cable systems. Although income for magazines is not reported separately, a company executive grants that the division has been performing "very well." Revenue for magazines includes sales of some books, primarily those associated with the magazine-related book clubs, such as Popular Science Book Club (the largest special interest book club in the U.S., claims the company).

The most recent addition to the magazine line-up was the 1977 acquisition of St. Louis-based The Sporting News Publishing Co., which publishes *The Sporting Goods Dealer* as well as the consumer title. Neither it nor *The Sporting News* has been integrated into the existing magazine organization.

Times Mirror executives admit that, all else being equal, they would prefer to have 100% newsstand sales. Nonetheless, all TM magazines showed a decrease in the proportion of single-copy sales during the 1970s. This paradox stems from the many imperfections TM management sees in the single-copy distribution network, including the months that elapse between end of sale of an issue and the report on the results.

The same executives believe that their magazines will have to be more judicious about price increases in coming years, compared to the rate of increase in the 1974-79 period. But they also feel that a moderate recession will not affect TM magazines very much. Book clubs do better, they feel, as do outdoor magazines. "The unemployed fish and hunt," is the reasoning advanced by a senior manager. Still, Times Mirror magazines tend to run behind their competitors in each category, supposedly because TM eschews the circulation "rat race." "If circulation is kept at a manageable level, our operating margins can improve."

While circulation prices may have to be moderated, Times Mirror sees more latitude for raising CPM charges to advertisers. The outdoor and the science magazine categories have CPMs that are "too low." At the same time, TM has been pushing its network buy, finding that it is still easier to sell advertising agencies numbers than a quality audience.

Times Mirror strives for considerable integration of magazine functions in the group, with the notable exception of *The Sporting News*. All circulation functions, production, data processing and financial services are centralized. The publishers of each magazine also meet regularly to discuss, among other things, new advertisers.

For the most part, Times Mirror runs its magazine operation conservatively. It has refused so far to get involved in high-priced bidding contests for acquisitions. *The Sporting News* was consistent with TM's mostly male-oriented magazines, but it does not have an active interest editorial focus, as do TM's other special interest magazines.

In staying out of the circulation wars necessary to become the leading magazine in the categories of its titles, TM is concerned about the saturation point for readers of special interest topics. For example, it sees the golf field as being saturated.

Still, real growth in TM magazine revenue has been strong with essentially the same line-up of publications.

TM magazine executives claim to be keeping an eye on developing video technologies. Editorially, TM's publications are compatible with special interest video programming. One possibility for TM is video producing, using the company's established editorial expertise.

TRIANGLE PUBLICATIONS, INC.

Consumer Magazines

TV Guide
Seventeen

Walter Annenberg may not have much of a media empire anymore, but he does have *TV Guide*, which by itself is larger than most other media conglomerates. It is the largest selling and greatest revenue producing magazine in the United States. It is also one of the most profitable.

The continued success of *TV Guide* with the public—selling almost 18 million copies per week, the bulk of them as single copies—is something of a mystery. Most newspapers have daily as well as weekly listing television guides. But people still plunk down 40 cents for one of the nearly 100 separate editions with local television listings, with a common editorial package wrapped around them. The national section has to be printed at four plants around the country and the listing sections photocomposed at 16 regional printing plants. It's been reported that only the inability to print more copies has prevented higher sales of some issues.

If people want to buy the magazine, it could not be easier. It is available at 300,000 check-out counters and newsstands. Supermarkets have long had an affection for *TV Guide:* it produces a 24% markup, is fully returnable if not sold, does not have to be price stamped, takes up no shelf space and does not even have to be handled (wholesalers take care of filling the racks). As a weekly, *TV Guide* produces at least a 52 time turnover, but with mid-week restocking, a magazine executive claims it yields a 117 time turnover. With its emphasis on single-copy sales, postal rate increases have had relatively little effect.

Advertisers also are pleased with the magazine, spending $62,000 for a four-color page (before discounts). Even regional editions are expensive, since the New York edition alone sells 1.2 million copies weekly. Gross advertising revenue for 1980 was $239 million.

The irony of *TV Guide* is that its editorial position is relatively critical of the programming its readers watch. (This was not always so; until the mid-1960s, the magazine tended to feature puff pieces and personality profiles.) Articles by prominent sociologists, historians, literary figures and others have examined the impact of television on society. *TV Guide* also covers FCC developments and even gets some true scoops, such as breaking the story of Barbara Walters' $1 million yearly contract with ABC. Nonetheless, the magazine is rarely cited by others.

Seventeen, which Annenberg purchased even before his acquisition of *TV Guide* in 1953, is a successful magazine in its own right. Circulation is 1.6 million monthly. Legally, it is not part of Triangle Publishing, although it is under the same top management.

Unlike others who are successful with a magazine, Annenberg has not run about acquiring or starting many new magazines. He did make an abortive attempt with *Good Food* in 1974. It too was designed for supermarket checkout sales and was a compact size. But it failed to survive for six months, although Triangle no doubt had the wherewithal to carry it for a longer time. Actually, Annenberg has sold off most of his media holdings, which once included two Philadelphia daily newspapers, the *Inquirer* and *Daily News* (now owned by Knight-Ridder) and several broadcast stations. The *Daily Racing Form* is Annenberg's only non-magazine property.

In early 1979 Triangle did announce another new publication. *Panorama* was a monthly about the television industry, including cable, pay TV, video cassettes and discs. It was aimed at a much smaller audience than *TV Guide*'s, consisting of readers who have a personal interest in the television medium. Although the subject matter was similar to that of *TV Guide,* the new magazine required very different marketing skills, since it was priced closer to *Seventeen* and relied primarily on subscription sales. Even with a modest circulation goal, it failed to appeal to even 200,000 monthly readers and was closed down after 17 issues.

Annenberg has also been adding locally originated cable television listings to some editions of *TV Guide* and as far back as 1967 registered the name *Cable TV Guide*. In the immediate future, *TV Guide* will continue to provide a healthy return. But its long-term future is tied to the current structure of broadcast television and the potential changes, including the proliferation of programming for cable and home video cassettes, may force *TV Guide* to either change or surrender to a slow decline.

THE WASHINGTON POST COMPANY

Consumer Magazines

Newsweek
Inside Sports

Although the combined circulation of the three major newsweeklies has shown little growth in recent years, revenues and profits have made healthy advances through a combination of sizable subscription and newsstand price increases, advertising linage gains and stiff increases in advertising rates. With all this, *Newsweek* has found itself unable to make circulation gains against rival *Time,* holding to just under a third of newsweekly combined circulation (3.0 million compared to *Time*'s 4.4 million and *U.S. News & World Report*'s 2.1 million). However, several syndicated studies have shown *Newsweek*'s estimated total *readership* proportionately closer to *Time*'s owing to a larger number of readers per copy.

On the other hand, *Newsweek* has maintained a slim edge in advertising pages, accounting for about 40% of the category total:

Year	Total Pages	Newsweek Pages	% of Total	Time Pages	% of Total	U.S. News & World Report Pages	% of Total
1980	7898	3117	39.5%	2849	36.1%	1932	24.5%
1979	8658	3436	39.7	3153	36.4	2069	23.9
1978	8476	3328	39.3	3166	37.4	1982	23.3
1977	7926	3131	39.5	2951	37.2	1844	23.3
1976	7174	2920	40.7	2485	34.6	1769	24.7
1975	6592	2630	39.9	2305	35.0	1657	25.1
1974	8335	3208	38.5	3082	37.0	2045	24.5

Source: *Advertising Age.*

Newsweek receives about 30% of its revenue from circulation. Its subscription price was raised 15% in 1978 while the cover price went up 25% to $1.25. According to the parent Washington Post Co., the second class postage costs used up more than half of the additional revenue provided by the price hikes. The cover price was raised to $1.50 and subscriptions to $39.00 in 1981.

Newsweek has been one of the leaders in promoting the magazine imperative concept, having initiated an aggressive program encouraging advertisers to adopt "Zero-Based Media Planning," essentially a strategy of increasing reach by switching some television dollars to magazine pages.

Newsweek, Inc. also publishes an international edition, using a separate staff. With separate overseas Atlantic and Pacific editions, it had a circulation of about 500,000 and provided about 18% of total magazine revenue.

The Washington Post Co.'s magazine operation has provided a remarkably constant 41%-42% of total revenues, even as the company's major newspaper has continued to prosper. Although operating margins have improved substantially since the slowdown of 1975, the contribution of the magazines to total operating income has fallen to below its proportionate revenue share. The start-up of *Inside Sports* has admittedly been a drag on overall company magazine performance. Circulation passed 550,000 in 1981, but a higher proportion than planned was coming from subscription rather than newsstand sales. The magazine was put up for sale in late 1981.

Newsweek may be an influential and profitable property, but it operates in a mature, highly competitive market segment. In *Time* it has a formidable competitor, so it cannot expect to improve its relative circulation position. It is clear that advertising pages are largely a function of total pages advertisers are allocating to the newsweekly group. *Inside Sports* failed to prove its necessity in a niche dominated by *Sports Illustrated* and *Sport,* as well as the *Sporting News.*

ZIFF-DAVIS PUBLISHING COMPANY

Consumer Magazines

Adventure Travel
Backpacker
Boating
Camera Arts
Car and Driver
Cycle
Flying
Fly Fisherman
Modern Bride
Popular Electronics
Popular Photography

Psychology Today
Skiing
Sport Diver
Stereo Review
US Air Magazine
Yachting

Ziff-Davis, best known for its stable of successful and well-managed special interest consumer publications and trade magazines, has been reorganized as a multi-media conglomerate. The largest subsidiary of the parent Ziff Corporation, it was joined by six television stations acquired as part of an $83 million deal for Rust Craft Greeting Cards in early 1979. Rust Craft also brought with it a money-losing greeting card operation, which was combined with another acquisition, Norcross, also a money loser. Ziff is now third in the greeting card market (behind Hallmark and American Greeting, just ahead of Gibson).

On its familiar consumer magazine turf, Ziff-Davis has continued to make acquisitions of small, special interest category periodicals such as *Fly Fisherman, Sport Diver* and *Backpacker*.

In general, Ziff-Davis publications tend to lead their competition in both circulation and advertising in each category. (One match-up where they are behind is in automotive, where *Car & Driver* trails CBS' *Road & Track*). Z-D's only non-active interest magazine is *Psychology Today,* which is also its largest, at over 1.2 million circulation monthly, about 86% by subscription. (Of the special interest publications, all but *Modern Bride* are predominately sold by subscription.)

The advertising to circulation revenue ratio varies among the magazines, from as high as 75% from advertising to as low as 50%.

As a privately held concern, Ziff must make its acquisitions for cash. The strength of its balance sheet was tested by its ability to pay the $83 million for the Rust Craft operation, followed by the smaller Norcross deal. After eschewing a move into cable television for many years, the firm has earmarked $20 to $30 million to buy into that booming arena, following the path of Time Inc., Times Mirror and other media giants.

At the same time, it is unlikely that Ziff will abandon further growth by acquisition in the magazine business. In 1979 it published the first edition of *USAir,* the new in-flight magazine for that airline (formerly Allegheny). Although technically a start-up situation, the captive nature of the in-flight magazine minimizes substantially the marketing risks.

Ziff's decision to finally branch out of publishing may have been due in part to the stiff competition in the bid for acquiring on-going magazines (not that TV stations come cheap). With ABC throwing around money, along with other U.S. and, increasingly, European competitors, Ziff has found it difficult to acquire magazines at decent prices. Nonetheless, Ziff-Davis can be expected to pick up selected trade as well as consumer magazines. While they might like to find another *Psychology Today* type of magazine, they have shown a continued willingness to acquire small magazines with limited circulation potential, but which fit into their niche of marketing know-how.

One acquisition that has moved them into a new market was Wharton Econometrics, the computer-based service bureau. It competes with Data Resources, Inc., a subsidiary of McGraw Hill, Inc.

Having used its editorial expertise in the past to produce profitable annuals and spin-offs related to existing titles, Ziff's new-found interest in the electronic media should logically lead to its move into video programming, distributed through cable networks as well as video discs. If the firm runs true to form, this development will be through the acquisition of an existing production house, with Z-D supplying the editorial know-how. This interest was signaled by the hiring of a former ABC executive whose charter was specifically to translate the magazine properties into other communications forms, i.e., video format.

Appendix A

Table A-1: Circulation for Selected General and Special Interest Consumer Magazines, 1973 and 1978

General Interest	Av. Circ. Per Issue	% Subscription	% Single-Copy	One Year Sub. Price	Single-Copy Price
New Yorker (W)					
1973	484,876	89.5%	10.5%	$15.00	$ .50
1978	498,128	91.4	8.6	24.00	1.00
% change	+2.7	+4.9	-15.7	+60.0	100.00
TV Guide (W)					
1973	18,702,249	36.3	64.7	8.00	.15
1978	19,495,113	38.5	61.5	9.50	.25
% change	+4.2	+10.4	-0.8	+18.8	+66.7
Newsweek (W)					
1973	2,898,743	90.4	9.6	16.00	.60
1978	2,925,694	91.3	8.7	29.95	1.25
% change	+0.9	+1.9	-8.6	+87.2	+108.3
Sports Illustrated (W)					
1973	2,270,731	96.1	3.9	12.00	.60
1978	2,272,905	95.5	4.5	25.00	1.25
% change	+0.1	-0.6	+16.6	+108.3	+108.3
Harper's (M)					
1973	334,728	89.1	10.9	8.50	1.00
1978	302,469	90.7	9.3	9.98	1.25
% change	-9.6	-8.0	-22.9	+17.4	+25.0
Reader's Digest (M)					
1973	18,198,402	90.2	9.8	4.97	.50
1978	17,978,238	92.7	7.3	8.93	.95
% change	-1.2	+1.5	+26.1	+79.7	+90.0
Playboy (M)					
1973	6,503,261	23.7	76.3	10.00	1.00
1978	5,248,309	38.0	62.0	14.00	2.00[a]
% change	-19.3	+29.4	-34.4	+40.0	+100.0
Mademoiselle (M)					
1973	850,205	47.6	52.4	5.00	.60
1978	1,017,907	69.6	30.4	10.00	1.50
% change	+19.7	-23.6	+59.1	+100.0	+150.0

Table A-1: continued

General Interest	Av. Circ. Per Issue	% Subscription	% Single-Copy	One Year Sub. Price	Single-Copy Price
Ladies' Home Journal (M)					
1973	7,081,855	82.7 %	17.3 %	$ 5.94	$ .60
1978	6,031,430	82.1	17.9	7.97	1.25
% change	−14.8	−15.4	−10.5	+34.2	+108.3
Family Circle (17x)[b]					
1973	8,075,095	0.0	100.0	—	.29
1978	8,380,582	0.0	100.0	—	.55 to .59
% change	+3.8	0.0	—	—	+89.7 to +103.4
Photoplay (M)					
1973	980,047	49.1	50.9	5.00	.50
1978	943,102	87.0	13.0	6.00	.60
% change	−3.8	+70.5	−75.5	+20.0	+20.0
National Geographic (M)					
1973	8,276,668	100.0	—	9.00	1.00
1978	10,134,530	100.0	nil	11.00	1.25
% change	+22.4	0.0	—	+22.2	+25.0
Total					
1973	74,656,860	60.8	39.2	9.04	.61
1978	75,228,407	63.7	36.3	14.21[b]	1.08
% change	+0.8	+5.5	−6.7	+57.2	+77.0

Special Interest

	Av. Circ. Per Issue	% Subscription	% Single-Copy	One Year Sub. Price	Single-Copy Price
Golf Digest (M)					
1973	654,865	88.5	11.5	7.50	.75
1978	943,520	91.3	8.7	11.95	1.25
% change	+44.1	+48.6	+9.0	+59.3	+66.7
Trains (M)					
1973	63,724	45.4	54.5	9.00	.75
1978	67,891	50.9	49.1	17.00	1.50
% change	+6.5	+19.4	−3.9	+88.9	+100.0
Popular Photography (M)					
1973	645,536	78.2	21.8	7.98	1.00
1978	820,459	78.1	21.9	13.98	1.25
% change	+27.1	+26.9	+27.8	+75.2	+25.0
Flying (M)					
1973	406,354	82.5	17.5	7.98	.75
1978	398,892	81.4	18.6	14.00	1.25
% change	−1.8	−3.1	+4.2	+75.4	+66.7

Note: Letter in ( ) following title is frequency: W = weekly; M = monthly; BM = bimonthly; 7x,17x = # issues per year

[a.] December issue is $2.50; January is +3.00.

Table A-1: continued

Special Interest	Av. Circ. Per Issue	% Subscription	% Single-Copy	One Year Sub. Price	Single-Copy Price
Yachting (M)					
1973	127,752	61.2 %	28.8 %	$ 10.00	$ 1.50
1978	142,017	63.9	26.1	12.00	2.00
% change	+ 11.2	+ 16.1	+ 39.3	+ 20.0	+ 33.3
Apartment Life (M)					
1973	442,935	72.4	27.6	3.00	1.00
1978	823,213	83.0	17.0	7.97	.95
% change	+ 85.8	+ 112.8	+ 15.0	+ 165.7	−5.0
Ski (7x)					
1973	394,441	81.2	18.8	5.00	.75
$978	413,991	78.2	21.8	7.94	1.00
% change	− 5.0	+ 1.1	+ 21.7	+ 58.8	+ 33.3
Bride's (BM)					
1973	292,229	38.7	61.3	5.00	1.00
1978	306,805	9.5	90.5	5.00	+ 1.50 to + 2.00
% change	+ 5.0	−74.2	+ 54.9	0.0	+ 50.0 to + 100.0
Camping Journal (M)					
1973	380,047	95.6	4.4	7.50	.50
1978	321,487	97.1	2.9	8.95	1.00
% change	+ 14.8	+ 16.6	−24.2	+ 29.3	+ 200.0
Hot Rod (M)					
1973	817,172	54.5	45.5	7.50	.75
1978	833,166	57.4	42.6	9.00	1.25
% change	+ 2.0	+ 7.3	4.5	+ 20.0	+ 66.7
The Magazine Antiques (M)					
1973	75,034	100.0	nil	16.00	2.00
1978	74,734	99.0	1.0	28.00	3.50
% change	−0.4	−1.3	N.M.	+ 75.0	+ 75.0
Skin Diver (M)					
1973	119,784	68.2	31.8	7.50	.75
1978	165,903	77.8	22.2	10.95	1.50
% change	+ 38.5	+ 58.0	−3.4	+ 46.0	+ 100.0
Totals					
1973	4,319,873	66.3	33.7	7.83	.96
1978	5,312,078	75.0	25.0	12.23	1.52
% change	+ 23.0	+ 39.1	−8.8	+ 56.2	+ 58.3

b. Monthly in 1973.
c. Does not include *National Geographic*.
N.M. Not Meaningful.
Source: Audit Bureau of Circulation statements for second six months, 1978.

Appendix B

Consumer Magazines Published by Major Groups*

American Broadcasting Companies, Inc. — 4

    High Fidelity (M), Modern Photography (M), Schwann Record & Tape Guide (M), Los Angeles (M).

    Total 1.2 million paid

CBS Inc. — 10

    Audio (M), American Photographer (M), Mechanix Illustrated (M), Woman's Day (15x), Cycle World (M), Pickup, Van & 4WD† (M), Road & Track (M), Field & Stream (M), World Tennis (M), Family Weekly (W).

    Total 13.6 million paid (not including 12.4 million for *Family Weekly*, Sunday newspaper supplement)

---

*Circulation for groups most current available to December 1980. Titles in group current, where changes known, to October 1981. May differ from previous tables which are based on earlier data.

† *Pickup, Van & 4WD* (circulation 265,000 in 1980) was sold by CBS in 1982.

Key: (M) monthly; (BM) bimonthly; (BW) biweekly; (W) weekly; (Q) quarterly; (10x, etc.) 10 times annually

Challenge Publications, Inc. — 10

Air Classics (M), Air Progress (M), Military Modeler (M), Minicycle/BMX Action (M), Modern Cycle (M), Popular Off Roading (M), Rod Action (M), Scale Modeler (M), Sport Flying (BM), Street Machine (BM).

Total 485,000 paid

Charlton Publications, Inc. — 9

Charlton Muscle Group (3 titles) (BM), Charlton Comics Group (16 titles) (BM), Charlton Crossword Group (5 titles) (BM), Country Song Roundup (M), Hit Parader Combination (M), Official Karate (8x), Real West (BM), Gung-Ho (M), Rock and Soul Songs (7x).

Total 4.1 million paid

Charter Co. — 2

Ladies' Home Journal (M), Redbook (M).

Total 10.0 million paid

Condé Nast Publications Inc. (Newhouse) — 7

Brides (BM), Gentlemen's Quarterly (M), Glamour (M), House & Garden (M), Self (M), Vogue (M), Mademoiselle (M).

Total 7.1 million paid

Davis Publications, Inc. — 8

Alfred Hitchcock Mystery (13x), Camping Journal (8x), Ellery Queen's Mystery Magazine (13x), Income Opportunities (M), Isaac Asimov's Science Fiction Magazine (13x), Science & Mechanics (Q), Computers and Programming (BM), Analog (13x).

Total 1.3 million paid

East/West Network, Inc. — 7

    Continental Extra (M), Amtrak Express (M), Eastern Review (M), Ozark Flighttime (M), PSA (M), Texas Flyer (M), United Mainliner (M).

    Total 881,722 unpaid

Hearst Corp. — 14

    Cosmopolitan (M), Cosmopolitan Living (Q), Good Housekeeping (M), Sports Afield (M), Connoisseur (M), Motor Boating & Sailing (M), Popular Mechanics (M), Science Digest (M), Harper's Bazaar (M), House Beautiful (M), Country Living (BM), House Beautiful's Home Decorating (Q), House Beautiful's Building Manual (Q), Town & Country (M).

    Total 12.9 million paid

Johnson Publishing Co. — 2

    Ebony (M), Jet (W).

    Total 2.1 million paid

Macfadden Group — 8

    True Story (M), True Confessions (M), Secrets (M), True Romance (M), True Experience (M), True Love (M), Modern Romances (M), Us (BW).

    Total 3.4 million paid

Meredith Corporation — 8

    Successful Farming (13x), Metropolitan Home (M), Better Homes and Gardens (M), Better Homes and Gardens Building Ideas (Q), Better Homes and Gardens Remodeling Ideas (Q), Better Homes and Gardens Country Living and Kitchen Ideas (Q), Better Homes and Gardens Decorating Ideas (Q), Sail (M).

    Total 12 million paid/unpaid

New York Times Company — 4

Family Circle (17x), Golf Digest (M), Tennis (M), New York Times Magazine (W).

Total 10.5 million paid

Parents' Magazine Enterprises, Inc. (Gruner & Jahr, U.S.A.) — 6

Baby Care (Q), Expecting (Q), Parents' Magazine (M), Young Miss (M), Children's Digest (10x), Humpty Dumpty (10x).

Total 4.1 million paid/unpaid

Petersen Publishing Co. — 13

Car Craft (M), 4 Wheel & Off-Road (M), Guns & Ammo (M), Hot Rod Magazine (M), Hunting (Petersen's) (M), Motorcyclist Magazine (M), Motor Trend (M), Petersen's Photographic Magazine (M), Skin Diver Magazine (M), Sea & Pacific Skipper (M), 'Teen (M), Lakeland Boating (M), Rudder (M).

Total 5 million paid

Playboy Enterprises Inc. — 2

Games (BM), Playboy (M).

Total 5.7 million paid

Scholastic Magazines, Inc. — 10

Co-ed (10x), Scholastic Coach (10x), Scholastic Newstime (W), Forecast for Home Economics (9x), Junior Scholastic (10x), Senior Scholastic (10x), Scholastic Voice (10x), Scholastic Search (10x), Scholastic Scope (10x), Scholastic World (10x).

Total 6.1 million paid

Time Inc. — 7

Fortune (BW), Life (M), Money (M), People (W), Sports Illustrated (W), Time (W), Discover (M).

Total 12.5 million paid

Times Mirror Magazines, Inc. — 6

Homeowners How To (BM), Golf Magazine (M), Outdoor Life (M), Popular Science (M), Sporting News (W), Ski (7x).

Total 6 million paid

Webb Company — 8

Consumer Life (Q), Family Handyman (10x), Passages (M), Snow Goer (5x), Snow Week (18x), TWA Ambassador (M), Family Food Garden (9x), Frontier Magazine (M).

Total 3.2 million paid/unpaid

Ziff-Davis Publishing Company, Inc. — 17

Adventure Travel (BM), Backpacker (BM), Boating (M), Camera Arts (BM), Car and Driver (M), Cycle (M), Flying (M), Fly Fisherman, Modern Bride (BM), Popular Electronics (M), Popular Photography (M), Psychology Today (M), Skiing (7x), Sport Diver (BM), Stereo Review (M), USAir Magazine (M), Yachting (M).

Total 6.3 million paid/unpaid

Selected Bibliography

The literature of memoirs, biographies and histories of individual publishers and magazines is rather rich. Far less so is the literature on the development and structure of the periodical industry. Among some of the more comprehensive works are:

Compaine, Benjamin M. *Who Owns the Media? Concentration of Ownership in the Mass Communication Industry.* White Plains, N.Y.: Knowledge Industry Publications, Inc., 1978.
Ford, James L.C. *Magazines for Millions.* Carbondale, Ill.: Southern Illinois University Press, 1969.
Mott, Frank Luther. *A History of American Magazines.* 5 vols. Cambridge, Mass.: Harvard University Press, 1968.
Peterson, Theodore. *Magazines in the Twentieth Century.* Urbana, Ill.: University of Illinois Press, 1964.
Servan-Schreiber, Jean-Jacques. *The Power to Inform.* New York: McGraw Hill, 1974.
Tebbel, John W. *The American Magazine: A Compact History.* New York: Hawthorne Books, 1969.
Wolseley, Roland E. *Understanding Magazines: Trends in Readership and Management.* New York: Hastings House, 1973.
Wood, James P. *Magazines in the United States.* New York: Ronald Press, 1971.

A running account of current developments and some statistics are available in several periodicals. One, *Folio,* is the trade magazine that covers the magazine industry, both consumer and trade. Its "Folio 400" issue is a wealth of statistical data on the 400 largest magazines. Periodicals to examine include:

Advertising Age, Chicago, Ill.
Folio, Norwalk, Conn.
Media and Marketing Decisions, New York, N.Y.
Media Industry Newsletter, New York, N.Y.

Among the most useful reference sources are:
Ayer Directory of Publications. Bala Cynwyd, Pa.: Ayer Press. Annual.
Bowker Annual of Library and Book Trade Information. New York: R.R. Bowker Co., Annual.
Consumer Magazine and Farm Publication Rates and Data. Skokie, Ill.: Standard Rate & Data Service. Monthly.
U.S. Industrial Outlook. U.S. Department of Commerce. Annual.

Finally, the Information Center at the Magazine Publishers Association, 575 Lexington Ave., New York, has a small library and is the source of the many statistical compilations made by the association. MPA also publishes newsletters on research, advertising and circulation.

About the Author

Benjamin M. Compaine is executive director, media and allied arenas, at the Program on Information Resources Policy at Harvard University. His current work involves research on the policy implications of changing information technology. He is editor of *Who Owns the Media? Concentration of Ownership in the Mass Communications Industry* and author of *The Newspaper Industry in the 1980s: An Assessment of Economics and Technology*, and *The Book Industry in Transition*, all published by Knowledge Industry Publications, Inc. Dr. Compaine has written many other studies and articles about mass communications and technology, including *A New Framework for the Media Arena: Content, Process and Format*, published by Harvard's Program on Information Resources Policy. A graduate of Dickinson College, he holds an M.B.A. from Harvard and a Ph.D. in mass communications from Temple University.

Index

ABC, 122, 129, 133, 135, 157-158
ARA Services, 39
ARF. *See* Advertising Research Foundation
Acquisitions, 133-135
Advertising
  effectiveness of, 68-73
  expenditures, 10-14
  in other media, 61-64
  leading advertisers, 64-66
  pages, 10, 15, 18, 19, 64, 67, 98, 99
  rates, 55-62
  research, 69-75
  revenue, 10, 18, 63, 64, 150
Advertising Research Foundation (ARF), 78, 79
Ambiance, 116, 117
American Photography, 115
American Stage, 116
Antitrust activities, 39-40
Apartment Life, 111, 121
Associated Newspapers Group, Ltd., 136
Audience research
  ad hoc studies, 81, 82
  readership surveys, 82-83
  syndicated research, 77-81
Audit Bureau of Circulation, 125
Audits and Surveys, Inc., 73, 81
Axiom Market Research Bureau, 78

Belden Communications, 82
Bennett, Alan, 115
Better Homes and Gardens, 46, 101, 121

Blair, William, 120
Block, Chip, 114
Bok, Edward, 106
Bonnier Magazine Group, 136
Brown, Helen Gurley, 106

CBS Publishing Co., 122, 126, 130, 133, 134, 135, 150, 159-161
Capital Distributors, 34
Charney, Nicholas, 106
Charter Publishing Co., 126, 161-162
Chicago Sun-Times, 36
Chilton Research Services, 82
Circulation, 9-10, 19, 95-98
  economics of, 26-31, 26-29, 63-64
  management of, 23, 24, 26-31
City magazines, 58, 101
Condé Nast, 30, 39, 45, 66, 106, 121, 126, 137, 142, 162-164
Consumer magazines
  definition of, 5
  largest circulation, 126, 127
  number of, 8, 9
Consumer Magazine and Farm Publications Rates and Data, 60
Cost per potential customer, 57-59
Cost per thousand (CPM), 23, 55-64, 126
  for selected magazines, 56-59
Cowles Communications, 109, 136
CPM. *See* Cost per thousand

Index

Curtis Circulation Co., 34, 39
Curtis, Cyrus, 106

Delacorte, George T., Jr., 106
Demographic editions, 58
Demographic profile, 84, 85
Demographic trends, 152-153
Distribution, 31-40, 42-49

East/West Networks, 66, 130
Economist, The, 137
Editorial/ad ratios, 19-20
Editorial trends, 20-21
Entrepreneurship, 105-122

Family Circle, 53, 119, 138, 141
Family Reading Centers, 38
Fawcett, Wilford, 106
Felker, Clay, 30, 107
Filipacchi, Daniel, 109, 120, 136
Flynt Publications, 39

Games, 114
General interest magazines, 57, 90-104
Group publishing, 123-138
Gruner & Jahr, 136
Guccione, Robert, 36, 107, 121

Harcourt Brace Jovanovich, 108
Harlequin Enterprises, 137
Hartford, Huntington, 115
Hearst Corp., 30, 66, 122, 126, 137, 141, 150, 164-165
Hefner, Hugh, 115, 117
Hirsch, George, 107, 114, 119, 121

ICD. *See* International Circulation Distributors
Independent News Company, 34
Inland Carriers, 46
International Circulation Distributors (ICD), 34
International publishing, 136-138

Jazz, 108, 119

Kops, Ronald, 38

Lane Publishing Co., 150
Levy Cooperative Ad Plan, 36-37
Life, 106
Look, 109
Luce, Henry, 106

Macfadden, Bernarr, 106
Magazine networks, 66
Magazine Publishers Association, 85
Magazine Research Inc. (MRI), 81
Mark Clements Research, 82
McCall's Publishing Co., 121
McClure, S.S., 106
Meredith Corporation, 89, 151, 165-167
Media imperative concept, 85-87
MRI. *See* Magazine Research Inc.
Munsey's Magazine, 17

National Association of Selective Distributors, Inc., 45-46

National distributors, 32, 33, 34
National Geographic, 49, 53, 126
National Geographic Society, 49
New Times, 114
New York, 132
New York Times Co., 39, 122, 130, 135, 150, 167-168
Newsweek, 122, 137
Nonprofit organizations, 48-49, 50, 53

Obis, Paul, 118
Omni, 36, 110
Operating costs, 16-19, 21
Opinion Research Corporation, 70

Paper
  costs, 142, 144-146
  manufacturers of, 139-142
  supply of, 139-140, 141, 142
Patricof, Alan, 115
People, 109
Periodical publishing industry, 7, 16-17, 123, 124, 138
Petersen Publishing Co., 111, 151, 168-169
Peterson, Theodore, 106
Playboy Enterprises, 114, 150, 151, 169-171
Postage costs, 42-48, 133
Pricing, 29-31, 97-98, 125
Print media shipments, 8
Printing
  costs of, 142, 144-146
  methods of, 142-144
Private delivery, 47, 48, 152
Production costs, 144-146
Profitability, 16

Publishers
  largest by circulation, 130
  largest by number of magazines, 129-130
  largest by revenue, 128-129
Publishers Clearing House, 84, 114

Reader's Digest, 45, 50, 117, 126, 137
Reader's Digest Association, 130, 149, 171-172
"Recent reading" technique, 79
Regional editions, 58-59
Regional magazines, 58-59, 101, 104
Retail Management Marketing Co., 39
Retailers, 32, 33, 35
Ross, Harold, 106

Scott, Jack, 38
Seagram Distillers Co., 73
Select Magazines, 34, 39
Self, 37, 121, 142
Simmons Market Research Bureau, 78-80, 81, 82
Simmons, W.R. & Associates, 78, 79
Single-copy sales, 24-40, 50, 51, 52, 53, 95, 96
Smithsonian, 49, 50
Smithsonian Associates, 49
Special interest magazines, 26, 58, 73, 89-104
Special issue magazines, 100-101, 102, 103
Spin-off activities, 149-151
Sports Illustrated, 91, 108
Standard Rate & Data Service, 125, 126

Starch/INRA/Hooper, 73, 80
Study of Media Involvement, 70
Styer, Warren, 36
Subscriptions, 40-49, 50, 51, 52, 53

Target Group Index (TGI), 78
TGI. *See* Target Group Index
3-Sigma, 80
"Through the book" method, 78, 79
Time Distribution Service, 39
Time Inc., 36, 45, 81, 109, 122, 126, 130, 133, 135, 149, 150, 172-174
Times Mirror Co., 29, 66, 126, 141, 150, 174-176
Triangle Publications, 6, 108, 110, 126, 130, 176-177
TvB, 87
TV Guide, 50, 123

U.S. Postal Service, 42-48, 152

Universal Product Code, 38
Us, 82, 83, 110

Vegetarian Times, 108, 118, 119
Veronis, John, 106
Video programming, 147-149

Wallace, DeWitt, 106, 117
Washington Post Co., 129, 178-179
Wenner, Jan, 109
Wilderness Camping, 91
Wholesalers, 32, 33, 34-35
Woman's Day, 101, 141

Your Place, 117, 121

Ziff-Davis, 66, 121, 122, 129, 179-181

Related Titles in the Communications Library . . .

Who Owns the Media? Concentration of Ownership in the Mass Communications Industry
edited by Benjamin M. Compaine
LC 79-15891   ISBN 0-914236-36-9   hardcover $24.95

The Newspaper Industry in the 1980s: An Assessment of Economics and Technology
by Benjamin M. Compaine
LC 80-10121   ISBN 0-914236-37-7   hardcover $29.95

U.S. Book Publishing Yearbook and Directory, 1981-1982
edited by Judith Duke
LC 79-649219   ISBN 0-914236-63-6   softcover $60.00

Guide to Electronic Publishing: Opportunities in Online and Viewdata Services
by Fran Spigai and Peter Sommer
LC 81-20787   ISBN 0-914236-87-3   softcover $95.00

The Shrinking Library Dollar
by Dantia Quirk and Patricia Whitestone
LC 81-12319   ISBN 0-914236-74-1   hardcover $24.95

The Print Publisher in an Electronic World
edited by Clare Green
LC 81-671   ISBN 0-914236-81-4   softcover $95.00

Knowledge Industry Publications, Inc.
White Plains, NY 10604